*i*China

NORDIC INSTITUTE OF ASIAN STUDIES
NIAS Studies in Asian Topics

*i*China

The Rise of the Individual in Modern Chinese Society

Edited by

Mette Halskov Hansen and Rune Svarverud

 niasPRESS

*i*China: The Rise of the Individual in Modern Chinese Society
Edited by Mette Halskov Hansen and Rune Svarverud

NIAS – Nordic Institute of Asian Studies
Studies in Asian Topics, no. 45

First published in 2010 by NIAS Press
Reprinted in 2011
Nordic Institute of Asian Studies (NIAS)
Leifsgade 33, DK-2300 Copenhagen S, Denmark
Email: books@nias.ku.dk
Online: http://www.niaspress.dk/

British Library Cataloguing in Publication Data
iChina : the rise of the individual in modern Chinese society. -- (NIAS studies in Asian topics ; 45)
1. Social change--China. 2. Individualism--China. 3. China--Social conditions--2000-
I. Series II. Hansen, Mette Halskov. III. Svarverud, Rune. IV. Nordic Institute of Asian Studies.
302.5'0951-dc22

ISBN: 978-87-7694-052-2 (Hbk)
ISBN: 978-87-7694-053-9 (Pbk)

Typesetting by Donald B. Wagner
Printed in the United Kingdom by Marston Digital

Contents

Contents

Tables

Contributors

Ulrich Beck is professor of sociology at the University of Munich, and the British Journal of Sociology Visiting Centennial Professor at the London School of Economics and Political Sciences. He is editor of *Soziale Welt* and the *Edition Second Modernity*. His interests focus on risk society, globalization, individualization, reflexive modernization and cosmopolitanism. He is founding director of a research centre at the University of Munich (in cooperation with four other universities in the area), *Reflexive Modernization*, financed since 1999 by the DFG (German Research Society). His books include: *Risk Society* (1992); *Reflexive Modernization* (with Anthony Giddens and Scott Lash) (1994); *The Reinvention of Politics* (1997); *Power in the Gobal Age* (2005); *The Cosmopolitan Vision* (2006); *The Cosmopolitan Europe* (2007, with Edgar Grande); *World Risk Society* (2008); *World at Risk* (2008). His books have been translated into 35 languages.

Elisabeth Beck-Gernsheim is professor of sociology at the University of Erlangen-Nuremberg and visiting professor at Trondheim University, Norway. Her current research areas are migration and ethnicity, gender, family, and reproduction technologies. Her latest book is *Wir und die anderen. Kopftuch, Zwangsheirat und andere Mißverständnisse* (Frankfurt: Suhrkamp 2007), and recent publications in English include 'Transnational lives, transnational marriages' in *Global networks*, 2007 and 'Seeing through the migrants eyes' in Gökçe Yurdakul (ed.) (2009), *From Guestworkers into Muslims: The Transformation of Turkish Immigrant Associations in Germany*, Cambridge Scholars Press.

Jørgen Delman is professor of China studies in the Department of Cross-Cultural and Regional Studies at Copenhagen University. He has worked with China as a researcher and consultant since 1978. He was Director of

NIAS Nordic Institute of Asian Studies 2002–2008. His research interest has focused on state-society interaction, in particular in relation to rural and agricultural development, knowledge systems and innovation, business and politics, and civil society development. Recent publications include: 'Nordic Collaboration with China in Energy Research and Development', NIAS, 2008 (with Chen Yong) and ' "Dog wags tail" or "tail wags dog"?', *Norwegian Journal of Geography*, 2005.

Mette Halskov Hansen is professor of China studies at the University of Oslo. She has published widely in the fields of minority education (e.g. *Lessons in Being Chinese*, University of Washington Press, 1999), Han migrations to minority areas (e.g. *Frontier People*, Hurst & Co. 2005), and Chinese rural society. Being interested in processes of individualization in China, she is currently engaged in an anthropological study of schools' ways of socializing citizens and individuals, and rural students' views on their world and themselves.

Li Minghuan is professor of sociology at Xiamen University. She has written extensively on transnational migration of Chinese people and has carried out research at both sending and receiving societies for decades. Publications include *'We Need Two Worlds': Chinese Immigrant Associations in a Western Society* (Amsterdam University Press, 1999) and 欧洲华侨华人史 [A history of Chinese immigrants in Europe] (Zhongguo huaqiao chubanshe, 2002).

Klaus Mühlhahn is professor of history at Indiana University, Bloomington. As an historian of modern China he has published widely on Chinese legal history and the history of criminal justice in China. Other areas of interest are Western colonialism, governance and the world of the treaty ports. His most recent publication is *Criminal Justice in China – A History* (Harvard University Press, 2009).

Ni Anru is associate professor of sociology at Shandong University. He has published extensively in Chinese on sociological research methods and rural issues.

Cuiming Pang is currently a PhD student at the University of Oslo. Based on fieldwork in East China, she writes about the emergence of civic-organized

Internet communities, the regulation of Chinese cyberspace, and state-society relations in the age of the Internet.

Unn Målfrid H. Rolandsen is associate professor of China studies in the Department of Culture Studies and Oriental Languages at the University of Oslo. She is currently writing a monograph on leisure and power in contemporary China.

Rune Svarverud is professor of China studies in the Department of Culture Studies and Oriental Languages at the University of Oslo. His main fields of interest are the intellectual history of China, Sino-Western relations and the East–West intellectual transfer of ideas. His research has focused on pre-Qin and Han intellectual history (e.g. *Methods of the Way: Early Chinese Ethical Thought*, Brill, 1998) and the translation and reception of ideas from the West in late imperial/early modern China (e.g. *International Law as World Order in Late Imperial China: Translation, Reception and Discourse, 1847–1911*, Brill, 2007).

Stig Thøgersen is professor of China studies at Aarhus University. He is the author of *A County of Culture – Twentieth Century China Seen From the Village Schools of Zouping, Shandong* (University of Michigan Press, 2002), *Doing Fieldwork in China* (ed. with Maria Heimer, NIAS Press 2006) and several articles on social, political and cultural change in rural China. He is presently interested in social organizations and rural reconstruction and has established a Chinese–Scandinavian network on this topic (http://www.ruralchina.au.dk/en/).

Anne Wedell-Wedellsborg is professor of modern Chinese Language and Culture at Aarhus University. She specializes in modern and contemporary Chinese literature and has published extensively in this field. Other research interests include the contemporary Chinese cultural scene and Sino-European cultural relations.

Yunxiang Yan is professor of anthropology at the University of California, Los Angeles. He is the author of *The Flow of Gifts: Reciprocity and Social Networks in a Chinese Village* (1996), *Private Life under Socialism: Love,*

Intimacy, and Family Change in a Chinese Village (2003), and *The Individualization of Chinese Society* (forthcoming, 2009). His research interests include family and kinship, social change, social inequality and hierarchy, cultural globalization, and the individualization process in China.

Yin Xiaoqing is associate professor of sociology in the Labor and Social Security Department at Nanjing Normal University. Her research has focused on social transformations and labour migration in China.

Preface

This book comes out of years of cooperative research into concepts and practices of the individual in China, relations between individual and collective, and – inspired by the works by Ulrich Beck and Elisabeth Beck-Gernsheim – the process of individualization in the specific context of the Chinese state and society. The project included scholars from Europe (most from the Nordic countries) and China: senior scholars and PhD students, scholars from the disciplines of history, literary studies, anthropology, political science, and sinology. The book reflects this diversity.

As highlighted in Yunxiang Yan's Introduction, all the authors contribute from their different perspectives and academic backgrounds with empirical research that (hopefully) brings us a step further in understanding not only changing Chinese perceptions of the individual, expressed for instance in literature and law, but also how rising demands and expectations for individual freedom, choice and individuality result in the emergence of new forms of collectivities and negotiations with the state. As argued by, for instance, Beck and Beck-Gernsheim, individualization is a social condition which is not arrived at by a free decision of individuals. One of the decisive features of the process of individualization is precisely that it not merely permits but demands an active contribution by individuals. How this process evolves in the context of a state and society that lacks two of the defining characteristics of European individualization – a culturally embedded democracy and a welfare system – is one of the questions that the articles in this volume engage with.

The book, and the research that led to it, was made possible by contributions from the various universities in Europe, China and the US that the participating scholars are affiliated with. It was first of all the generous support from The Research Council of Norway in the period 2006–2009 that made it possible to bring these scholars together in order to develop the research and this book into more than just the sum of the individual contributions. Our hope is that the volume will help to spur further research into the processes of individualization in China, and contribute to new comparative research where Chinese experiences may serve to redefine theories developed in the European or North American context, as pointed out also by Ulrick Beck and Elisabeth Beck-Gernsheim in their Foreword to this book.

Four of the articles (by Thøgersen and Ni; Delman and Yin; Rolandsen; Hansen and Pang) have previously been published in somewhat different versions in the *European Journal of East Asian Studies*, vol. 7 no. 1, 2008, and we thank the journal for granting the right to republish. We would also like to point out that all the articles have been going through long processes of revisions based on constructive debates and comments from all the other participants in the project and network.

Last but not least, the collaborative research project and the present book have been greatly facilitated by the support and help from a number of individuals and institutions in addition to those mentioned above. Ane Husstad-Nedberg has assisted the project in various practical ways, and has been of tremendous help in the process of formatting the manuscripts and structuring the individual contributions into a book manuscript. Ann Kunish has greatly contributed to the manuscript with her meticulous work with the language and style of the English text. The Danish–Norwegian Collaboration Foundation gave the project a generous grant to hold a workshop at Schæffergården in Copenhagen. And finally, we want to express our gratitude to Gerald Jackson and the NIAS Press for their encouragement, and for taking on the task of editing and publishing this volume.

Mette Halskov Hansen and Rune Svarverud
University of Oslo

Foreword: Varieties of Individualization

Ulrich Beck and Elisabeth Beck-Gernsheim

Two accomplishments in particular set this multifaceted and intellectually stimulating book apart. On the one hand, its authors succeed in depicting the Chinese path towards individualization in conceptually acute and empirically sensitive terms. The highly sophisticated and multidimensional analyses in this book provide impressive proof of the fact that the individual has become a basic social category in China. A development has begun that permeates all areas of social life and determines not just the private sphere, family structures and relations between the sexes, but also the organization of the economy and flexible employment and, last but not least, the relation between individuals and the authoritarian state. At the same time the different chapters also make clear from different angles that this Chinese individualization process has its own distinctive profile: it does not simply represent a copy of the European path of individualization but must be understood as Chinese-style individualization. Therefore this book must be read by all those who want to understand the basic constitution of present-day Chinese society, with all of its ambivalences, contingencies and contradictions.

Moreover – and this constitutes the second major accomplishment of this book – it also makes an essential contribution to the current debate over theoretical developments in sociology. For what emerges as a recurring underlying motif in the various chapters is currently being debated within theoretical approaches as a central task of sociology. The issue is how the meaning of 'modernity' should be conceptualized and redefined from a cosmopolitan perspective. The theory of individualization which we and others have developed is not tied rigidly to the frame of reference of Western societies but is open in principle to different historical constellations. In this respect the authors of this volume prove to be pioneers who shine a spotlight on unexplored varieties of individualization. To develop them further in the future is among the most important tasks of a sociology and theory of modernization with a cosmopolitan orientation.[1] In what follows we offer some remarks on this issue. In particular, we first point out some conceptual and methodological problems which such a shift in perspective can be expected to raise; and, second, we offer a concrete presentation of these problems through a comparison between the Chinese and European paths to individualization.

I

The theory of individualization is part of the theory of reflexive modernization or, alternatively, of the second modernity. One can break this theory down accordingly into three complex arguments: the theorem of enforced individualization, the theorem of (world) risk society and the theorem of multidimensional globalization (cosmopolitanization). All three develop the same line of argumentation and thus mutually reinforce one another. 'Risk society', 'individualization' and 'cosmopolitanization' represent the radicalized forms of a dynamic of modernization that, at the beginning of the twenty-first century and applied to itself, supersedes the era of the first modernity. The first modernity exhibited a logic of order and action marked by sharp boundaries and distinctions – between categories of people, groups, activities, spheres of action and forms of life – which made possible unequivocal institutional ascriptions of jurisdictions, competences and responsibilities. This *logic of unequivocalness* – one could speak metaphorically in terms of a *Newtonian* social and political theory of the first modernity – is being increasingly superseded by a logic of ambiguity or, to vary the metaphor, a *Heisenbergian* uncertainty principle of social and political reality. Therefore it is precisely the victory march of modernity that is shaking its principles to the core. Modernity is radicalizing itself as a conscious response to the myriad risks and unanticipated side effects to which the process of modernization gives rise. In other words, modernity seems to have reached the limits of its current development and is entering a new phase that can be appropriately called the second modernity. Unlike the earlier phase, the second modernity challenges rather than takes for granted the foundations of modern growth which are now being undermined by events defined as ambiguous, fluid and uncertain.

This view of modernity seeks to demonstrate the significance of *reflexivity* in the process of social change. It has been rightly objected against this that it presupposes a European or Western frame of reference, while ignoring the question of what reflexivity means in those regions of the world in which modernity is only now gaining a foothold. The theory of the second modernity must be developed further in a systematic way in order to avoid this blinkering of our angle of vision. In what follows we suggest what this might imply for the individualization thesis.

First and foremost we must develop a comparative perspective that expressly includes the extra-European countries and, taking this as a basis, explores different varieties of individualization. This means that we cannot simply assume that the process of individualization exhibits the same basic pattern in all regions of the world, that it everywhere takes the same institutional forms, that it everywhere translates into the same biographical patterns and gives rise to the same social contradictions and conflicts. On the contrary, it must be shown at the theoretical level that the specificity of the European path towards individualization becomes visible only when it is juxtaposed with extra-European paths towards individualization. This approach must be developed in turn in three steps.

The first step is to demonstrate why different variants of individualization arise in the first place. This is rooted first in the process of individualization itself, which almost by its very nature is open to new styles and forms of social life that are neither recapitulations nor extrapolations of the European model of individualization. To be more precise, the multidimensionality of the process of individualization must liberate itself from the constraints of a national, European outlook which regards itself as the centre of innovation. It was colonialism which drew sharp dividing lines between the centre of the first modernity and the colonized peripheries, positing 'the West and the rest' as a pair of opposites. In the postcolonial era, by contrast, the discourse of the second modernity has annulled these very boundary constructions and attaches central importance instead to the linkages, lines of communication and interrelations between the global regions.

The theory of the second modernity, and thus also of individualization, in effect opens up European social theory to the postcolonial experiences of the adaptation and variation of the components of modernization. If one follows this line of thought through consistently, we can no longer assume as a matter of course that the European path of individualization is the original, true and authentic one. We must instead develop a perspective that starts from the opposite premise, namely from the parallel existence of European and extra-European varieties of individualization which are interconnected in a whole variety of ways.

Taking this as our basis, we then work out in the second step the differences between varieties of modernity and individualization. These varieties could be represented in three dimensions: economic production and reproduction (capitalism), the nature of political authority, and sociocultural integration (individualization, cosmopolitanization and religion). On this basis it may be possible to develop ideal-typical definitions of four different basic types of historical constellations of modernity:

> **Type 1**: *European modernity* – regulated or coordinated capitalism; developed democracy; institutionalized individualization (welfare state); secularized society.
>
> **Type 2**: *US American modernity* – liberal or uncoordinated capitalism; developed democracy; institutionalized individualization; post-secular religiosity.
>
> **Type 3**: *Chinese modernity* – state-regulated capitalism; post-traditional authoritarian government; truncated institutionalized individualization and plural-religious society.
>
> **Type 4**: *Islamic modernity* – regulated capitalism; traditional authoritarian government; prohibition of individualization; mono-religious society.

The third step is to identify combinations or 'hybrid forms' of the pre-modern, first-modern, second-modern and post-modern structural principles, with particular reference to processes of individualization within the above-mentioned European, American, Chinese and Islamic conceptions of modernity. The present book is a paradigmatic example of such a procedure, for its multidimensional analyses reveal the thoroughly contradictory and open character of the Chinese path towards individualization.

II

Something for which this book calls and for which it provides much stimulating material, even though it does not develop it explicitly, is an inversion of our point of view, namely a redefinition and specification of the European model of individualization by comparison with the Chinese model. A number of the contributions correctly point out that we simply took for granted that the instrumental relations of capitalist markets under the conditions of the post-welfare state have produced something no one really imagined they would, namely an individualization infused with ideas of cultural democratization. Manifestly this does *not* hold for Chinese individualization: in China there is neither a culturally embedded democracy nor a welfare state. Likewise, to date individualization in China, in contrast to Europe, has not been institutionally anchored in a system of basic rights (for instance family law and labour law).

This makes it clear, however, that what is presented in the European context as the 'universalistic logic' of individualization – namely the concurrence of the institutionalized legal forms and the biographical patterns of individualization – is in fact a historically and culturally limited special form, the result of a particular amalgamation of modernization and individualization. As the Chinese example shows, these two developments can also be uncoupled from one another or can combine to form different paths towards individualization.

There is in principle a close connection between individualization and the state in both the European and the Chinese contexts. However, this connection can assume completely different forms, indeed it can even point in diametrically opposed directions. If, as this book consistently shows, the individual is also acquiring increased importance in China, this is not occurring, as in Europe, within an institutionally secured framework and based on the civil, political and social basic rights which were won through political struggles in Europe during the first modernity. Instead the very thing which sets the Chinese process of individualization apart is the fact that these goals are still objects of struggles whose outcomes remain open. In other words, a key difference concerns whether there is a domain of inviolable individual basic rights in the relation between individual and state.

That said, it is the Chinese state which, since the 1970s, has put a programme of reform into effect that follows a common guideline. Its aim is to 'emancipate' the economy from the controlling socialist mechanisms of the state by loosening state controls on commodities, labour and the capital markets, while simultaneously liberating individuals from the all-encompassing socialist institutions of the urban work units and the agricultural collectives. This has led to a kind of limited, state-sanctioned individualization in which individuals are condemned to take their own initiatives, while the social safety nets of Chinese state socialism have disappeared. This opens the door to the individual assignment of responsibility which is one of the general features of individualization, albeit within the constraints of a restricted geographical mobility and the strict regulation of the opportunity to emigrate from the country into the cities.

The irony is that, in the course of the market reforms of the past decades, an individualized society of a kind has emerged in China, one which is by no means as uniform as the European image of China would have us believe, but which also corresponds to the official presentation (as during the Olympic Games) and has long since begun to shape and restrict the scope for action of the dominant party. If one considers this Chinese society of individuals in all of its different facets – held together by a pronounced nationalism and a breathtaking economic growth, hence by a dramatic 'lift effect' (*Fahrstuhleffekt*), but at the same time subject to the control and censorship of the government – one gains a much more realistic, differentiated, and also more positive image, of a 'Chinese modernity', with all of its contradictions on the scale between anarchy and state authoritarianism.

A commentator on a reformist weekly newspaper recently wrote that the country's 'soft power', on which the government sets so much store, depends primarily on the freedom and quality of the press. In this sense, the scope for expression within this partially individualized society has indeed expanded – but only as long as it does not directly affect the Party's monopoly on power.

This highlights a further outstanding feature of Chinese individualization, one which in our Western European understanding seems at very least unstable, if not altogether impossible. The Chinese reform of the market-economic individualization *truncates* – or, to put it bluntly, *castrates* – the process of individualization in its claims to democratic political participation. Individualization is possible, indeed is welcome and is even being enforced, in order to ensure the dream rates of growth with which the Chinese economy is storming the global markets. However, this process of liberation is supposed to remain within clear limits. In particular, it is supposed to be confined to the sphere of economic activities and private lifestyles. Should these developments lead to calls for participation and democracy, they will be prohibited, if possible preventively, through rigorous state controls and corresponding demarcations between the private and public spheres. At the same time, today the Internet offers access to a collectively individualized public arena in which even claims to political participation can be tested and effectively articulated. At present it is an open question to what extent this contradiction can actually be quashed in the long run.

It is striking that the Chinese path towards individualization, by comparison with the European, is unfolding in a characteristically different, indeed a reverse, temporal sequence. In China the neoliberal deregulation of the economy and the labour market of everyday culture and consumerism is being initiated *before* and *without* the constitutional anchoring of individualization as we know it in Europe. As a result political and social basic rights are being won on the basis of a neoliberal market-based individualization. One consequence of this inversion (as a number of the contributors to this volume show) is that the authoritarian state, which has revoked its social guarantees together with its obligation to the collective, is now trying to set clear limits to the claim to political participation which is inherent in the process of individualization by spreading a tight net of controls around the individual. Individual rights are being accorded as privileges, not as inviolable basic rights that everyone possesses as a birthright. Thus the government is trying to banish the individualism that it needs by linking it with officially celebrated values such as the nation and the family.

To sum up, one could say that whereas in Europe rights and law speak the language of individualization, in China a practice of tolerated, even enforced, individualization is occurring, coupled with an official ideological stigmatization of this same individualization. This book deals with the 'rise of the Chinese individual'. In doing so it offers impressive evidence for how those elements of the process of individualization that appear from a European point of view to be logically inherent in this process can be combined in completely different ways both as regards their temporal sequence and as regards their contents.

Notes

1   On this see Ulrich Beck, *The Cosmopolitan Vision*, Cambridge: Polity Press, 2006; and, 'Cosmopolitan Sociology', *British Journal of Sociology*, special issue, vol. 1, 2006.

Introduction: Conflicting Images of the Individual and Contested Process of Individualization

Yunxiang Yan

A transition perspective is frequently examined in studies of contemporary China, such as the transition from central planning to a free market in the economy (Naughton 2007), from totalitarianism to authoritarianism and/or to democracy in the political regime (Pei 2006; Zheng 2004) or from asceticism to hedonism in ethics (Ci 1994; Wang 2002). Marketization, privatization, liberalization, democratization and secularization/de-ideologization are among the most frequently used paradigms to study these transitions. Interestingly, there is no widely agreed theoretical concept by which scholars can make sense of the equally radical and rapid changes in Chinese society. In the 1990s, the notion of civil society was adopted but after a few years it became less attractive, mainly due to unexpected developments in China that did not fit the prevailing understanding of civil society in the West.[1]

Chinese society has never stopped changing, and, in a number of respects, radical changes have recently altered society beyond recognition in comparison to the Mao era. The rise of the individual is one such transformative change. As my previous research in rural north China shows (Yan 2003 and 2009), the private life of Chinese villagers has undergone a profound transformation in a dual sense: the rise of the private family within which the private lives of individuals are thriving. This transformation, which took clear shape by the end of the 1990s, is characterized by the relatively weak influence of public forces on the family, the greater control of the individual over her or his life, the centrality of companionate marriage and conjugal relationships, and an emphasis on personal well-being and affective ties. The essence of this transformation, I stress, lies in the rise of the individual, rather than in household size or family structure, albeit the latter have changed significantly. The rise of the individual alters the structure of social relations to a great extent, resulting in the individualization of Chinese society (Yan 2009). My findings also reveal that, due to the hostility of the Chinese state toward self-organizations and an autonomous society, the rising individual has shown a tendency to emphasize rights while overlooking obligations and other individuals' rights, running the risk of becoming what I refer to the 'uncivil individual'. Consequently, the rising individual is primarily confined to the sphere of private life, and egotism prevails when uncivil individuals interact with one another (Yan 2003).

Turning to the public sphere, especially in the urban context since the late 1990s, the role of the rising individual has become both more complicated and more important. The development of volunteerism and philanthropy, the growth of various NGOs and the appearance of rights movements in various domains of social life all testify to the impact of the rising individual on Chinese society (see Chan 2005; Economy 2004; Jankowiak 2004; Li 2006; Linebaugh and Spencer 2007; Thelle 2004; Wonacott 2004). For the current generation of Chinese youth, the primacy of personal happiness and individual realization has without doubt become the ultimate goal in life, indicating that society has undergone an ethical shift from collective-oriented values to individual-oriented values (Ci 1994; Wang 2002). Although most rights-assertion movements are *ad hoc* actions to protect the self-interests of the participants against the encroachment of greedy and often brutal capitalism (O'Brien and Li 2006; Lee 2007), some individuals have surpassed the level of materialism and have taken extraordinary steps to challenge the authoritarian state. For instance, Zeng Jinyan, a 23-year-old woman married to the political dissident Hu Jia, stood up to openly protest against police brutality and government-sponsored oppression. (As a result, she was featured as one of the *Time* magazine's 100 most influential people in 2007.)

The challenge is how to understand the rise of the Chinese individual and its wide and profound implications in China and beyond. A fundamental question arises: is Chinese society, like its counterparts in the West, undergoing a process of individualization? To answer this question, the first step is to map the rising individual in various domains of Chinese life – private and public alike – and then to analyze the Chinese cases using the appropriate theoretical tools. It is therefore both timely and critically important that a group of Nordic and Chinese scholars from different disciplines have met this challenge by examining the rise of the Chinese individual through empirical research. Moreover, it is to their credit that they examine the China case in light of the individualization thesis in European social theories, especially the framework of institutionalized individualism of Ulrich Beck and Elisabeth Beck-Gernsheim (2003), thus creating a dialogue between China studies and Western theories.

In the following pages, I begin with a brief account of the individualization thesis, highlighting the major points that appear to be relevant to our understanding of the Chinese case or that have been addressed by the authors in this volume. Next I take a close look at a recent case of identity politics, which reveals several features of the individualizing process in Chinese society. Chief among them is the defining role of the state, which is also a common thread that links the chapters in this volume. In the third section, I briefly comment on the contributions of these chapters by examining several themes that emerge from the collective effort. In the conclusion, I explore the possibility that Chinese society is following a different path to become individualized, which may shed new light on our understanding of the universality of the individualization thesis.

The Individualization Thesis

Admittedly, the rising importance of the individual in social life is not a new phenomenon, and one can argue that it began with industrialization or even earlier (MacFarlane 1978). The individual–society relationship occupied a central place in the classic theories of Durkheim and Weber nearly a century ago and continues to do so in contemporary social theories. What is new in the contemporary individualization thesis, however, is the scholarly effort to address the tensions between the increasing demands for individuality, choice and freedom being imposed on individuals on the one hand and the complex and unavoidable dependence of these same individuals on social institutions on the other. Unlike neoliberal theories that assume humans to be naturally autonomous and self-determining agents and in an ideal situation to be able to perform best without the constraints of social institutions (Harvey 2005), the new interpretative framework emphasizes the critical role of contemporary social institutions and relationships in form-ing the independence-seeking individual and re-shaping the individualizing society.[2]

The individualization thesis, which developed from the theories of Zygmunt Bauman, Anthony Giddens, and Beck and Beck-Gernsheim, highlights the following features of contemporary life (see Howard 2007). The first might be called differentiation and disembedment from the social. Increasingly, individuals are disembedded from external social constraints, which include both cultural traditions in general and some encompassing categories in particular, such as the family, kinship, community and social class. As a result, society has become further differentiated and diversified. Yet, this does not mean that tradition and social groups no longer play a role; instead, they still may be important if they serve as resources for the individual.

The second feature is a paradoxical phenomenon referred to by Bauman as 'compulsive and obligatory self-determination' (Bauman 2000: 32). This means that modern social structures compel people to become proactive and self-determining individuals who must take full responsibility for their own problems and develop a reflexive self (Giddens 1991). This is done through a set of new social institutions such as the education system, labour market and state regulations. By removing the option to seek the protection of tradition, family or community, the influence of modern social insti-tutions on the individual has actually increased.

The third feature is characterized as 'life of one's own through conform-ity' (Beck and Beck-Gernsheim 2003: 151), meaning that the promotion of choice, freedom and individuality does not necessarily make every individual unique. On the contrary, because the dependence on social institutions determines that contemporary individuals cannot float free in the search for and construction of a unique self, contemporary individuals must construct their own biographies through guidelines and regulations, and thus they end up with a life of individual conformity.

Finally, the individualization process relies on what Beck calls 'cultural democratization', meaning that democracy is widely accepted and practised as a principle in everyday life and social relations. Cultural democratization, in Beck's view, is one step farther from political and social democracy be-cause of the internalization of democratic culture: 'We are living under the preconditions of internalized democracy: the belief in equality in relationships, in dialogue not violence or the imposition of authority as the main element for reaching agreement' (Beck and Beck-Gernsheim 2003: 205).

It should be noted that the individualization thesis as a theoretical construction captures the particular changes in the nature of social relations in Western European societies, changes which have certain features that do not exist in China. Most noticeably, in European societies individual rights and freedom are regarded as a given and have long been protected by political democracy; the inequality gap is under the control of the welfare state; and individual identity is increasingly defined by lifestyle and an individual biography instead of by social groups such as the family or social class. Consequently, the increasingly institutionally defined individual must rely on the security and wealth provided by the welfare state to maintain 'ontological security' (Giddens 1991), a paradoxical development categorized as institutional individualism by Beck and Beck-Gernsheim (2003). Yet, the globalization of the world economy has radicalized the competition for profit and raised the bar much higher for efficient individuals. As a result, the social democratic countries in Western Europe have had to reduce the dependence of individuals on the support of the welfare state by promoting individual choice, agency, responsibility and a 'do-it-yourself-biography'. Consequently, the individualization of society and social relations under postmodern conditions has been accelerated and intensified, leading to a risk society full of precarious freedom (Beck 1992) and uncertainty/fluidity of many sorts (Bauman 2001).

To what extent can the individualization thesis be applied to other types of societies, such as that in China, which is still undergoing the modernization process? Alternatively, is Chinese society moving toward individualization? If so, in what specific ways has individualization occurred in the modernizing, non-Western society of China? These questions by no means derive merely from scholarly interest; instead, they arise directly from the changing life experiences of Chinese individuals, and they pose a challenge to existing scholarly accounts. Now let us turn to a common case of identity politics and highlight certain features of the individualization process in China.

The Politics of a Temporary Residence Permit

On 2 April 2008, Mr Liu Shuhong, a 38-year-old freelancer who is better known by his pen name *Laodan* (老蛋, 'old egg') through his essays, commentaries and short stories published on the Internet, posted a personal statement on his blog entitled 'A Statement on my Beijing Temporary Residence Permit' (Liu 2008). Liu had moved to Beijing in 2006 and since then has been holding a C-type temporary residence permit. Liu argued that the temporary residence permit, as part of the household registration (*hukou* 户口) system, perpetuated the low status of migrants in Beijing, subjecting them to a variety of open and institutionalized discriminations. Moreover, because the temporary residence permit was issued in three types (A, B and C types in different colours) in accordance with a migrant's economic status and history of living in the city and because the migrants were forced to carry the permit at all times, the Beijing government openly discriminated against and humiliated migrants, similar to the government discrimination against Indian immigrants in South Africa at the turn of the last century. These practices, argued Liu, violated the Chinese constitution and several residence regulations and thus should be ended immediate by collective action. A good example to follow was that of Mahatma Gandhi who, in 1906, began his Satyagraha movement by publicly burning the discriminatory identity card that the government of Natal forced Indian immigrants to carry. However, because burning a government-issued identity card is a criminal act in China, Liu decided to wear a big letter 'C' on his left arm to protest against the inhuman government policy and illegal practice of temporary residence cards issued by the Beijing government. At the end of his statement, Liu also posted two photos of himself, holding his government-issued C-type temporary residence permit and wearing an armband bearing the letter 'C'.

Within three days, Liu's statement had been read by 22,400 people and 668 people had submitted follow-up commentaries on the Internet, effectively making Liu's personal politics both public and collective (Liu 2008). The majority agreed with Liu and supported his protest, and some even called Liu a Martin Luther King hero and wanted to join him in further collective action. About 20 per cent of readers, however, disagreed with Liu, calling him an ungrateful migrant who merely wanted to take advantage of the social welfare in Beijing, an opportunist who wanted to create his 15 seconds of fame and to find business opportunities. Most of the opponents identified themselves as Beijing residents and complained about the high crime rate, crowdedness, poor hygiene and other social vices that the large influx of migrants had brought to their lovely hometown. These views were countered by more arguments from migrants who emphasized their contributions to the city through their hard work and who complained about the local discrimination. A war of words quickly accelerated into a hostile confrontation between Beijing residents and migrants in the virtual world. The importance and rich meanings of this debate, however, can only be fully understood in a larger social context.

It is widely known that the infamous household registration system established in 1958 created a caste-like social stratification that deprived the rural population of almost all the social welfare benefits that the urban population could enjoy under radical socialism. To maintain this rural–urban divide, beginning in the late 1950s rural to urban migration without an official permit was legally banned and strictly policed. Those who travelled were required to carry their family's household registration booklet (more on this below) and report to the local police within three days; without a local household registration, they could not rent rooms. After the economic reforms began in 1978, the obstacles that these restrictions created to social mobility became increasingly obvious, and gradually the system was loosened by a number of new regulations. Among them was the 1985 regulation on temporary residence that for the first time introduced an official temporary urban residence permit (*zanzhuzheng* 暂住证) and also lifted the legal ban on renting rooms to outsiders. Along with the rapid increase in rural to urban migration, the regulations on temporary urban residence were frequently changed with local variations.

In Beijing, the government issued new regulations in 2001 which require all migrants (*wailai renkou* 外来人口, which means literally people from outside) to obtain a new temporary residence permit (Zhongguo renkou yu fazhan yanjiu zhongxin 2001). This new temporary residence permit is issued in three types: an A-type is given to those who have lived in the city for three years, are legally employed and have no criminal records; a B permit is given to those who have lived between one and three years in the city but meet the latter two conditions; a C permit is for those who have lived in Beijing for less than one year. Because the A permit is green, the B permit yellow and the C permit red, some migrants also refer to the A permit as a 'Beijing green card', after the popular usage of the US legal alien card.

The 2001 regulation makes it clear that holders of the different types of temporary residence permits will be treated differently. 'The government will mainly protect and serve the A permit holders; for the B permit holders, the government focuses on increasing their capacity for self-management, self-education and self-control; the government regards the C permit holders as the key objects of government control and thus it must increase the inspection, prevention and control of this population' (Zhongguo renkou yu fazhan yanjiu zhongxin 2001). Additional requirements were added in 2007 by the Bureau of Public Security in Beijing (Beijing zhengfu wang 2007). For example, the mandatory residence in Beijing for an A permit was increased to five years. But the new policy also opened the A permit to five categories of people who do not have to meet the five-year requirement: managerial and technical talent hired by Beijing enterprises, those who have purchased real estate in Beijing or who have invested at least 300,000 yuan, staff in offices of various regional governments, spouses of Beijing household registration holders, and migrants who have been recognized and honoured by district-level governments in Beijing.

Obviously, the temporary residence permit separates the migrants from Beijing residents in a hierarchically arranged social space; the distinctions of the three permit types differentiate the migrants and create a hierarchical identity among them. For the migrants, it is a double attack on their identity and individual rights. Although the Beijing government claims that the regulations were enacted to better serve the migrant population because the migrants have become a much differentiated population, the real purpose is to control the migrants, especially those at the lower rungs of society, namely, the C permit holders. The rope of control can be tightened at the discretion of the Beijing government at any time. For example, fewer migrants received an A permit in 2008 even though they qualified either by the length of their residence or by the property ownership requirement (Liu Shuhong belongs to latter case). To answer Liu's question in this regard, one individual revealed that he had been told by local cadres that no A permits would be distributed in 2008 because of the Olympics, as a massive clean-up of migrants from Beijing was expected. The arbitrary implementation of the regulation, as in many other cases, provoked strong reactions among migrants who felt insulted, humiliated and angry. A related problem is official corruption. As the A permit is highly desirable, some local officials reject qualified applicants but offer the permit to others who have the *guanxi* (关系) connections to offer bribes. In any case, as Liu pointed out in his online statement, the policy of three types of residence permits simply added a new layer of open discrimination and humiliation to the migrants, causing serious damage to their daily life, psychology and self-identity. Liu's blog statement was endorsed by many readers who then engaged in a heated debate with the supporters of the government policy.

This debate among anonymous bloggers and Web readers, like many other debates that appear on the Internet daily, should not be taken at surface value because some participants may not be serious about what they write or may purposely make extreme remarks to attract attention. Nevertheless, a careful and close reading of this case reveals four informative clues about the individualization of Chinese society and about the connections and disjunctions between the European individualization thesis and the social changes in China.

First of all, it is noteworthy that the individual has become the basic unit of discourse by which both Liu presents his views in his statements and others engage in the online debate. As more readers participate in the debate with more personal stories, the notion of self-identity emerges as another important category. Echoing Liu's complaint that he was arbitrarily given a C-type temporary residence permit even though he qualified for an A permit because of his ownership of real estate in Beijing, a number of migrants offered similar personal accounts and then raised a question that bears a strong flavour of possessive individualism (Macpherson 1962): 'Who am I if by law I can only temporarily reside in my own house?' They further questioned the legality of temporary residence: 'Why do I have to live temporarily in my own country given that freedom of travel and residence is a citizen right guaranteed by the Chinese constitution?'

The second implication of the Liu case of a temporary residence card is the increasing awareness of individual rights and the centrality of individual happiness among Chinese citizens. Liu's statement revolves around the idea of equal individual rights to pursue a happy life in Beijing, and this remains the focal point in the debate, albeit being articulated differently by participants of different backgrounds. Most supporters of Liu's position maintain that freedom of travel and residence are universal human rights and should extend to all Chinese citizens. By this logic, not only the temporary residence permits but the entire household registration system should be abolished. It is in this context that Gandhi and Martin Luther King are brought up by some commentators. Those who oppose Liu's statement argue that the rights and privileges of Beijing residents derive from their hard work and/or their parents' hard work in the city, indicating that individual rights are earned, not given at birth. Interestingly, to this argument that effectively turns individual rights into earned privileges, some migrants counter-argued that they had already made a contribution by paying taxes or by working in the city. They went into great detail to show how they had contributed to the city by paying taxes, creating employment opportunities and purchasing commodities and property. This line of argument infuriated the other side because, as they complained, the purchasing power of successful migrants is the real reason why so many Beijing natives have been driven out of the market.

This rather instrumental argument is revealed in Liu Shuhong's statement when he noted that the most intolerable injustice was that although he had purchased property in Beijing, which in theory would have qualified him for an A-type card, he was still given the lower-level C-type card that was only given to new immigrants who had only worked in the city for less than one year. Following the same logic of individual rights as earned instead of given, some successful migrants used their biographies to show how they eventually earned a Beijing household registration due to their extraordinary achievements. While the notion of equal rights for everyone was a good one, they tried to convince their former fellow migrants that the notion could not be realized in China, due to the huge population and other problems. For the sake of social order, it was justifiable that the government maintained the household registration system, but it should grant more rights (namely, earned privileges) to individuals who deserve rewards. It is noteworthy that both sides seem to perceive the individual pursuit of happiness as a zero-sum game and regard the legal right to live in the city as a limited resource. From such a perspective, the migrants have gained what the Beijing locals have lost.

Third, the assertion of individual rights most often involves negotiation with the state, usually taking the form of public appeal. The conflicting views show that the rising awareness of individual rights in China is not based on a universal notion of natural rights that apply to every individual; both the migrants and their opponents in this online debate seem to confuse rights with earned privileges and thus they often disagree over who deserves what. Such an understanding of individual rights will eventually lead competing individuals to seek an authority that has the power and resources to grant the earned privileges to individuals. This is still in line with the traditional Chinese mode of the individual–state relationship, in which the state is bestowed with both virtues and absolute authority, and the individual is dependent on the state for protection and well-being (Pye 1996).

In his personal statement Liu clearly asserts: 'I hope that my action can push the government to reform the household registration system and make improvements to the temporary residence regulation, . . . so that more Chinese people, instead of only the residents of a few metropolitan cities, can enjoy the fruitful results of China's reform' (Liu 2008). Although most migrants supported Liu's appeal by adding personal stories about being discriminated against and humiliated by the temporary residence permit regulation and demanding better treatment, the other side (including Beijing natives, new Beijing residents and migrants with green cards) defended the Beijing government's policy and supported the status quo. In other words, this case can be viewed as individuals making a public appeal to the Chinese government to change or not to change a policy that determines the redistribution of privileges.

This case is by no means exceptional. For example, a consumer rights consciousness is perhaps the most developed in the area of rights awareness in China, as there has been a well-organized consumer protection movement since the 1980s, with the rapid growth of both consumer associations and individual advocates of consumer rights (Croll 2006; Hooper 2005; Palmer 2006). Beverley Hooper, a veteran scholar who has studied Chinese consumers and consumerism, suggests that the term 'consumer citizen' captures this development in individual rights. Yet, the entire consumer protection movement has developed within government-created structures, and both the consumer rights protectors as well as their opponents, such as merchants and manufacturers, must appeal to government-sponsored agencies to settle disputes. As Hooper sharply notes, consumer citizens in China are asserting rights not vis-à-vis the state, but vis-à-vis the market, with the endorsement and encouragement of the state (Hooper 2005).

The fourth and final implication of this case can be called Internet individualism and activism, an important feature of the rise of the individual in Chinese society. Due to the anonymous nature of activities on the Internet and, more importantly, the decreased control by the state, the virtual world has become an increasingly important public space for hundreds of millions of Chinese, or 'Netizens'. Some choose to express their individuality by exposing their private lives, such as Mu Zimei who became famous in 2003 for posting on the Internet detailed accounts of her sexual encounters with a number of men. Many others found blogging the best way to express themselves, and by 2006 China had 30 million bloggers who were eager to share their most personal and individualistic ideas with faceless and nameless persons in the virtual world. Through discussion boards, forums and personal blogs, Chinese netizens have formed a force of public opinion, which, as in the 2003 Sun Zhigang case below, can have a significant impact on the real world.

Among all the discriminating restrictions imposed on rural migrants, the most infamous is the requirement always to carry three identity documents, known as the *sanzheng* (三证), i.e., a national identity card, a temporary residence permit issued by the local police department, and a work permit issued by the local labour bureau. A migrant who fails to carry any one of the three documents will be labelled a *sanwu renyuan* (三无人员, a person without the three) and may be subject to detention and expulsion from the city. In 2003, a young migrant named Sun Zhigang was caught by the police in Guangzhou city without an identity card and temporary residence permit. He was sent to a local detention centre but was later allegedly beaten to death by fellow detainees. Detaining migrants and sending them home have been practices that can be traced back to the pre-reform era, and police brutality in the practices is not uncommon. Yet, because Sun was a college graduate and because his classmates quickly spread his tragic story on the Internet, his case became headline news, a national sensation, and soon caused a huge wave of public protests both on the Internet and in printed media against the inhuman treatment of rural migrants. Public opinion pressure was so strong that it eventually forced the central government to abolish the practice of detaining rural migrants. Similarly, during the second half of the same year, strong public opinion expressed on the Internet forced the central government to intervene in a case of organized crime when the issue of whether the mafia leader Liu Yong should receive the death penalty became the focal point of a heated debate. Due to the strong pressure of public opinion that claimed that Liu had saved his life by bribing high-ranking provincial government and law enforcement officials, the central authorities overruled the decision of the provincial court and re-sentenced Liu to death. These two cases are regarded as Netizen victories in 2003, leading many others to follow suit in using the Internet as a weapon to assert individual rights or to seek justice through public opinion. Some attempts were successful, others worked to no avail, and still others were crushed by the state, the results mainly depending on how much the subversive power of the case threatened the government. Liu Shuhong's blog statement and the debate it provoked on the Internet should also be understood in this context of Internet individualism and activism.

To summarize, the case of Liu's blog statement on the temporary residence permit system reveals the following: the individual has emerged as a key unit in both discourse and action in everyday life, but consciousness of individual rights is based on a Chinese understanding of rights as earned privileges through individual efforts. Such an understanding of rights and the limitations to political freedom in public life are mutually reinforcing; consequently, the assertion of individual rights is primarily achieved through public appeals to the state. When an issue is politically sensitive, the Internet provides a unique social space for the rising individual to contest and negotiate with the powerful state because (in most cases) the individual is protected by the anonymity of the Internet and the size of mass participation, thus leading to the popularity of Internet activism in China.

The political sensitivity of the case of the temporary residence permit policy, like many other cases, derives from the simple fact that, judged by the principles of justice and equality for all individuals, some individuals or social groups are illegitimately dominated by others in contemporary Beijing, and such illegitimate domination is officially sanctioned by the state. The individual migrants are engaged in what Giddens calls 'emancipatory politics', a feature of the modernization age in Europe and a precondition for the shift to the life politics of the postmodern individual in the age of high modernity (Giddens 1991: 210–213). Historically speaking, it is this emancipatory politics that eventually internalized the values of modern individualism and democracy, including the basic understanding that individual rights are given at birth, hence forming the precondition for individualization, that is, 'cultural democratization' as Beck put it (Beck and Beck-Gernsheim 2003). Such a precondition obviously does not exist in China today.

Moreover, because the existing structure of inequality and domination is sanctioned by the state and in turn is supportive of state power, the changing individual–state relationship constitutes the central axis in the rise of the individual and the individualization of society. It is important to view this relationship as a fluid process of discourse and practices, because the state, as Frank Pieke (2004) points out, does not sit above society as an abstract entity of power and authority. There has yet to emerge in China the kind of life politics or self-politics that defines the individualization trend in European societies, because for the majority of Chinese individuals the dominant goal of everyday life is to improve life chances instead of self-realization through choice of lifestyles. In other words, the rising individual in China acts within the parameters set by both the state and the market, and the exercise of individual agency in turn reshapes the dynamisms among the individual, the state and the market, as indicated by the Liu Shuhong case and clearly shown in the complex picture presented by the chapters in this volume.

Understanding the Rising Individual in China

Obviously I cannot do justice to the rich contents of the empirical research presented in this book, nor do I intend to offer a balanced review or summary. Instead, I will highlight the themes and important findings in these chapters that are helpful for our understanding of the rising individual in China and the individualization thesis in general.

Each chapter in this book stands well on its own in addressing various issues, yet together they depict the contours of an individualizing society by deploying three general themes. First, the rise of the individual, a revolutionary call by the reform-minded Chinese elite at the turn of the twentieth century, has become a social reality in the everyday life of ordinary people at the beginning of the twenty-first century, which, in turn, is transforming Chinese society. Second, central to this transformation is the ongoing negotiation and contestation between the rising individual and the various forms of collectivity, including the Chinese state. The family, which historically was an important intermediary between the individual and the imperial state, plays a more influential role than society in fostering individual identity. Third, to date the individual is still perceived by the state and society (and often self-perceives) as a means to a greater end and thus cannot gain fully autonomous and indivisible status. Individualism, a core value of individualization in Western societies and a fundamental principle of a free market economy, remains underdeveloped among the rising Chinese individuals. At the same time, there is also a counter trend, that is, individuals who want to hang onto the protective collectives and exercise their agency to resist the changes of individualization. Either way, the individual seems to be a highly contested notion in contemporary Chinese society.

The rise of the individual

Throughout this volume, there is ample evidence showing the rise of the Chinese individual, such as the emphasis on individual rights and freedom in life aspirations, the greater exercise of individual choice in social practices, and the disembedment of individuals from previously encompassing social categories, such as the family, kinship and community. Most of the new ideas opposing the collective-oriented, Confucianism-based traditional culture appeared in the writings of reform-minded Chinese intellectuals in the early twentieth century. The most influential figure in this respect is Liang Qichao, who not only introduced these ideas to China but also added new meanings to a set of ideas associated with the rise of the individual, such as individual freedom, independence and happiness (see Chapter 6 in this volume). The realization of these ideas in the everyday life of ordinary people, however, arrived much later and became obvious only in the post-reform era.

According to Mette Halskov Hansen and Cuiming Pang (Chapter 1), notions of freedom, independence, free love and personal development are widespread and popular among young villagers, due to the influence of pop culture via the mass media and the fluid labour market at the end of the twentieth century. Inspired by individualistic ideas and aspirations for a freer and more self-fulfilling life, rural youth in millions from all corners of China leave their parents, families and communities for temporary and unpredictable work in the cities, an obvious step in the direction of disembedment. A significant number of these young migrant workers, instead of being driven by sheer poverty, are motivated to leave home by the excitement of seeing and experiencing the outside world. Fascinated by the promises of freedom and choice, they often refuse to sign the labour contract that is designed to protect their basic rights; instead, they want to have the freedom of quitting their job and move to a new place at any time. However, due to the persistence of the household registration system, rural villagers are denied the right to become permanent city dwellers and therefore remain permanent second-class citizens. Yet these villagers blame themselves for failing in their education rather than complaining about the institutionalized injustices generated by the social system. This strong sense of individual responsibility for success or failure, Hansen and Pang argue, derives from the individualization of the labour market and the lack of a comprehensive state system of social security, and eventually leads to the idealization of individual choice.

Individual choice is also important among the rural elderly, who by received wisdom should be the least individualistic sector of the rural population. In their study of the waning of patrilocal post-marital co-residence (i.e., the custom that a young couple lives with the husband's parents for an extended period of time), Stig Thøgersen and Ni Anru (Chapter 2) discover that many elderly villagers quickly adapt to the more individualized lifestyle in an empty nest family, and a number of elderly villagers single out autonomy and individual space as the most desirable aspects of this new arrangement. Although some still equate old age with dependency, others regard it as a time of leisure to enjoy oneself after a long working life. The notion of filial piety has been negotiated and modified as well so that the senior generation no longer expects to be the centre of attention, care and respect from their adult children. The statement 'he is he, and I am I' made by one of Thøgersen and Ni's elder informants obviously confirms a preference for freedom and choice.

The aspiration to make an individual choice and the courage to abide by it takes a rather extreme political form in the case of Mr Sun Dawu, a self-made entrepreneur who grew up in a peasant family but left his village for the outside world in his youth. Making a fortune in a successful agro-business,

Sun became a national celebrity by choosing not to bribe local officials to make business deals and by criticizing the prevalence of social injustices and the prolonged suffering of Chinese villagers. Sun propagated his own political ideas, derived from a variety of sources including Confucianism and constitutional democracy, in speeches and Internet writings. In their detailed account of Sun's saga, including his 2003 imprisonment and the campaign by his supporters to win his release, Jørgen Delman and Yin Xiaoqing (Chapter 3) present a telling case of the 'do-it-yourself' biography, in which an individual aspires to make the choice to disembed from the old social categories and to take risks to create his own world through a new type of 'self-politics' (Beck and Beck-Gernsheim 2003: 44–46). In the Chinese context where the Communist Party and state still monopolize political power and control most aspects of public life, Sun's self-politics inevitably challenged state politics and went far beyond the remaking of an individual identity. Delman and Yin rightly note that Sun Dawu represents the emergence of a new social segment of private business people who, after disembedding from the state-controlled economic sector, must find ways to establish new 'peg communities' to defend their identity and self-politics, which in turn creates a new dimension in the state–private business nexus and a new form of political activism in the era of individualization in China.

Needless to say, individuals are conditioned by their immediate social environment and thus have different priorities in terms of making choices and pursuing freedom. In contrast to rural residents who make more basic choices about work and life and in an even sharper contrast to Sun Dawu and individuals like him who chose to expand self-politics into emancipatory politics, better-off urbanities, especially urban youth, often display a different set of life aspirations and pursue their individual freedom and choices through different consumerist practices. The majority of urban youth grew up drinking Coke and eating McDonald's hamburgers and quickly developed a taste for listening to hip hop and watching NBA games. While being pushed by their parents to study hard, they want to live a first-world, postmodern life in China (Fong 2004). Defying parental advice, they dye their hair, pierce their ears and wear trendy clothing in a restless pursuit of being cool. Those who have achieved the respected status of successful professionals often have to make 'difficult' choices regarding dinner parties in fashionable restaurants or vacations at exotic foreign destinations (Elegant 2007).

Perhaps the most famous and influential self-choosing and self-made young idol is Han Han, a high-school dropout who, at the age of 17, published a best-selling novel depicting the dark side of China's exam-oriented education system. The fact that Han sold more than two million copies of his book and was hence able to afford five cars made him the ultimate symbol of instant individual gratification, not only for youth but also for the general public. So much so that his often exaggerated rebellious and arrogant behaviour is praised as individualistic and creative by the Chinese media, and his not-so-unique statement that 'It is my choice to do whatever I want and to go wherever I want' is widely quoted as the motto of the new individuals (Beech 2004).

The disembedment of the individual from the former encompassing social categories is a defining feature of the individualization process (Beck and Beck-Gernsheim 2003). This is also a primary finding common to the chapters by Hansen and Pang; Thøgersen and Ni; Delman and Yin; and Li. Particularly noteworthy is that, unlike in the postmodern welfare states of Western Europe, the current trend of disembedment in China, especially in the sphere of public life, is closely related to the market-oriented reforms sponsored by the Chinese state since the 1970s. Although differing from one another in specific ways, these reform programmes share a common feature, that is, to loosen state control over the product, labour and capital markets on the one hand and to liberate the individuals from the previous all-encompassing socialist institutions of the rural collectives and urban work units on the other. These programmes have been praised by some commentators as the state's increasing commitment to a free market economy and have been criticized or opposed by others for the state's shirking of its responsibilities. The entire reform era since the late 1970s, to a certain extent, can be viewed as a process in which the state is untying the individuals by either eliminating or reducing its previous institutional support and at the same time maintaining control over the individual. Such a disembedment from socialism has been perceived as either liberating and thus welcomed by individuals in search of new opportunities or as abandoning and thus resisted by individuals trying to maintain their old privileges. Thus, a distinction can be made between voluntary and involuntary or forced disembedment.

The best known example of voluntary disembedment from socialism is the story of how eighteen men in Xiaogang village, Anhui province, started the first spark of rural reform in 1978. Driven by poverty and deeply disappointed with collective farming, these villagers decided to divide up the collective land and assign individual plots to each family. They would take individual responsibility to make sure the state-imposed quota of grain procurement would be met and, thereafter, they would have freedom to sell the surplus at a higher price on the black market. This was illegal at the time and could be easily punished as a counter-revolutionary act. To share the risk, the villagers signed a secret compact with their fingerprints, promising that if their leader or any others were to be incarcerated by the state, all the others would support their families until the children reaching adulthood. Luckily, some local government leaders strongly supported these villagers when their experiment was hugely successful, and the local leaders' additional reform efforts, later known as the reform of the household farming responsibility system, were accepted by the central authorities and then implemented elsewhere (see Zhou 1996).

One of the reasons why the Xiaogang villagers were willing to take so much responsibility and even risk being imprisoned was the extreme poverty and near-collapse of the rural economy. In this respect, they were by no means alone at the time. Therefore, when the state did not punish the Xiaogang villagers and villagers in other areas who carried out similar experiments, the majority of the rural population quickly followed suit. Their strong will to leave the socialist collective institution not only accelerated the initial reforms but also changed their course and eventually led to nationwide decollectivization in 1982–1983. The successful rural reform from 1978 to 1983 benefited both the villagers and the state and also provided a strong push for urban reforms along the same lines.

The disembedment from socialism in the cities, however, turned out to be a very different story, one that was full of resistance and social discontent.[3] The fundamental difference lies in the fact that the urban residents were much better protected under socialism, enjoying life-time employment, retirement pensions, free medical care, heavily subsidized housing and education, and other perks and benefits provided by their employers, known as work units, all of which belonged to the state. Workers and other state employees relied on their respective work unit so much that they even developed a work-unit identity and a culture of personal dependence on their work unit and their leaders, dubbed an 'organized dependency' by Andrew Walder (1983). Their benefits, privileges and sense of superiority were institutionally established and secured by the household registration system that legally banned rural to urban migration and thus separated the countryside from the cities for more than two decades. Therefore, urban reform actually meant that the state had to force the disembedment of workers from socialist institutions, hardly a popular move. The widespread and strong resistance by workers in state-owned enterprises to the downsizing reform and privatization of the SOEs since the 1990s was the most publicized resistance because it took the form of public protests (Lee 2007).

The individual in and out of the collective

Interestingly, several chapters in the volume also depict a picture of the individual constantly moving in and out of the collective, particularly the family institution.

First and foremost, the family serves as a key resource for the rising individual. For instance, the fact that rural elderly choose to live alone in an empty nest household (see Chapter 2) does not necessarily imply the withering away of the family as an important and encompassing unit of meanings for individual villagers in China, old and young alike. An alternative reading of the older villagers' choice to live alone is that they strategize the move so that they can maintain a good relationship with their married sons and can eventually move back into the latter's family when they become too old to take care of themselves. This may explain why the majority of independent-minded villagers in Thøgersen and Ni's study are the 'young old' who can still take care of themselves, a phenomenon that is also found elsewhere (see Yan 2003: 178–182). The bottom line is that the family remains the sole source of elderly support, regardless of the specific type of residence; at the same time, the traditional ideal family has lost its constraining power, so much so that individuals can make a variety of residence arrangements to meet their individual needs.

The family can also serve as an 'imagined community' and still play an important role in the construction of individual identity. As Hansen and Pang note, the high mobility, unpredictable employment and emphasis on individual choice among young migrant workers have not done away with the family as a unit of life meanings. For example, although insisting on their individual right to find a spouse through free love, rural youth also seek parental support and take family interests into serious consideration. Because of their marginal status in the cities, they are indifferent to public politics or official organizational life, which in turn makes the family stand out as a collective of pragmatic, symbolic and emotional importance.

There is, however, an important change in the individual's relationship to the family institution. In the traditional pattern of the relationship, the individual exists for the sake of perpetuating his (or her husband's) family, instead of the family being created to serve the needs of the individual. At a higher level, individual families exist to perpetuate the descent line, not the other way around (Baker 1979). As a result, the collectivity (be it the family or the lineage organization) designates individual choices by way of tradition. What we see from the chapter by Thøgersen and Ni or the chapter by Hansen and Pang are almost the opposite. The family is mobilized to serve the needs of an individual who exercises his or her agency in how to engage in the family institution, and tradition has lost its absolute authority. These cases actually echo an important argument of the individualization thesis, that is, as the individual disembeds from encompassing social categories, neither tradition nor the collective has to disappear; instead, both can be used as a resource by the rising individual.

For urban people who enjoy more and freer social space, the family is not the only collective to which the individual can relate. Rolandsen (Chapter 4) presents the individual experiences of a group of urban youths who try to create their individual biographies by helping others in the form of volunteerism, a new social phenomenon that emerged in the mid-1990s (Jankowiak 2004). At first glance, these young volunteers seem to make an effort to re-embed rather than to disembed. But the precondition for undergoing this new collective experience in the form of a semi-autonomous civil association is the disembedment of volunteerism from the work units which, as Rolandsen shows, formerly monopolized the organization of all social activities, including voluntary work. The socialist legacy of 'organized dependency' (Walder 1983), however, has not entirely disappeared. While consciously introducing an individual perspective, Rolandsen unpacks a multivocal, multilayered and multifunctional process of voluntary work chosen and participated in by white-collar urban youth yet organized by the local Youth Volunteers' Association, which is led and financially supported by the Chinese Communist Youth League. The emphasis on individual choice by both the organizers and the young volunteers distinguishes this new form of volunteerism from the organized and mandatory non-paid work during the period of high socialism. The motivations and purposes of doing volunteer work among the youth are highly individualistic, varying from efforts to expand one's social network, searching for a meaningful life in a different domain and self-training for leadership skills, to the more opportunistic concerns of obtaining party membership. Yet they all have to pursue their goals through the leadership and organization of the Volunteers' Association, which, in turn, has close links with the party–state apparatus. As a result, the young volunteers must attend study sessions, carry out party–state propaganda programmes in their volunteer work, and organize activities on special days designated by the party–state apparatus.

In Chapter 5, Anne Wedell-Wedellsborg sets out to examine how the individual is defined and developed in contemporary China. At a rather abstract level, most Chinese intellectuals agree that the emancipation of the human being (*rende jiefang* 人的解放) constitutes one of the most important achievements of the reform era since the late 1970s. Fewer attempts have been made, however, to explore and specify the traits and nature of the liberated human being. Is it the individual, the humanistic self, the role-playing person, or a generic substitute of the plural notion of the people? Wedell-Wedellsborg notes that a major trend in Chinese literature during the last three decades has been the reflection and construction of the individual under conditions of modernity.

Unlike most authors in this book, Wedell-Wedellsborg does not adopt the individualization framework of Beck and Beck-Gernsheim, which emphasizes certain features of second or late modernity. Instead, she examines the Chinese literary individual in light of a modernist framework and builds her arguments on the dual model of personhood. Citing the work of Steven Lukes (1985), Wedell-Wedellsborg aims to identify the rising Chinese individual. Is this an autonomous, self-directing, independent agent who relates to others as no less autonomous agents, or a relational person whose self-identity is mostly defined by the inherited social framework and social positions the person has acquired or achieved? It should be noted that the cultural construction of the person has long been a central concern in anthropology, and Marcel Mauss has made the distinction between the indivisible individual in the modern West and the relational person in most non-Western societies, in an effort to trace the evolutionary development of personhood in human societies (see Mauss 1985). Despite its essentialist shortcomings, this model may still provide a counter-balance to the current Euro-American theories of the individual, such as those of liberalism, neo-liberalism, and the individualization thesis of second modernity.

According to Wedell-Wedellsborg, literary work in the 1980s is pre-occupied with the (re)establishment of the individual within the framework of the Chinese nation/state and history, asserting the individual by way of social roles, long-held virtues, and goals with historical significance. In the 1990s, the trend turned toward the personal and private, and the individual is portrayed mainly as a free-running and lonely subject, full of desire and pain. Yet the inner strength of the materialistic and private individual can only derive from negotiation with the family and the network of friends, showing that the individual can hardly bear the burden of autonomy without making constant reference to the collective. The impact of globalization, argues Wedell-Wedellsborg, may explain why since the late 1990s there has been the parallel development of two trends: an increasing focus on individual orientation in the private sphere along with renewed concern with the Chinese nation and culture.

In the end, Wedell-Wedellsborg finds that there has always been an emphasis on the link – be it negative or positive – between the individual and the collectivity or social group. As a result, the truly autonomous and independent individual as an indivisible entity has yet to emerge in contemporary Chinese literature. Yet, the literary individual is on the move and thus different from the traditional role-binding person. As an example of this on-the-move individual, Wedell-Wedellsborg pinpoints the type of ideal individual promoted in *Wolf Totem*, an extremely popular novel published in 2004, which was quickly dubbed as the 'way of the wolf' (*langdao* 狼道) and widely celebrated in China.

According to this way of the wolf, the ideal individual is both a self-reliant and proactive person and also a member of her/his group, and is self-disciplined and beholden to authority. Wedell-Wedellsborg notes that interactions within the pack of wolves represent an ideal relationship between individual and group. 'Each member is independent, wild and free at the same time as loyal to its pack and willing to be sacrificed if needed for the survival of the group. It is a strictly hierarchical formation with a strong and wise leader, whose authority is unquestioned.'

This way of the wolf, or the disciplined individuality promoted by the author Jiang Rong and widely cheered by the Chinese media and public alike, is hardly a new idea; actually, to a great extent it recycles the early discourse and understanding of Western individualism among the Chinese elite at the beginning of the twentieth century, as shown in Svarverud's chapter in this book.

The individual contested in discourse and practice

Focusing on the work of Liang Qichao, the most important enlightenment figure in modern China, Svarverud (Chapter 6) argues that the altruistic individualism in the second modernity, another important element in the individualization thesis of Beck and Beck-Gernsheim, in some respects was long promoted by Chinese intellectuals in the context of the first modernity, because the autonomous individual in Chinese discourse is always defined in relation to the society or the nation. Particularly noteworthy is Svarverud's analysis of Liang Qichao's changing views about individual freedom. In a number of essays published in 1899, Liang regarded unfettered freedom as the key to survival in the Darwinian sense, and such a notion of freedom applied to any entity – be it the individual, group, or society in general. Three years later, Liang began to interpret individual freedom as the limited liberty enjoyed by citizens, with the purpose of achieving this liberty being to enable the individual to contribute to the benefits of the collective, particularly the survival and strengthening of the Chinese nation. After visiting the United States and witnessing the factionalism among Chinese groups there, Liang decided that excessive individual freedom was harmful to the interest of the nation and he thus became a strong critic of individualism.

Regardless of his different interpretations of the notion of individual freedom, Liang always assessed the value of individual freedom in accordance with its contribution to the group interest. Even at the early stages when he believed in the importance of freedom for individual survival, the ultimate goal of individual survival was still the national interest, namely, the survival of the Chinese race (*zhongde shengcun* 种的生存). Liang stated this most clearly in a passage quoted by Svarverud: 'Collective freedom is the accumulation of individual freedom. The individual may not leave the collective and exist on his own, and if the collective is not able to protect its freedom then there will be other collectives coming from the outside to infringe on, suppress and seize this collective. And then, what about the freedom of the individual?' It is in the same logic that, argues Svarverud, Liang interpreted the notion of autonomy as *zizhi* (自治 self-discipline), regarding it as the most important quality of the modern individual.

It should be noted that when Liang Qichao made these statements about individual freedom and autonomy China was facing a serious challenge from the Western powers and being forced to search for new ways to defend its survival; otherwise, it would become another victim of colonialism. However, in an entirely different context, Mao Zedong, the leader of the Communist victory in China, also emphasized the importance of disciplining the individual for the interest of the collective, as Klaus Mühlhahn quotes at the beginning of his chapter: 'We must affirm anew the discipline of the Party, namely: (1) the individual is subordinate to the organization; (2) the minority is subordinate to the majority; (3) the lower level is subordinate to the higher level; and (4) the entire membership is subordinate to the Central Committee. Whoever violates these articles of discipline disrupts Party unity' (Mao 1968, quoted in Mühlhahn's chapter).

To juxtapose Liang's interpretation of liberty and autonomy with Mao's emphasis on party discipline (also taking into consideration the above-mentioned wolf-like individuality in Jiang Rong's novel), what do we find in common? First, the value of the individual – as free, disciplined, or wild – is defined by the individual's contribution to a given group; consequently, the identity of the individual is constructed in a hierarchical relationship to a group. The nature and boundary of the given group may vary greatly in different contexts, ranging from the family to the nation-state, but the relationship between the individual and the group remains the same. Throughout the twentieth century, this relationship between the individual and the group is often elaborated by Chinese intellectuals as the relationship between the small self (*xiaowo* 小我) and big self (*dawo* 大我), and the value of the small self is defined in relation to the big self (see Liu 1995). This discourse on small self versus big self warrants a separate study in its own right; suffice to say that the Chinese understanding of the self in this discourse is mostly defined by the utilitarian functions and material interests of the individual and the group, instead of by ontological or existential terms. (It would not make much sense for an ontological self to be split into two parts – one small and one big.)

Moreover, through an analysis of Liang's changing views, Svarverud also reveals that Liang's understanding, acceptance, or rejection of Western thoughts are all driven by the pragmatic concern of how to strengthen the nation and restore China's lost glory on the world stage. From such a pragmatic perspective, the standard of judging the value of any thought (including individualism) is its effect, usage and practical power. In other words, efficacy is the ultimate standard by which to evaluate the imported ideas and thoughts. In this connection, Liang Qichao is by no means alone; most Chinese intellectuals follow the same path to deal with Western thoughts and theories.[4] The time-compressed nature of modernization has made the testing time of Western thought increasingly short, allowing almost no room for Chinese intellectuals to truly understand notions like individual autonomy, individual rights, or freedom. The result is what I call the 'flipping fate' of individualism in modern Chinese discourse (Yan 2005): that is, these notions have been alternately called upon to save the nation or have been condemned for the same purpose.

Shortly after Liang Qichao's interpretation of the self-disciplined individual whose freedom must yield to the interest of the nation-state, a number of Chinese intellectuals in the 1910s began to place the individual in opposition to the state and other collectivities. For them, the most important thing was the self-realization of the individual; the state, society, community and family should all work to provide the conditions for the development of the individual. This new, positive image of individualism contributed to the May Fourth New Cultural Movement in 1917, during which the liberation of the self and humanistic literature were central issues. But then the tide began to turn rapidly. Starting from 1920, leftist theories began to criticize individualism as a negative, passive and destructive value to the society. For example, in 1922, Chen Duxiu, one of the most famous advocates of individualism during the May Fourth Movement made a 180-degree turn, denouncing individualism as a socially irresponsible, nihilist idea, and these views became quite influential (see Liu 1995).

The Chinese Communist Party naturally viewed Western individualism as the ideological enemy of socialist collectivism. After repeated propaganda and political campaigns sponsored by the party from the 1920s to the 1970s, individualism was thoroughly demonized as a corrupt, irresponsible and antisocial value of the dying capitalist culture, which was characterized by selfishness, lack of concern for others, aversion to group discipline and runaway hedonism. This evil image of individualism was suddenly turned on its head during the post-Mao reform era of the 1980s, because it was rediscovered to be one of the engines of modernization in the West, stimulating individual incentives and economic growth. Yet, there has been no serious effort by Chinese intellectuals to explore what individualism actually means and how it works in Western culture, thus the earlier understanding of individualism remains unchanged in China today. Individualism is still regarded as a selfish, utilitarian and hedonistic morality that places self-interest above that of the group or other people. The only change is that the previous denouncement and critique of these traits of individualism have now been replaced by outright praise and admiration (Wang 2002).

The Chinese understanding of individualism, in my opinion, is incomplete, to say the least, because of the original instrumental purpose of introducing individualism along with other Western thoughts to strengthen the nation and to build China into a modern nation-state. Defined as an autonomous, self-directing, independent agent who relates to others as no less autonomous agents, such an individual did not exist on the horizon of the reform-minded Chinese elite at the beginning of the last century, as the Liang Qichao case shows, and it remained a bourgeois subject to be condemned and rejected in the Marxist-Leninist-Maoist discourse of post-1949 China. It is no wonder that Wedell-Wedellsborg cannot locate the true individual in Chinese literature, and it is also understandable why in social practices during the post-Mao reform era, the individual appears to be quite independent in some respects of social practice but remains dependent in the moral universe of values, beliefs and self-identity (see also chapters by Hansen and Pang; and Li), a particular yet important feature of the rising individual in contemporary China, which I refer to as the rise of the incomplete and uncivil individual (Yan 2003).

Unlike Wedell-Wedellsborg, who reveals the lack of true autonomy of the individual in Chinese literature, Mühlhahn (Chapter 7) examines the individual from a legal perspective and quite convincingly demonstrates the absence of social-cultural-political recognition of individual autonomy in Chinese law. Based on liberal notions of legality that maintain that all rights and duties must originate from the individual and that the encounter between the individual and the state is the most intimate and intricate in criminal justice practice, Mühlhahn identifies two basic models in criminal law systems. The crime control model emphasizes the role of law to repress individual violations for the sake of maintaining social order, and the due process model focuses on the containment of state power for the sake of protecting the inalienable rights of individual citizens. In other words, the key difference is the presence or absence of the notion of inalienable individual rights in the context of the individual–state (or any powerful group) relationship.

Taking a closer look at the criminal law systems of late imperial, Republican and Maoist China, Mühlhahn concludes that, although the importance of the individual in criminal justice has been emphasized for various reasons, none of the three systems developed a concept of individual rights that could shield the individual from excesses in the use of state power. The basic reference point of traditional Chinese law is not the individual, but rather the collectivity. During the Republican period, although the traditional practice of imposing corporal punishment on the collectivity to which an individual offender belonged was replaced by a modern prison system that punished only the individual offender, the individual remained an object of concern for social order, not as a holder of inalienable rights. However, the individual approach during the Republican period was generally abandoned under the radical socialism of the Mao era when criminal law was used by the state to create a coherent and unified society in which individual interests were compelled to merge with the interests of the socialist state.

Mühlhahn's analysis of criminal justice and criminal law in China is most illuminating because, as a system of enforceable rules governing social relations and legislated by a political regime, the law is intrinsically connected to the dominant ideology. With respect to the notion of the individual, the absence of a legal notion of inalienable individual rights actually reflects how notions of the self and the individual are culturally constructed and politically enforced in social practice. Because of the absence of the notion of inalienable rights, the individual will not be able to obtain true autonomy. As a result, Western individualism has never been understood in China as an oppositional mode of thinking to emancipate the Chinese individual; instead, it was introduced and has been used as an instrument to save the nation and to build a strong nation-state, as noted in the chapters by Svarverud and Wedell-Wedellsborg.

From a historical perspective, Li Minghuan's study of a special group of farm workers from the Songping Farm in southeast China (Chapter 8) examines how individuals resist the imposed individualization process by reinventing a new collective identity. This case study is particularly noteworthy because it reveals not only the counter-movement to individualization but also the highly contested nature of the notion of the individual.

As returned overseas Chinese, most of these farm workers were former refugees in Southeast Asia in the 1960s. The state established a number of state-owned farms and recruited the returned overseas Chinese as non-agricultural employees, meaning they were given welfare benefits similar to those of urban workers, a privilege strongly coveted by the local villagers from whom the state took the land for the establishment of these farms. As the market-oriented reforms proceeded further and competition became more intense, the state decided to stop subsidizing the money-losing farms in the 1990s and then redistributed the land among the farm workers, turning them into self-employed and independent farmers. Stripped of all state-sponsored protection and welfare privileges, the farm workers were initially shocked, feeling like 'a baby suddenly losing her mother', but then they reacted in a different manner. Some of them seized various opportunities offered by the market and state and became quite successful private entrepreneurs, moving to the cities or leaving the country. Others appealed to the state for their lost privileges. Emphasizing their collective identity as patriotic overseas Chinese by remaking their history and cultural legacy, this group of farm workers effectively played the political card because the state had a huge vested interest in the power of the millions of overseas Chinese whose investment in China plays a decisive role in the economy. Ultimately, the group was able to exert sufficient pressure that the state changed some of its policies and re-conferred some of their privileges.

This case is the epitome of a much larger trend of forced disembedment from socialism in the name of reforming state-owned enterprises, resulting

in numerous such enterprises being closed down or sold to private entrepreneurs and millions of workers being laid off. Having been bought off
cheaply or completely losing the pensions, medical care and other benefits
that they had enjoyed under socialism, these laid-off workers, like the
returned overseas Chinese in Li's study, appealed to the state in various
ways, ranging from personal appeals to leaders to public protests on the
streets. Similarly, they also resorted to their previous collective identity,
namely, as a member of the proletarian class, to make the strong moral
claim that as the masters of socialist society and the primary force of the
revolution, they deserved much better treatment from the state.

What can we learn from Li's chapter? First, forced disembedment tends
to have serious negative consequences as it simply shifts the previous responsibilities of social institutions onto individuals who are unprepared
or unwilling to leave the protective umbrella of these institutions. These
individuals tend to belong to disadvantaged social groups. If choice-making
is one of the primary indicators of individualization, forced disembedment
practically deprives individuals in the disadvantaged groups of making a
choice. As a result, the individualization process creates both rising and
losing individuals, and the negative consequence of this dual effect is
particularly acute in China because the majority of Chinese individuals
are still fighting to improve their life chances rather than to diversify their
lifestyles. Losing in this context often means losing one's life chances.

Second, at least in the eyes of the losing individuals, the collective
identities of Maoist socialism remain the best way to pursue individual
interests vis-à-vis a state that is determined to cast them out from the
protective net of the socialist family, so to speak. It is highly questionable
that Chinese individuals uphold the core values of social collectivism, such
as the primacy of collective interests over those of individuals. Yet, when
needed, as in the case presented by Li, they can easily invoke the socialist
collective identity to pursue their individual interests without seeing the
contradictions between the two. In other words, while losing its previous
all-encompassing power, socialist collective identity can serve as a resource
to be exploited by individuals. Such an instrumental usage of collective
identity by no means belongs only to the older generations. Recent research
shows that Communist Party membership is highly desirable among many
ambitious Chinese youth, who make great efforts to join the party only for

the purpose of career advancement and social status enhancement (see Rolandsen's chapter in this volume).

Third, the Songping farm case points out that the relationships between individual identity and collective identity and between individual action and collective interest are often negotiated through the interactions between individuals and the representatives of the state. As Pieke (2004) suggests, the state is in nature a set of institutions, networks of agents and practices within society. Individuals may find different ways to engage state agents and agencies at different levels, and, in the Songping case, individuals achieved their goals by engaging the state through the discourse of socialist collective identity.

Conclusion

To summarize, the chapters in this book capture important characteristics of the rising Chinese individual in contemporary China and, based on detailed empirical findings, vividly reveal how the individual on the rise exercises agency in claiming and defending her/his rights against the constraints of the encompassing social categories, including the powerful state. The rise of the Chinese individual, however, does not necessarily reinforce the ideology of Western individualism in China. Individual rights are chiefly understood as earned privileges instead of inalienable rights given at birth (see the Liu Shuhong case that I examined in the section The Politics of a Temporary Residence Permit above), and individual identity remains to be defined in relation to a collectivity, albeit increasingly an individually chosen collectivity, such as the more democratized and privatized family. More importantly, the individual–state relationship remains the central axis in the changing structure of social relations, and societal forces have yet to grow sufficiently strong to form an alternative for the rising individual to re-embed herself. As shown in some of the chapters (see Hansen and Pang; Li; Rolandsen; and Wedell-Wedellsborg), the challenge of being uprooted and disconnected in the context of marketization will likely force the rising individual to seek protection and meaning in the existing collectivities, that is, either the family or the state (see also Pye 1996).

Therefore, viewed as a whole, this book presents conflicting portraits of the rising Chinese individual, with two interesting contrasts. First, the three chapters on the Chinese individual in discourse, representation and law inform us that the Chinese individual has yet to rise as a truly autonomous, independent and self-directing agent. This makes an interesting contrast with the findings in other chapters on contemporary social practices, which present the Chinese individual as able to exercise a great deal of agency and thus as indeed actively on the rise. How can we make sense of this disjunction between ideology and practice?

A clue to addressing this question is to take a closer look at the individualized practices. We can see that the pursuit of individual choice and personal freedom in most cases appears to be a discrete act, carefully avoiding politically sensitive areas of individual autonomy in relation to state power and inalienable rights in public life. For example, in her analysis of the most individualistic Chinese youth, such as Chun Shu, a high-school dropout-turned-young-writer and the cover girl for the February issue of *Asia Times* in 2004, Hannah Beech notes: 'Chun writes bluntly about her own life, but she stays away from the grander ideologies such as democracy, freedom and equality that have often motivated her alternative brethren in the West.' In an exchange with the reporter, Chun clearly explains her choice: 'Our concept of freedom is different from the West's. We want the physical freedom to travel where we want, work where we want, have the friends we want. But right now we can't be so concerned with spiritual freedom' (Beech 2004). In a similar vein, the self-disciplined individual described in the novel *Wolf Totem* (see the chapter by Wedell-Wedellsborg) reflects a similar choice made by the elite. The rational strategies chosen by the young volunteers in Quanzhou (Rolandsen's chapter) present another concrete example of the same cultural twist in the development of individuality.

The second contrast lies between the chapters on rural individuals (by Delman and Yin; Hansen and Pang; and Thøgersen and Ni) and those on urban individuals (Rolandsen; Wedell-Wedellsborg; Svarverud; and Li). One may intuitively assume that urban individuals would be more likely than their counterparts in the countryside to disembed themselves from the constraints of the existing social categories and to be more willing to take risks and responsibilities in exchange for personal freedom and opportunities. The chapters in this book, quite interestingly, present the opposite findings, namely that it is the urban individual who tends to resist the individualization trend by either defending her collective identity or by seeking the protection of the state. Such a contrast is intriguing if one takes into consideration that rural individuals are poorly educated and possess much less financial and social capital.

Recent research also shows that support for the elderly appears to be much less of a social problem in the cities than it is in the countryside, and more urban elderly tend to live with their adult children in stem families (see e.g. Ding 2003). A similar rural–urban difference is also reflected in the increasing number of public protests. In most cases, villagers claim their individual rights for farmland and other important means of production by resorting to the law and challenging local government (O'Brien and Li 2006). In contrast, urban workers who organize themselves to seek compensation for their lost jobs and benefits from state-owned enterprises often use the socialist ideology of workers as the masters of the new society to appeal to the party-state (Lee 2007). Only Sun Dawu, a self-made private entrepreneur from the countryside dared to openly challenge the local government and question the national policies of the party-state, and it was not accidental that he always identified himself as a peasant. Here, the more individualistic rural Chinese defy our received wisdom that the better-educated, well-informed and economically safer and stronger urbanities are more individualistic.

Why is the rural individual embracing individualization more than her urban counterpart? Perhaps a short answer here is that the prolonged rural–urban dual structure in Chinese socialism, which made rural residents second-class citizens and deprived them of most of the social welfare entitlements enjoyed by urban residents, effectively made Chinese villagers into a proletariat who, to borrow from Marx, have nothing to lose but their chains. Having gained little from their previous embedment in the socialist collectives, they have stronger motivations for disembedment. Because in the post-reform era by and large they remain outside the state-sponsored social welfare systems, they must rely on themselves for their own and their family's survival and well-being and can only blame themselves for failure in market competition. By contrast, urbanities were and remain protected by the state through social welfare programs, so they naturally have weaker motivations to disembed themselves from the existing social categories. The case presented in Li's chapter is quite illuminating in this connection. The returned overseas Chinese whom she studies live in the countryside and make a living by farming, and thus would generally be regarded as rural individuals. Yet, merely because they are classified as urban residents in the official household registration system, they distinguish themselves from other villagers in the area and strongly resist the trend of marketization and individualization, attempting various political strategies to maintain their status quo as members of the old collective state farm. In other words, the rising individual in rural China should be understood more as a self-protective reaction to systematic discrimination by state socialism than as a development inspired by ideas of autonomy and freedom. This may explain why the family remains a meaningful unit of the collective and the ultimate goal of the pursuit by the rising individual.

The conflicting images of the rising Chinese individual problematize the applicability of the individualization thesis in China. As Beck and Beck-Gernsheim clearly state, social democracy and the welfare state constitute the most important preconditions for the individualization process in Western Europe. To clarify the various misunderstandings about his theory, in a 2000 interview Ulrich Beck asserts: 'The capitalist market of instrumental relations under the conditions of the post-welfare state has produced something no one really imagined it would – an individualization which is infused with ideas of cultural democratization' (Beck and Beck-Gernsheim 2003: 205). Obviously, neither an internalized democracy nor a welfare state currently exists in China. Moreover, if the term 'second modernity' indicates, as Beck and Beck-Gernsheim maintain, the new era of post-democracy and a post-welfare state, the rising Chinese individuals examined in this book are still working to achieve goals that belong to the first modernity of Western Europe, such as comfortable material lives, secure employment, welfare benefits and freedom to travel, speak and engage in public activities (for more details on this argument, see the Conclusion chapter in Yan 2009).

Yet, Chinese individuals are also living in a post-modern environment where a fluid labour market, flexible employment, increasing personal risks and isolation, a culture of intimacy and self-expression, and a greater emphasis on individuality and self-reliance are created by the trend of globalization in the context of the political authoritarianism of the party-state. In other words, the Chinese case simultaneously demonstrates pre-modern, modern and post-modern conditions, and the rising Chinese individual must deal with all of them simultaneously. This multi-layered and multi-temporal mixture characterizes the complex process of the rise of the Chinese individual as presented in this book. More importantly, the Chinese state, like many other states in a market economy, has been playing an active role in supporting institutional changes that shift more responsibilities to the individual and promote social changes that favours individual choice and creativity, except for those that might challenge the state's monopoly of power. In this sense, one may argue that China is indeed undergoing a process of individualization on a uniquely Chinese path, and the individualization thesis in European social theories introduces a useful lens for observation and a powerful tool of analysis, providing that we keep in mind that the Chinese path toward individualization is different in a number of important ways, thus warranting more systematic study.

Notes

1   A good example in this connection is the rise and fall of Western attention to, enthusiasm for and support of the development of NGOs in China, as many newly established Chinese NGOs turned out to be sponsored by the government, earning them the nickname of GONGO, see e.g. Chan 2005. For an insightful discussion of civil society in China's past and present, see the articles in a special issue of *Modern China, vol. 19, no. 2.*

2   For an excellent overview of the individualization thesis, see Cosmo Howard's introduction essay to his 2007 edited volume. Howard made the distinction between individualization as a discursive field in which a number of theoretical frameworks competing with one another and the individualization thesis as one of the frameworks that aims to challenge the dominant neoliberalism model of individualization.

3   For a well-balanced account of rural and urban reforms from the late 1970s to the early 1990s, see White 1993.

4   Mao Zedong was perhaps the most successful because he not only utilized the effective tool – Marxism – but also remade it according to the practical needs of the Chinese Communist revolution.

Bibliography

Baker, Hugh (1979) *Chinese Family and Kinship.* New York: Columbia University Press.

Bauman, Zygmunt (2000) *Liquid Modernity*. Cambridge: Polity Press.
—— (2001) *The Individualized Society*. Cambridge: Polity Press.
Beck, Ulrich (1992) *Risk Society: Towards a New Modernity*. (Trans. Mark Ritter.) London: Sage.
Beck, Ulrich and Elisabeth Beck-Gernsheim (2003) *Individualization: Institutionalized Individualism and its Social and Political Consequences*. London: Sage.
Beech, Hannah (2004) 'China's new radicals'. *Asian Times*, 26.1.04.
Beijing zhengfu wang (北京政府网) [Beijing government official website] (2007) '暂住证的种类' Zanzhuzheng de zhonglei [The different types of temporary residence permit], 17.7.07, http://shzbj.beijing.cn/sxzjblyzs/sfz/zzz/n214035760.shtml. Accessed 6 May 2008.
Chan, Kin-Man (2005) 'The development of NGOs under a post-totalitarian regime: the case of China.' In Robert Weller (ed.), *Civil Life, Globalization, and Political Change in Asia: Organizing Between Family and State*. London: Routledge, pp. 20–41.
Ci, Jiwei (1994) *Dialectic of the Chinese Revolution: From Utopianism to Hedonism*. Stanford: Stanford University Press.
Croll, Elisabeth (2006) 'Conjuring goods, identities, and cultures'. In Kevin Latham, Stuart Thompson and Jakob Klein (eds.), *Consuming China: Approaches to Cultural Change in Contemporary China*. London: Routledge, pp. 22–41.
Ding Shijun (丁士军) (2003) 中国农村家庭养老问题分析 *Zhongguo nongcun jiating yanglao wenti fenxi* [An analysis of the elderly support problem in Chinese rural families]. Beijing: Zhongguo nongye chubanshe.
Economy, Elizabeth (2004) *The River Runs Black: the Environmental Challenge to China's Future*. Ithaca: Cornell University Press.
Elegant, Simon (2007) 'China's me generation: the new middle class is young, rich, and happy. Just don't mention politics'. *Time*, 5.11.07, pp. 47–51.
Fong, Vanessa (2004) *Only Hope: Coming of Age under China's One-Child Policy*. Stanford: Stanford University Press.
Giddens, Anthony (1991) *Modernity and Self-Identity: Self and Society in the Late Modern Age*. Cambridge: Polity Press.
Harvey, David (2005) *A Brief History of Neoliberalism*. Oxford: Oxford University Press.
Hooper, Beverley (2005) 'The consumer citizen in contemporary China' Working paper #12, Centre for East and South-East Asian Studies, Lund University, Sweden.
Howard, Cosmo (2007) 'Introducing individualization'. In Cosmo Howard (ed.), *Contested Individualization: Debates about Contemporary Personhood*. New York: Palgrave MacMillan, pp. 1–24.

Jankowiak, William (2004) 'Market reforms, nationalism and the expansion of urban China's moral horizon'. *Journal of Urban Anthropology*, vol. 33, no. 1–3, pp. 167–210.

Lee, Ching Kwan (2007) *Against the Law: Labour Protests in China's Rustbelt and Sunbelt*. Berkeley: University of California Press.

Li, Jing (2006) 'Steam own: charity China'. *China Business Weekly*, 21.8.06, pp. 10.

Linebaugh, K. and J. Spencer (2007) 'The revolution of chairman Li: China's richest man leads others to give, bucking nation's taboos'. *Wall Street Journal*, 2.11.07, W1.

Liu, Lydia H. (1995) *Translingual Practice: Literature, National Culture, and Translated Modernity – China, 1900–1937*. Stanford: Stanford University Press.

Liu Shuhong (刘书宏) (2008) '我对我持有的北京 C 类暂住证的声明' Wo dui wo chiyou de Beijing C-lei zanzhuzheng de shengming [A Statement on my Beijing Temporary Residence Permit], 2.4.08, http://liushuhong.blog.sohu.com/83552839.html. Accessed 6 May 2008.

Lukes, Steven (1985) 'Conclusion'. In Michael Carrithers, Steven Collins and Steven Lukes (eds.) *The Category of the Person*. Cambridge: Cambridge University Press, pp. 282–301.

Macfarlane, A. (1978) *The Origin of English Individualism: The Family, Property and Social Transition*. Cambridge: Cambridge University Press.

Macpherson, C. B. (1962) *The Political Theory of Possessive Individualism: Hobbes to Locke*. Oxford: Clarendon Press.

Mauss, Marcel (1985) [1938] 'A category of the human mind: the notion of person; the notion of self'. In Michael Carrithers, Steven Collins, and Steven Lukes (eds.), *The Category of the Person*. Cambridge: Cambridge University Press, pp. 1–25.

Naughton, Barry (2007) *The Chinese Economy: Transition and Growth*. Cambridge: MIT Press.

O'Brien, Kevin J. and Lianjiang Li (2006) *Rightful Resistance in Rural China*. Cambridge: Cambridge University Press.

Palmer, Michael (2006) 'The emergence of consumer rights: legal protection of the consumer in the PRC'. In Kevin Latham, Stuart Thompson and Jakob Klein (eds.), *Consuming China: Approaches to Cultural Change in Contemporary China*. London: Routledge, pp. 56–81.

Pei, Minxin (2006) *China's Trapped Transition: The Limits of Developmental Autocracy*. Cambridge: Harvard University Press.

Pieke, Frank (2004) 'Contours of an anthropology of the Chinese state: political structure, agency and economic development in rural China'. *Journal of Royal Anthropological Institute*, vol. 10, no. 3, pp. 517–538.

Pye, Lucian W. (1996) 'The state and the individual: an overview interpretation'. In Brian Hook (ed.), *The Individual and the State in China*. Oxford: Clarendon Press, pp. 16–42.

Thelle, Hatla (2004) *Better to Rely on Ourselves: Changing Social Rights in Urban China Since 1979*. Copenhagen: NIAS Press.

Walder, Andrew (1983) 'Organized dependency and cultures of authority in Chinese industry'. *Journal of Asian Studies*, vol. 43, no. 1, pp. 51–76.

Wang, Xiaoying (2002) 'The post-Communist personality: the spectre of China's capitalist market reforms'. *The China Journal*, vol. 47, pp. 1–17.

White, Gordon (1993) *Riding the Tiger: The Politics of Economic Reform in Post-Mao China*. Stanford: Stanford University Press.

Wonacott, Patrick (2004) 'Green groups bloom in China'. *Wall Street Journal*, 15.6.04, A13.

Yan, Yunxiang (2003) *Private Life under Socialism: Love, Intimacy, and Family Change in a Chinese Village, 1949–1999*. Stanford: Stanford University Press.

—— (2005) 'The Individual and Transformation of Bridewealth in Rural North China'. *Journal of the Royal Anthropological Institute*, vol. 11, no. 4, pp. 637–657.

—— (2009) *The Individualization of Chinese Society*. Oxford: Berg.

Zheng, Yongnian (2004) *Globalization and State Transformation in China*. Cambridge: Cambridge University Press.

Zhongguo renkou yu fazhan yanjiu zhongxin 中国人口与发展研究中心 [China Population and Development Research Center] (2001) '首都新型暂住证：要分ABC' Shoudu xinxeng zanzhuzheng: yaofen ABC [New types of temporary residence permit in the capital: A, B, C], 23.3.01, http://www.cpirc.org.cn/news/rkxw_gn_detail.asp?id=413. Accessed 6 May 2008.

Zhou, Kate (1996) *How the Farmers Changed China: The Power of the People*. Boulder: Westview Press.

1

Idealizing Individual Choice: Work, Love and Family in the Eyes of Young, Rural Chinese

Mette Halskov Hansen and Cuiming Pang

In one of the most inspiring recent ethnographies about family life and relations in rural China, Yunxiang Yan concluded that since the period of de-collectivization and the gradual introduction of a market economy, the high price paid for increased individual space and determination among younger people was a loss of civility and the growth of ego-centered consumerism (Yan 2003). Having gained insight into intriguing and complex relationships between parents and children, lovers and spouses over a long time span, Yan showed that the dismantling of state collectives and the collapse of socialist morals in the 1990s left young Chinese villagers in an ideological vacuum. With first Confucian and then communist structures of mutual obligations and responsibilities lying in ruins, the every-man-for-himself values of the market economy and globalized consumerism came to dominate family life and relationships among people.

The research presented in this chapter supports many of Yan's findings, but we emphasize two main results that serve to further nuance and add to the picture provided by Yan. One of them is the remarkable sense of personal responsibility expressed by the young people we studied. The other is a tendency towards a discursive emphasis of the importance of family alliances, while individual autonomy vis-à-vis the family was constantly under negotiation. This research contributes to our understanding of how a process of individualization, discussed by proponents of the 'individualization thesis' (such as Giddens 1991; Beck 1997; Beck and Willms 2004; Beck and Beck-Gernsheim 2003; Howard 2007; Bauman 2001), evolves in the Chinese context and influences people's behaviour and perceptions of self. In his theories of risk society and individualization, Ulrich Beck focuses for the most part on individualization in late forms of modernity ('second modernity').[1] In Beck's view, democracy and a welfare system are prerequisites for the emergence of a type of individualization during second modernity that may provide people with the means to break with existent dependencies, disembed from clear-cut social categories, and develop new kinds of voluntary collectivism and societal engagement (Beck and Beck-Gernsheim 2003).[2]

In China, changes in the legal, social and economic fields during the period of de-collectivization have had a particularly strong influence on the rate at which the process of individualization has occurred, as is also shown in other articles in this volume. Collective forms of production have been abolished, the individual has become responsible for finding work, laws have increasingly set the individual in focus, pensions and other forms of social security are directed towards the individual, and the media promote individual consumption. The rapid changes in family relations, the demands on the individual to establish a livelihood outside the village and support family members, and the high awareness of unequal lifestyles disseminated through the media have all contributed to people's subjective experiences of social risk, uncertainty and need to make choices. Choices regarding such areas as social engagement and collective activism are obviously not made freely. They are, as proponents of the individualization thesis acknowledge, shaped by the way the government exercises its control, the government's definition of the possible field of action and its governing techniques, and structures such as class and gender, all of which continue to play a significant role in the social production of people's lives (Henman 2007; Howard 2007; Furlong and Cartmel 2007).

In the case of China, one of the direct and explicit limitations on the exercise of choice and on experiments with the type of collective engagements which Beck and Beck-Gernsheim argue are characteristic of the 'second modernity', is the lack of legal, non-governmental forms of organizations which can provide villagers with real possibilities to participate actively in public life. This, Yan has argued, strengthens the negative social results of individualization in China:

> If there were autonomous societal organizations and if villagers were able
> to participate in public life, a more balanced individualism might have

developed, in which the individual obligations to the public and to other people could be emphasized as well. But just the opposite has happened.

(Yan 2003: 234)

This chapter builds on Yan's research by continuing with a discussion of how younger people born and socialized in rural families in China account for their own roles as individuals who relate to the family as a collective, to other collectives such as workplaces and Party organizations, and thereby to the very Party-state. We present our analysis of data concerning (1) young people's negotiations of 'free love' (*ziyou lianai* 自由恋爱) and 'freedom' (*ziyou* 自由) in relation to their families, (2) their concepts of individual responsibility, and (3) their views of themselves as individuals and family members in relation to both state and non-state organizations. We conclude the article with a discussion of how and why young people from rural areas do not simply resort to self-indulgence and a destructive loss of solidarity as a response to the process of individualization. They do in many ways experience disembedding from the family, which is one of the characteristics of an individualizing society, but at the same time they respond to the social and personal uncertainties and risks that accompany individualization by employing and engaging in a discourse on the family as the individual's main, and often only, collective unit of direct importance.

Fieldwork and the Biographical Approach

The fieldwork data presented and discussed in the following were mainly collected between 2004 and 2006 when we carried out longer semi-structured interviews in villages in Shaanxi and Fujian Provinces. Our subjects included 100 young people (most between the ages of 16 and 28), and 70 people belonging to the older generations. Interviews were supplemented by many other forms of conversations that took place while participating in and observing local activities, including work and social life in two factories, in small shops and workshops, agitated village meetings about the distribution of land, and one local election. In Shaanxi we stayed in a private home in an agricultural village where most of the young people had temporarily migrated out to find work. We carried out interviews in periods when many of the young people were gone, and during the New

Year Festival in 2005 when nearly all of them returned home. In Fujian we stayed for several periods in the private home of a previous village head, in a larger semi-industrialized area made up of several administrative villages. In this area we also lived for several weeks during two different periods in a dormitory of a local factory where many of our interviews were carried out with young workers who came from other places in Fujian and other provinces, to work as unskilled labourers.

People's biographical narratives, when collected in this way, are seldom consistent, linear or neatly organized accounts. They provide scattered glimpses into people's own analyses of experiences, their memories of episodes of special importance to them, opinions on certain topics, all mixed with daily observations. The data we analyze in this article consist for the most part of what people *told* us, which topics they preferred to talk about, and the words they chose to express their ideas, experiences and opinions. We cannot, and do not, claim to know too much about how ideals and perceptions of social practices actually reflected people's own actions. While we argue that 'the family' was discursively constructed as the main – and for many the only – relevant 'collective', we do not thereby imply that the young people who work away from home necessarily send money back to their families, or that they for instance take better care of their grandparents than others do.

We do argue, however, that by comparing and analyzing people's bio-graphical accounts and the ways in which they choose to engage in discussions about topics of importance to themselves, we gained insight into some important aspects of how young people in rural China today perceive their own roles as individuals in a society which increasingly forces the individual to make choices, and to respond to the immediate and increasing experience of risks related to uncertain livelihoods and rapidly changing relations in the family and village communities. By using the biographical approach, we learned quite a bit about young people's own interpretations of these experiences, and how they 'put together the pieces of life's jigsaw' (Furlong and Cartmel 2007: 7).

Although Paul Henman claims that 'The individualization literature has clearly demonstrated the ways in which individuals in contemporary society conceive of and act on themselves' (Henman 2007: 183), this does not hold true in many parts of the world, and certainly not in the Chinese contexts of rapid individualization and recent historical experiences of state collectivization. However, as also pointed out by Furlong and Cartmel, when employing a biographical interpretation, as we have in this chapter, one runs the risk of underplaying structure, and of taking people's own interpretations at face value (Furlong and Cartmel 2007: 7). While we obviously have attempted not to fall into this trap, we are aware that the material we present is first and foremost based on people's stories and self-interpretations, and that there may be a larger disjunction between subjective perceptions and objective conditions than we have managed to grasp.

Dilemmas of Individual Space, 'Free Love' and Family Commitments

During one of our interviews with a young man of 17, a text message from one of his two girlfriends ticked in. The man had just related how he had dropped out of his ninth school year, and that he was now trying to become a hairdresser. Getting serious about partnership was a bit too early at 17, he explained, 'you should wait till you have passed 20'. This was in accordance with his parents' views, as was the opinion that a good steady partner should not be one of those girls who 'spend a lot of money and go out to have fun all day'. The girlfriend who had sent the text message was in her second year of junior high school and only 15 years old. Nevertheless, according to our interviewee, the couple was now 'sincere' (*zhenxinde* 真心的), and he was able to make the choice between the two girls he had been dating for some time. He therefore also became quite excited when we translated the content of the message, which was written in the language of fashion – English – of which he did not understand a single word: 'I fall in love with you' [sic].

Like most of our other young interviewees, both male and female, this man genuinely enjoyed talking about the challenges and excitement of love and partnership, and he regarded the choice of partner as one of the major decisions in any person's life. There were girlfriends/boyfriends, and there were wives/husbands. They belonged to two different categories, and the criteria for choosing them were therefore also different. It was one thing to date for fun, but something else entirely to plan to find someone to marry. And while parents played a minor role in the first case, they became very important as advisers or even judges in the second. The concepts of 'talking about love' or dating (*tan lianai* 谈恋爱) and 'free love' (*ziyou lianai* 自由恋爱) were often brought up by our young interviewees, whether in the rural village of Shaanxi or in the more urbanized villages of Fujian. When talking about the ideals and practices of engaging in intimate relationships and finding marriage partners, about 40 per cent of our 100 young interviewees would spontaneously bring up the concept of 'freedom' (*ziyou* 自由), and often specifically in connection with the expression of free love. The young interviewees often insisted that the ideal of free love was a modern (*xiandaide* 现代的), and for them very important practice which their parents and grandparents did not necessarily understand, and had certainly not been able to live according to.

Based on fieldwork in 1986–1987 regarding marriage practices in rural North China, Myron L. Cohen found that free love in the Chinese context 'simply means that husband and wife became acquainted and romantically attached on their own, or at least apart from any actions by their families' (Cohen 2005: 87). Listening to isolated accounts by young people discussing the concept nearly 20 years later could easily give the impression that they were indeed also mostly concerned with choosing their own partners without having to consider parents, practicalities, economy, or other earthly matters. Love was a matter of destiny (*yuanfen* 缘分), we were often told. However, the social implications of free love in practice turned out to be more complex than this. Implicit in the notion are both wishes and hopes specifically connected to an idealization of the individual and individual choice, but in practice free love involves very pragmatic considerations involving the family, mainly parents and siblings, as a collective of decisive importance.

Within the small Shaanxi village we studied, the rapid changes in marriage practices were reflected in the experiences accounted for by people from different generations, and we were also able to witness negotiations among family members on this issue.[3] Teacher Yuan, for instance, was born in 1925, and when he was 9 years old his marriage was arranged by parents and a matchmaker. The couple met for the first time on their wedding day, when Yuan was 18 years old. 'I did not give this any special thought,' Yuan explained, 'this was just how it was and it was the same for everybody.' His neighbour, Mrs Jia, was born 45 years later in 1969, and her experience was characteristic of a large number of people both older and much younger than she. Mrs Jia was introduced to a man whom the family and the matchmaker found appropriate. They too did not know each other, but unlike the Yuan couple they were given the chance to meet briefly before the final decision of engagement was made. In 1989 when Mrs Jia was 20 years old the couple married. 'Were you nervous at the time?', we asked Mrs Jia, who was normally a very talkative woman. 'No!' 'Were you happy?' 'What was there to be happy about?!' (*gaoxing shenme* 高兴什么?!).

This did not mean that Mrs Jia was *un*happy in her marriage. On the contrary, during the weeks that we lived in her family, we saw that she was by and large satisfied with her husband and their relationship. However, she also realized that it was unlikely that her two daughters and one son would accept a similar form of semi-arranged marriage. She and many other adults in the village were aware that the younger generation, born from the 1980s on, emphasized so-called free love. Particularly those who left the villages to work in the cities would 'find somebody by themselves' (*ziji zhao* 自己找), and they would date several people before finally deciding to introduce one of them to their parents. As we observed in the village, the introduction to parents resulted in the parents acting as consultants, and sometimes intense negotiations with parents about the potential son- or daughter-in-law arose. This practice did not seem to raise any serious moral concerns or strong disapproval from the older generation. The right in principle to choose one's own partner was obviously much more accepted in this village in 2005 than in the village surveyed nearly 20 years earlier by Cohen. At that time, 'free love marriages' were regarded as being in conflict with family interests, and they generally raised a lot of talk and agitation among villagers (Cohen 2005: 87).

In 2005 'everybody talks about free love', as one our informants said, and as we also experienced during fieldwork. This reflects the changes, also described by Yan, in the power balance between the generations in stem families. Unlike in the traditional patriarchal family, it is now to a much larger extent the horizontal, conjugal ties that are at the centre of family relations (Yan 2003). In connection with this change we found that the notion of free love – understood as individual choice of partner through negotiation with parents – has become widely accepted as an ideal practice. It is even accepted – albeit sometimes as a necessary evil – by people who themselves had very different, but not necessarily bad, experiences of arranged or semi-arranged marriages.

It was the experiences of people above approximately 30 years of age to which the youngest interviewees compared their own ideal of free love and their role as individuals in the process of finding and eventually deciding upon a spouse. The final outcome of this process was determined by an undefined notion of 'destiny' combined with parents' advice, but up to this point it was the *individual*, not the family or the parents, who was the main actor in the process. Parents became increasingly important as thoughts moved towards the serious consideration of engaging in a lasting relationship. At this point, individual choice was in reality inseparable from family negotiations in the practice of the free love ideal. In this respect there were striking similarities among nearly all the groups of young people we interviewed, whether they had grown up in the northern village of Shaanxi, in the more industrialized villages of Fujian, or had come to factories in Fujian from throughout China to take up unskilled labour.

Gender differences were reflected in the fact that men tended to emphasize the ideal of free love even more strongly than women, who on the other hand often spoke more about their family responsibilities. Nevertheless, nearly everyone agreed that before deciding upon marriage they would ideally meet with several persons of the opposite sex, date them for a longer or shorter period of time depending on age, and then reach a final decision. A sense of panic of not being able to settle down and marry in 'due time' set in at around 22–24 years of age for women and 24–26 for men. And while it was widely acknowledged that one could have 'fun' (not necessarily meaning sex) dating different people, interviewees agreed that one would certainly end up using a set of relatively clear criteria before making the final decision of whom to actually marry. In the period when identifying a marriage partner was not yet considered truly urgent, the young people stressed their own individual role and right to engage in personal relationships. However, as soon as they started to consider marriage and talk about their considerations and criteria for choosing a partner, parents and often also siblings were brought onto the stage.[4]

People become 'wild at heart' (*xin yele* 心野了) when leaving the villages to take up work in factories in the South or in the larger cities, we were often told. 'We live our lives on our own and we have freedom', a group of young workers explained, and indeed several of them were engaged in romantic relationships of which their parents were not aware. Nevertheless, it was remarkable to hear and observe how important feelings and acts of obligations towards parents and siblings were among many of those who left the villages for work. It was not uncommon that siblings pooled their money to share the expenses for the education of one of their brothers or sisters, and although it was hardly possible to get completely reliable information about how wages were spent, nearly all interviewees claimed that they regularly sent money home to parents and siblings, or at least brought home money for New Year. This was confirmed in some instances by parents, but finding reliable information about issues of private economy proved to be almost impossible.

The young people's sense of obligation should not be mistaken for altruism. It was based on practical and realistic assessments of how to live a life with room for individual choices and the pursuit of individual interests, while at the same time ensuring that the family remained a stable source of security. The family was crucial as it was usually the sole source of social security for the individual in case of disease, the need for care, loss of property or unemployment, and it constituted a collective of indisputable social, emotional and psychological importance for the young people.

Traditionally the responsibility for taking care of parents was delegated to sons, while daughters married out of the family (Watson and Ebrey 1991). In our research material, we saw a clear tendency that many parents now rely to a large extent on their daughters' support, and daughters in general expressed a high degree of responsibility towards their parents. Very often both parents and daughters wanted to ensure that the daughter would marry a man who lived relatively near her own family. This was an especially important factor in the wealthier villages of Fujian when parents and daughters negotiated about possible and suitable husbands. With more parents in villages having daughters and no sons, interviewees also emphasized that it was becoming less of a stigma to take a son-in-law into the house.[5] Several families had already done so, and people in other villages rarely spoke negatively about this.

This structural change also meant that daughters were often under a lot of pressure to fulfil their filial duties. Older parents frequently mentioned to us that they actually felt more assured that daughters, rather than sons, would help them during old age, and those who only had sons sometimes expressed worry that daughters would in fact have proven more reliable caretakers than their own sons. There were also numerous examples in our data of how young women eventually gave up dating men from other provinces whom they had met at work, out of concern for their parents or to follow the will of their parents. However, daughters were rarely directly *forced* to give up such relationships. More often, a young woman would go through a long period of consideration and negotiation with her parents, and would reach the conclusion that everyone, including she herself, would be better off if she married another man. While conflicts in families over such issues were mentioned quite frequently, especially by neighbours and friends, but also by the implied parties themselves, it was nevertheless clear that most parents and young couples tried hard to reach a consensus for their preferred choices. Sometimes parents would tell us that in order to avoid escalating conflict they simply had to agree to what they thought was a bad choice of partner. Just as their children did, they expressed in various ways that their closest family made up a small collective which was so significant both for emotional and practical reasons that conflict over such an important issue as whom to marry should be avoided. Such perceptions were probably strengthened by the fact that in both of the areas we studied, divorce was still considered a near-disaster, a loss of face, dignity and opportunity, especially for women but also for men, who often had even greater difficulties finding a new partner in the home region due to the shortage of women.

Yan's study of families in rural North China pointed to a degeneration of social relations due to the rise of the individual which had negatively manifested itself in egoistic, consumption-obsessed behaviour among young villagers (Yan 2003: 234). Yan's examples of such behaviour are numerous, and in our material we also recognized similar cases of young people's self-centered behaviour and disregard for parents. At the same time, we were surprised to learn how strongly nearly all of our interviewees emphasized, directly or indirectly, in their accounts or actions, the importance of their family (not the traditional Chinese extended family, but mainly their parents, grandparents, and siblings) as their main collective – a collective the individual needed to cater to and to safeguard. This is not necessarily in contradiction to Yan's findings, but it adds another dimension. Many of the young people we interviewed told of how they experienced the demands and possibilities that the rapidly modernizing society offered in terms of jobs in ever-shifting places, encounters with people from very different areas of China, moving out of their parents' homes at an early age, sex before marriage, and patterns of consumption. While all these options and demands seemed to promote a strong degree of individualism and focus on individual choices, our data nevertheless show that many of the young people put special weight on the importance of close family ties in their own biographical narratives. Data concerning topics of conversation other than family and partners, for instance concerning work experiences, relations to friends and colleagues, and views on organizational life and political authority, suggested that the role of the family as a collective has changed, but that it remains strong, especially due to the lack of common welfare and alternative collective opportunities for these rural young people without education or secure jobs. As we show below, young people were highly individualistic in their perceptions of success and failure, but they were also very conscious of their own dependence on family support and on their need to nurture the family collective.

The Burden of Individual Responsibility

Among our 100 young interviewees, 22 were currently students or had studied beyond the compulsory nine years of junior secondary school. Nearly 80 per cent had nine years or fewer of schooling. The well-documented prestige and status connected to higher education in China was, not surprisingly, visible in the attitudes of the young people with whom we spoke. Among virtually all our interviewees, regardless of age, gender, education and place of origin, there was a strong perception that the young generation in rural China could be divided into two main groups: those who studied at the level of high school and beyond, or had a job based on such an education, versus those who left school after nine years or earlier and had to work as unskilled labourers, peasants, or remain unemployed. This dominant perception of education as the major criterion for how to define different groups of young people, and as a marker of success versus failure, is disseminated through the media as well as in the schools, and was also largely internalized by interviewees. Among those who had failed to continue school after nine years, or had dropped out earlier, it was common to describe this as an unfortunate event, not necessarily at the time when it happened but seen in the longer perspective of a personal working career and income. It was especially those in their 30s or older who looked back on their time in school with regrets of not having succeeded to continue to higher levels of education. Few, if any, of those above 30 years of age were proud of having chosen or been forced onto a path other than that of schooling, something which was hardly surprising considering the strong emphasis on formal education in Chinese society.

The same perception of a deep divide between those who have studied and those who left school to work was expressed by young people currently within the educational system. One 24-year-old female student from a rural village told us that she (unlike many other students we talked to) had in fact maintained contact with friends who had dropped out of school. She consciously avoided speaking about school with them, however, because this 'just put psychological pressure on them':

> I can put myself on their level, although I am not like them (. . .). They envy all of us who study, they feel that they do not share our language, and therefore they do not want to be with university students. Many students feel that they are more important than them, or maybe they express it without knowing it.

Not all of our interviewees without education were embarrassed about it. After all, they shared this experience with the majority of villagers, and several expressed a sense of pride about how and why they *themselves* chose to quit school and find work instead. Regardless of what really happened when people dropped out of school, we were surprised to observe the extent to which the majority of our young interviewees tended to take individual responsibility for both failure and success in work as well as education. While some would mention the bad economic situation in their families as a reason for their own individual lack of educational opportunities, there was a remarkable tendency among the young people to place responsibility almost entirely on their own shoulders. Some emphasized how the decision to quit school was entirely their own, and others blamed themselves for not having worked hard enough to make it possible to continue through the educational system. In either case, the main responsibility was first and foremost attached to the individual rather than to other legitimate external factors, such as the lack of proper schools, costly education, fierce competition, parents lacking the abilities to help their children with homework, long distance to school, to name a few. 'In love you rely on destiny, in work on your own efforts', one young man concluded mainly about himself, but many of our other interviewees would probably have agreed.

Nearly 80 per cent of our young interviewees were working in factories, shops or agriculture, or they were temporarily without work. In our interviews and conversations with them, the most common topics were therefore those directly related to their working lives. 'Why do you work?' and 'What is important when looking for a job?' were questions we tried to raise in interviews, initially with the feeling of asking very stupid questions to which the answers might be so self-evident that respondents would find them meaningless. However, it turned out that many young people had a variety of opinions on the topic of what working life might, and ideally should, provide for them as individuals and for their family. The answers went far beyond the simple issue of having to make money for a living. From our observations in the factory where we spent time talking to people while they were at work and when they were resting in their dormitories or outside, it was also clear that working life often created the very situations where friendship and partnership were developed, where people amused themselves, and where new ideas and aspirations for how to live were formed.[6]

'Freedom' was certainly not what came to our minds first when we started spending our days with female workers who worked up to 12 hours a day in a factory, enduring a terrible chemical stench, and ruining the skin on their hands making small packages of incense sticks. But the concept of freedom was nevertheless often brought up by interviewees when talking about work. The longing for 'freedom' was sometimes used to explain either why interviewees dropped out of school to work, or to account for a certain job or a certain work place. The incense factory, for instance, was dirty, of low prestige, and had low wages, but it was described by many as having the great advantage of allowing workers to come and go freely, and to work when they wanted to (because all wages were calculated on the basis of production).

Notions such as freedom, independence (*duli* 独立) and personal development (*geren fazhan* 个人发展) were all used to express variations on the importance of being able to *move* – move away from and back to family, move from the village to a city, move from the familiar to the unknown, and back. It was especially the youngest interviewees (with little work experience and not yet engaged or married) who emphasized notions of freedom and the importance of their own personal choices. They often moved from one place to another:

> I did not want to continue school. It was not my parents who did not want me to study. I told them that this was the road I chose to walk and there was nothing to be done about it. I have never regretted it. I had always envied those who went out to work and came back with money. I felt that by leaving, they had some freedom (*ziyou yidian* 自由一点).
>
> (18-year-old factory worker)

This woman expressed a commonly encountered perception of freedom, namely something which allows you to leave the village, leave your parents, find work wherever you see the opportunity, and make your own money. Others of her age would agree that 'freedom' was to 'come and go' (*paolai paoqu* 跑来跑去) as you pleased, or that 'freedom is when you have a job where you can simply leave if something more important turns up', as a 17-year-old male worker explained.

The youngest people had the greatest tendency to idealize choice, even when it was recognized that the choice resulted in long hours of tedious and physically hard, sometimes even hazardous, work.[7] In clandestine Internet cafés[8] in villages and small towns in Fujian we often met young male workers who were travelling around the country from factory to factory, leaving for a new place whenever they got tired of the work and location. They explained that they enjoyed this kind of 'freedom' and the opportunity to see the country, although the work in itself was uninteresting, sometimes dangerous, and wages far too low. Both men and women in this category explained that they experienced a sense of freedom because they could engage with new friends in circumstances similar to their own, have romantic relations without their parents knowing about it, make their own money, and if they got too fed up with work they could move on to a new place.

This perception of freedom may also help to explain the deep mistrust many of them had for signing labour contracts: 'A contract is a way of binding workers. It is just a system to the advantage of the enterprise. If you sign a contract they will "fry you till you drop"; one young man explained. While we assumed that a labour contract would be a kind of insurance for workers, guaranteeing stable and predictable working conditions, our interviewees rejected this assumption almost without exception, and claimed that the employer was in full control once the contract was signed. By emphasizing their 'freedom to come and go' workers who were bound to carry out manual labour for long hours discursively manifested themselves as subjects in power, rather than as the mere objects of misfortune, deprived of pride, opportunity and dignity – an image that dominates the official, as well as popular, discourse on migrant labourers and school drop-outs.

While the youngest workers (15 to 19 years old) often emphasized personal choice and freedom as important aspects of their current lives as workers away from home, workers above the age of 20 seemed much more conscious of the restraints and pressures related to their work situation. These idealized versions of personal choice and the possibilities to 'tour the country' paled considerably with experience. From around the age of 20, the majority started to express a strong sense of worry for their future:

> I try out different kinds of work looking for something that suits me. It is anyway all more or less the same. There is no future in it. It is different for the people from universities who look for jobs. They have a future. They find jobs which suit them. Compared to them we are illiterates.
> (Male worker in his early 20s)

In their 20s, most of our interviewees had realized that their job prospects would probably not change considerably in the future, that their wages (to the extent that they were paid out at all) were hardly enough to save money for building a house, sending children to school, keeping a reserve in case of illness, or supporting aging parents with no form of health insurance or pension, not to mention providing for themselves or their closest family members in case of illness. At the same time, they had started to seriously consider establishing their own families. Those who had remained within the educational system were somewhat less worried about the future for themselves and their families, but in general everyone, regardless of education, gave voice to feelings of obligation and responsibility towards one major collective, namely the closest family. In addition to how to choose an appropriate partner, there were three main topics young interviewees brought up which emphasized the importance of family and family obligation: whether or not to provide economic support for siblings and parents, where and how to find work, and what constitutes proper behaviour in relation to parents, children and siblings.

One of many examples of young people worrying about family relations was a young man who was only 17 years when we got to know him. He was a worker in the incense factory, and with his reddish-dyed, longish hair and fashionable clothes, he looked like most of the other young men from the neighbouring Fujian villages who had only nine years of schooling and were often hanging around in the streets. He was popular with the girls, and very self-conscious in his first meetings with us. At first he also seemed very egocentric, and concerned only about his own future and career. However, he was also an only child, and after some time it became clear that he had a deep concern for his parents and the state of his family. When he talked about his own personal hopes and aspirations, he always emphasized the desire to leave the village and find better work elsewhere, but he could not help starting to cry when speaking of the difficulties this would create for his parents and grandparents. His parents often fought, and he wanted peace (*hemu* 和睦) in his family even more than he wanted money. Like many other of our young interviewees, this man felt personally responsible for ensuring peace and a basic standard of living for his elders, and he felt that eventual failure or success was first and foremost determined by his own efforts and abilities.

Many other interviewees stressed that since they had missed out on the opportunity to get an education, the least they could do was to support their siblings' schooling. One 26-year-old unmarried female worker explained:

> A daughter is responsible for giving money to her family. The individual is just one part of a family, and you have to make yourself useful. My younger brother is a good student, and this year I bought him a Western suit for 1,000 Yuan. For myself, I never buy anything that costs more than 100 Yuan. He is now doing his 'practice period', and I said that we had to get him something good, otherwise he would not make a good impression on people. My aunt said that spending all my money on my little brother will get me into trouble when I have to marry and leave the family. I do not think that is a problem. Maybe our family will be a little

bit poorer, but the most important thing is that the family is harmonious. I am an older sister, I have this responsibility. I have strong ideas about family.

Our material contains numerous other examples of how young people argued that since one of their siblings performed better than they themselves did in school, they should help support his or her education, and we have examples where this also happened in practice. Most would also argue that since their parents had brought them up, they were responsible for taking care of their parents during old age. Hardly any of them expected the state to take any responsibility for the old, and they took it for granted that they would have to support the elderly. For many, supporting their siblings or taking care of their parents during old age was the 'custom' (*xiguan* 习惯), something expected from them and not to be further explained or discussed, and many interviewees, regardless of age, were concerned with the fact that other people might 'talk about them' if they did not behave properly as family members.

The degree to which the family constituted the most (or even only) significant collective for people was obviously contextual, and differed among individuals as well as between people in different stages of life. The family was also by no means the only collective institution or unit that people spoke of or engaged in. However, as we return to in the following, we found that even in situations where people decided to act collectively as villagers, it was first and foremost because family interests were at stake.

Collective Engagement and Family Interests

One of the issues we wanted to study during our periods of fieldwork was how young rural people perceived the Chinese Communist Party (CCP), its youth associations and different forms of societal collectives. We were interested in learning with which organizations they were familiar, and which they found relevant for themselves. Were there collective units or activities of any kind, permanent or temporary, in which young people with a rural background, no education, and low-paid jobs if any, could and would engage?

The unequivocal perception of the CCP and its youth organizations among our young interviewees (with or without a longer education) was that membership was completely irrelevant unless you had a higher education or were employed in a state unit. Also, when discussing this topic, those interviewees who were the most interested in it tended to emphasize personal *choice*, rather than the obvious, strong structural barriers preventing their own enrolment. It was not so surprising that all the students in higher education planned to enrol in the Party. The Party was explicitly trying to recruit them, and they knew that there were advantages connected to membership. However, in spite of the CCP's lack of interest in including uneducated peasants and migrant workers into the Party ranks, some of our interviewees in this category also emphasized personal choice when talking about membership.

The views on the role of the Party were clearly related to differences in status, education and age. Most of our interviewees above the age of 50 viewed the Party in its historical context as the vanguard of a popular movement to promote equality and ensure land for the peasants. Many displayed a high esteem for Mao Zedong's leadership, regardless of their negative memories of the Cultural Revolution, and they were also generally in favour of Hu Jintao and Wen Jiabao whom they first and foremost praised for abolishing the unpopular taxes for peasants. The central government as represented by the president and prime minister was 'good', while local representatives of the state were mostly 'corrupt'. Our younger interviewees had less to say on the topic of Party membership and Party associations. Most would simply say that they 'were not interested' (*bu gan xingqu* 不感兴趣), or they would argue that their opinion on this did not matter. Others had a more pragmatic attitude, and explained that the Party as a collective had nothing to offer them – it was the efforts of the individual which counted:

> I would certainly not join the youth organization even if I could. After all, they [the CCP] have never done anything to help me. My family is poor and they have not helped us. Why would I rely on them? It is much better to rely on yourself!
>
> (23-year-old immigrant worker from Guangzhou)

This same attitude was reflected in many young people's scepticism towards village cadres and Party secretaries, and sometimes village collectives in general:

I do not care about village affairs. I care about my own affairs. (. . .).
What would it help to join the Party? Those with jobs can advance if
they are Party members. Even if we peasants join the Party, we remain
peasants! (28-year-old female shop attendant)

Our data contain numerous stories illustrating how our young interviewees, to a much larger extent than their parents, lack trust in the Party as a
collective where peasants, migrant workers and people without education
can bring their concerns to the forefront and find help. Their first concern
was whether or not the Party's local institutions could give them, or their
family, any advantages or support, and nearly all of them concluded that
they could not. Party membership was only seen as being advantageous
for university students, especially job-wise. The vast majority of peasants
and workers considered membership to be something for the educated,
for the local officials, or for the older activists in their villages, but it was
not relevant for themselves. They probably realized that the Party would
not really want them as members, but they nevertheless argued that they
personally lacked interest in membership.

Village elections were of only slightly more interest to young people than
Party politics and membership. Many of our 100 younger interviewees
regarded village elections as uninteresting (*mei you yisi* 没有意思), but here
there were clear differences between people in Fujian and Shaanxi, which
again were related to whether or not elections were seen as being advantageous to individuals and their families. In the Shaanxi village, most
young people had left for other parts of the country to work, and the
village was poor. Land was not a big issue because no one was interested
in buying it for industrializing purposes, and among the younger people
no one paid attention to the elections. In the Fujian village, on the other
hand, most young people had stayed in the province and were either
students, workers in factories and shops nearby, or unemployed. The
village was only a few hours from Xiamen, and much of the arable land
had been bought up for industrializing purposes. Practically all local
families took part in the elections and attended numerous meetings
where people gathered to discuss, even argue, with the officials who were
held responsible for selling out the land too cheaply years ago, and for
having benefited personally from the sale. People were paid 15 Yuan each

for their participation in each meeting and for voting, and this obviously added to people's interest in joining in.

In the Fujian villages, unlike the Shaanxi village, there were a few alternative organizations and collectives in which people could engage. The reactivated lineage organizations, and the officially established Old People's Association (OPA, *Laonianren Xiehui* 老年人协会) attracted members, especially among retirees with previous connections to the Party and government (Hansen 2008). None of these organizations had engaged the interest of the young people we interviewed, and even the lineage organizations were for the most part regarded as being of interest only to older people. The result of the government's repression of truly autonomous societal organizations, Yan has argued, is that young villagers come to disregard the need to work for larger collective interests, and instead indulge in a destructive type of individualism built on growing demands for consumption (Yan 2003: 234). Our research supports some of Yan's findings, but also suggests that this individualism remains to a large extent inseparable from the individual's identification with his or her family. Therefore, it was especially in cases where the interests of the family collective – not merely the individual – were threatened, that people spontaneously became involved in collective actions beyond the family.

In the Shaanxi village, this happened when the provincial government decided that all graveyards were to be transformed into fields, and people were forced to follow the rules of cremation. Using large sections of land for family graveyards was considered a waste of arable fields, and in February 2004 the county government enforced the levelling of graveyards in the villages. Villagers responded directly to this threat against family traditions by organizing a collective rebuilding of the all the graveyards during the Qingming festival in April, when many young people came home. In some of the villages in Fujian, on the other hand, many young people joined their families in expressing strong dissatisfaction with local officials selling the sections of land that were collectively owned. A conflict regarding this issue had been going on for years, and it intensified in connection with the unauthorized local 'redistribution of land' in 2003. Large groups of villagers – old and young – gathered during village meetings where land was supposed to be redistributed based on the current size and composition of families. Intense disputes erupted because villagers had been lured into selling land very cheaply, while large sums of money had disappeared, seemingly into the pockets of previous officials. The current officials had had nothing to do with the sale, but they were nevertheless held responsible, and villagers directed all their discontent towards these representatives of local government who were considered to be as corrupt as their predecessors. Local young people whom we interviewed and watched taking part in meetings were outraged; they expressed a very high degree of distrust in the officials' motives. They normally did not care much about the village as a community and they did not support attempts to collect money for common public goods in the village, but in this case issues of family property were at stake, and this engaged everyone.

Conclusion

We have assumed in this article that China is undergoing a process of individualization whereby more and more of society's demands, controls and constraints are directed towards and imposed on the individual, whereby people tend to disembed from family and village communities, and whereby they are tied into new networks through the labour market, the legal system and social welfare, which is also for the most part designed for individuals. Most of the scholars who develop or employ the 'individualization thesis' do so in the context of European or North American societies. They refer to late developments of modernity ('second modernity', 'reflexive modernity', or 'high modernity') where democracy, welfare systems and wide access to education are both characteristics of and prerequisites for the development of the kind of new alliances and societal engagements that at least Beck and Beck-Gernsheim argue are positive results of individualization in second modernity. One of the decisive features of individualization processes, according to Beck and Beck-Gernsheim, is that they not only permit but demand contribution and choices by the individual (Beck and Beck-Gernsheim 2003: 4). The individualization thesis does not reject the continuing power of, for instance, gender and class to inform and direct individual life opportunities, nor does it claim that people become free to 're-create the world in increasingly diverse forms' (Furlong and Cartmel 2007: 5). Individualization, rather than being a precise definition of a certain type of society or stage of development, is presented as a 'designating trend' that calls for investigation into how it manifests itself in certain groups, milieus, or regions, and how people respond to it (Beck and Beck-Gernsheim 2003: 5).

Proponents of the individualization thesis also argue – and this is particularly relevant in our study of rural Chinese perceptions of the individual – that in highly individualized societies people increasingly come to regard failure and success, setbacks or progress, as individually determined, rather than as results of structures or situations beyond their own control. In a modernized society, characterized by the experience of risks, individual subjectivity becomes an important force. In their study of young people in Western individualized societies, Andy Furlong and Fred Cartmel argue that, in spite of the fact that young people's experiences continue to be shaped by class and gender, the wider range of choices available creates in them an impression that 'their own route is unique and that the risks they face are to be overcome as individuals rather than as members of a collectivity' (Furlong and Cartmel 2007: 9). In our study of one delimited aspect related to the individualization of Chinese society, namely young rural people's perceptions of self and family, two results came to the forefront: first, the degree to which the young people who came from often poor villages tended to take individual responsibility for what they saw as social failure, although they in reality did not have that many options or choices; and second, the way they emphasized their closest family as the only collective of importance to them, while at the same time arguing strongly for their own interests, rights and aspirations as individuals. Unlike their parents or grandparents, the young people had not experienced the collectivization period, and relationships within families were changing rapidly, partly due to the fact that most individuals – men or women – often had to seek work far away from home, and therefore also became involved in new relationships, and experienced life in cities.

The individualization of Chinese society has led to a range of new varieties of relationships between the generations, and they take very different forms in different areas, not merely following the increasingly artificial rural/urban divide. However, one of the general trends seems to be that old people can no longer take for granted that children or grandchildren will provide for them, nor would they necessarily want them to, had they any choice (see Thøgersen and Ni in this volume). Furthermore, neither village collectives nor the state have emerged as stable providers of social security for individuals in rural areas who fall ill, have no children to take care of them, or are disabled. There are also no autonomous societal organizations available to the majority of the rural population, through which they can legally and with an impact express their interests collectively. In a rapidly individualizing society and economy, this, according to Yan, has created an extreme form of individualism and an egoistic concern for personal interests and consumption among young rural people (Yan 2003).

In this chapter we have argued that individualism among the young people we studied – reflected in their life choices, behaviour and personal narratives of freedom, free love and independence – remains entangled with their perceptions of the family as a collective of indisputable economic, social and emotional importance. The individualism they exhibited was to a large extent indistinguishable from their concern with collective family interests. Each person needed to find an appropriate partner, but the process involved negotiations with family, and broader family interests were taken seriously into account. Much was done on both sides – parents and children – to avoid conflict, and young people were often willing to abandon a partner if the relationship could not fulfil the common interests of the family.

Collectives consisting of colleagues at work or friends, not to mention official collectives such as Party youth organizations or village communities, played on the other hand a very small role in the personal accounts of our interviewees. Again and again we were struck by the interviewees' expressions of concern, about their parents' opinions and support, about their siblings' opportunities for education or their own contribution with an income, and about their own wishes to find partners who were both desirable from the individual's point of view and appropriate from a broader family perspective. In conversations and interviews with young people, they often emphasized the sense of insecurity they experienced when facing necessary choices of where to work, what to do, how to save money, whether or not to send money home, how to find a partner, and on more general level how to perform as members of the socio-economic collective that their families still constituted. They were very explicit in their expectations as individuals, with dreams, hopes and aspirations to create meaningful lives for themselves and their families. They emphasized, often even idealized, the power of personal choice, and they tended to blame themselves, rather than the Party-state, the school, or their families, for failure to succeed, such as in achieving the education they all believed would have provided themselves and their families with more comfortable, secure and, not least, respected lives.

Notes

1 Matthew Kohrman, in an interesting article about smoking in urban China, is one of the few scholars who has employed Ulrich Beck's theory of risk society directly to a Chinese case, Kohrman 2004.

2 See also Howard 2007: 40.

3 A number of publications have described and analyzed changing marriage practices and changes in family law, for instance Croll 1981; Cohen 2005; Yan 2003; Davis and Harrell 1993.

4 Unlike some other rural areas, for instance in Zhejiang Province, it was very uncommon in the villages we studied that young people lived together and had children before marriage. It happened in a few instances when families could not afford an appropriate wedding ceremony, and in those cases people largely tried to keep it secret.

5 Couples with rural household registrations were allowed to have a second child if the first was a girl. Due to widespread use of unofficial adoption of girls to relatives or friends, mostly in other provinces, and the use of ultrasound to determine the gender of a foetus, there were in the Shaanxi village about one third more boys than girls. Only six of 150 households had only daughters and no sons, and out of 128 women of the official child bearing age (up to 49) there were only four who had two girls and had been sterilized. There were 12 who had only one girl, but none of these were sterilized, and would most likely have one or more children later.

6 See also Ngai 2005: 152–163.

7 The exploitation of migrant workers is not a topic in this article, but it has been thoroughly documented, for instance in Chan 2001; Unger and Chan 2004; and recently in a report from Amnesty International 2007.

8 During our fieldwork in 2004, villages in Fujian were still under the influence of the 2002 national crackdown on Internet cafés with fewer than 100 computers, and in the villages we studied access to Internet cafés was only possible by personal agreement and in secrecy during the evenings.

Bibliography

Amnesty International (March 2007) 'People's Republic of China. Internal migrants: discrimination and abuse. The human cost of an economic "miracle"', http://web.amnesty.org/library/index/engasa170082007. Accessed 8 May 2007.

Bauman, Zygmunt (2001) *The Individualized Society.* Cambridge: Polity.

Beck, Ulrich (1992) *Risk Society: Towards a New Modernity.* London: Sage.

—— (1997) *The Reinvention of Politics: Rethinking Modernity in the Global Social Order.* Cambridge: Polity.

—— (2002) *What is Globalization?* Cambridge: Polity.

Beck, Ulrich and Elisabeth Beck-Gernsheim (2003) *Individualization: Institutionalized Individualism and its Social and Political Consequences.* London: Sage.

Beck, Ulrich and J. Willms (2004) *Conversations with Ulrich Beck.* Cambridge: Polity.

Chan, Anita (2001) *China's Workers under Assault: the Exploitation of Labor in a Globalizing Economy.* Armonk: East Gate Books.

Cohen, Myron L. (2005) *Kinship, Contract, Community, and State: Anthropological Perspectives on China.* Stanford: Stanford University Press.

Croll, Elisabeth (1981) *The Politics of Marriage in Contemporary China.* Cambridge: Cambridge University Press.

Davis, Deborah and Stevan Harrell (1993) *Chinese Families in the Post-Mao Era.* Berkeley: University of California Press.

Furlong, Andy and Fred Cartmel (2007) *Young People and Social Change. New Perspectives.* Milton Keynes: Open University Press.

Giddens, Anthony (1991) *Modernity and Self-identity: Self and Society in the late Modern Age.* Cambridge: Polity.

Goldman, Merle (2005) *From Comrade to Citizen: The Struggle for Political Rights in China.* Cambridge: Harvard University Press.

Hansen, Mette Halskov (2008) 'Organising the old: senior authority and the political significance of a rural Chinese "NGO" '. *Modern Asian Studies*, vol. 42, no. 5, pp. 1057–1078.

Henman, Paul (2007) 'Governing individuality'. In Cosmo Howard (ed.), *Contested Individualization: Debates about Contemporary Personhood.* New York: Palgrave Macmillan.

Howard, Cosmo (2007) 'Three models of individualized biography'. In Cosmo Howard (ed.), *Contested Individualization: Debates about Contemporary Personhood.* New York: Palgrave Macmillan.

Kohrman, Matthew (2004) 'Should I quit? Tobacco, fraught identity, and the risks of governmentality in urban China'. In *Urban anthropology and studies of cultural systems and world economic development,* June, http://www.accessmylibrary.com/coms2/summary_0286-6603468_ITM. Accessed 26 February 2008.

Ngai, Pun (2005) *Made in China: Women Factory Workers in a Global Workplace.* Durham: Duke University Press.

O'Brien, Kevin J. and Li Lianjiang (2006) *Rightful Resistance in Rural China.* Cambridge: Cambridge University Press.

Unger, Jonathan and Anita Chan (2004) 'The internal politics of an urban Chinese work community: a case study of employee influence on decision-making at a state-owned factory'. *The China Journal,* no. 52, pp. 1–24.

Watson, Rubie S. and Patricia Buckley Ebrey (1991) *Marriage and Inequality in Chinese Society.* Berkeley: University of California Press.

Yan, Yunxiang (1999): 'Rural youth and youth culture in North China'. *Culture, Medicine and Psychiatry,* vol. 23, no.1, pp. 75–97.

—— (2003) *Private Life under Socialism: Love, Intimacy, and Family Change in a Chinese Village, 1949–1999.* Stanford: Stanford University Press.

2

He Is He and I Am I: Individual and Collective among China's Elderly

Stig Thøgersen and Ni Anru

Old women sitting on their small stools along a Chinese village street, keeping an eye on their grandchildren and chatting about the passers-by, may seem almost untouched by the dramatic changes that have swept through China over the last decades. However, China's rural elderly have been just as strongly affected by recent economic, social and mental trans-formations as other groups, and they acutely feel the tension that has emerged between the life patterns they had expected to follow and the new risks and possibilities presented by a more dynamic and individualized society.

This chapter discusses how the elderly react to the rapid transformation of their social environment and particularly to changes in intergenerational relations. Its first part focuses on their preferences and strategies in regard to the two most common types of living arrangements during old age: maintaining an independent household, or living with a son's family. That every elderly person now can and has to choose between these two options is an example of the 'disintegration of social forms' that Beck and Beck-Gernsheim (2003: 2) see as one of the two main aspects of individualization. Earlier generations of elderly perceived cohabitation with a son as the only natural arrangement, and people who deviated from this norm were looked upon with pity or suspicion by their fellow villagers. Our interviews in two Shandong villages indicate that this is no longer the case. Living alone is sometimes a forced choice, a way of coping with changing family relations, but it has become a generally accepted alternative, and many appreciate the freedom it gives them. This illustrates that China's rural elderly are not just victims of modernization, or steeped in tradition, but are able to accept changes in family relations and create new life patterns. Their problems are generated by the lack of social services in rural areas rather than by any culturally determined resistance to change on their part.

The second part of the chapter discusses strategies for re-embedding the elderly in rural society. Not only are the elderly themselves concerned about their future, but the aging of the population is also perceived as a serious problem by social scientists and policy-makers (Ikels 2006), and the problems faced by the rural elderly have become a symbol in the Chinese debate of a more general social anxiety and insecurity. One solution to the problem of how the rural elderly can express their collective interests, increase their social status, and live more satisfactory lives has been to establish Old People's Associations, and we shall look at some of these initiatives as examples of the difficulties involved in rural community building.

Old Age in Rural China

Over the last decades, old age care in the rural areas has been identified as a major problem in China's social development. The Chinese population is greying, and this is not least evident in the villages. Thanks to substantial progress in rural health care after 1949, life expectancy has been rapidly rising, and strict birth control policies keep the number of children low. Many young people migrate to the cities, either permanently or in temporary jobs, and are therefore unable to personally care for their parents. The rural elderly of the present generation normally have several children, but it will not be long before one- and two-child parents reach the age when they will need care. By the end of 2008, 160 million Chinese, or 12 per cent of the population, were over 60 (China Daily 2009), and a 2007 report from China National Committee on Ageing predicted that by 2020 the elderly population will have swollen to 248 million. The problem of who will support them is going to be massive. According to the report, there will be only two working people for every retiree in the years between 2030 and 2050, while the current ratio is 6:1 (Wu 2007).

There is little public care for the elderly in rural China, as opposed to the cities, where many people receive pensions and have some sort of health insurance.[1] Instead, children are legally obliged to take care of their parents. Childless elderly may receive support through the 'five guarantees' system, which secures their basic livelihood (food, housing, clothing, health care and burial), but this system is only geared to meet needs at the lowest subsistence level, it only functions in some places, and it is only for those who have no children. By 2008 only 4.6 million people nationwide benefited from the 'five guarantees' (China National 2008). Experiments with introducing old age insurance in rural areas have generally been unsuccessful (Li and Shan 2004), and by 2008 only three million farmers received pensions (China National 2008). The privatization of rural health care means that medical expenses for elderly parents are a heavy burden on many families, and the hospital bill of a grandmother often has to compete with education fees for a son or daughter when the family plans its budget. Wealthy villages may provide old age support for their inhabitants (Joseph and Phillips 1999: 153–168), and a rural health insurance system has recently been introduced. However, the insurance only covers around one third of the expenses in case of serious illness, and many peasants cannot afford to buy it. In sum, the task of caring for elderly villagers is left mainly to themselves and their children, and the latter are an unreliable source of support because they are few, may live far from their parents, and often are under great economic pressure.

The main source of income for most rural elderly is the land they received when the collectives were dissolved in the early 1980s, and this land gives them some economic independence. However, the plots are normally very small, often only around one *mu* per person, and many types of farming are not profitable in China today. The land can be rented out, but the rent is low. Normally the land is turned over to a son, who in return promises to support his parents.

The present predicament of the rural elderly can be seen as the result of a double disembedding process from both collective and family that has been progressing since the early 1980s. The dissolution of the rural collectives left Chinese villages without a social safety net, and Beck and Beck-Gernsheim correctly mention China as an example of how people also outside the Western industrialized world 'are now expected to take their lives into their own hands and to pay a market price for services they receive' (Beck and Beck-Gernsheim 2003: 1). However, the social services provided by the rural collectives were limited in scope and, in contrast to the situation in urban state enterprises, never included pensions. For the elderly, the lack of mobility that characterized the Mao era was probably an even more important factor for old age care than collective welfare provisions. The household registration (*hukou* 户口) system meant that while daughters normally married out of the village, sons and daughters-in-law would almost certainly be around when parents grew old and needed care. By nailing peasants to their native village the collective system actually tied the family together and delayed the effects of modernization on intergenerational relations. Old villagers today, however, can no longer take it for granted that their sons will remain in the village.

Disembedded fully from the collectives by political decree and partly from the family by market forces, and still excluded from most of the social services provided by the state to urban dwellers, the rural elderly can be said to bear the full brunt of the uncertainties of modern life in post-reform China. How are they tackling this situation, practically and mentally? We try to answer this question by focusing on one concrete and fundamental issue faced by the elderly: should they maintain a separate residence or rather live with one of their children? This choice is made within a specific social and cultural framework and has to be considered in the more general context of the tradition for multigenerational co-residence that exists not just in China but in much of Asia.

Co-Residence in Asia and in China

One of the main characteristics of the modern family in the industrialized Western countries is that emotional ties inside the nuclear family (husband, wife and their dependent children) have grown stronger, while the bonds between the older generation and their adult children have been weakened. As a consequence, old people in the West now tend to live by themselves rather than with a married son or daughter. The causes of this transformation are changes in fundamental economic and occupational structures: the role of the family as the primary economic group is reduced in modern industrialized societies, as most individuals can make their own living without having to depend on the family land or family business, or on skills transmitted inside the family. Increased geographical and social mobility leads to a general decrease in the degree of dependency between generations, and with the declining frequency of *actual* co-residence, according to modernization theory, comes a gradual transformation of the *norms and preferences* for living arrangements.

In Western Europe and North America most people have apparently adapted their expectations to the new mode of life so that there seems to be a preference almost everywhere for elders who are losing physical and mental competence to continue to live separately from their offspring, but to have some regular contact with them, perhaps increasing as the parents need help with more aspects of daily life.[2] It is important to note that such changes in living arrangements have not destroyed the emotional ties inside the family. The generations continue to provide significant emotional and practical support for each other (Phillipson and Allan 2004).

Intergenerational relations are also changing in Asia, although these societies do not simply follow the Western model. Elisabeth Croll found ample evidence in the literature of 'an accelerated breakdown of the larger co-residential two- or three-generational joint-family form' which was attributed to a 'growing generation gap and an increasing preference of the young to live separately from the older generation'. Across Asia, the older generation feels deprived of authority and respect, while the role of the state in old age support remains minimal. However: 'Studies of old-age care across Asia emphasize that the resource flows hitherto associated with co-residence are not constrained by the physical boundaries of separate households and that living near, as opposed to with, children does not necessarily mean that there are fewer resource flows between the generations.' The intergenerational contract, according to Croll, has been 'renegotiated and reinterpreted to accommodate changes in the distinctive socio-cultural context that is Asia today', but intergenerational ties remain very strong even after this renegotiation (Croll 2006).

If we focus on co-residence, living with an adult child has been a significant and almost emblematic feature of successful family life in East Asia, where ratios of co-residence have remained much higher than in Western countries at corresponding levels of social development. According to the authors of a comparative study, the co-residence ratios in the 1980s were 71 per cent in Taiwan, 74 per cent in the Philippines, 77 per cent in Thailand and 88 per cent in Singapore, and co-residence was not only the most common but also the most commonly preferred living arrangement (Asis et al. 1995). Over the following years there has been some decline in the frequency of co-residence in East Asian countries. In Singapore, for example, the ratio dropped from 88 per cent in the late 1980s to 74 per cent in 2000 and 69 per cent in 2005 (Singapore Department of Statistics 2006), although this is still an extraordinarily high figure for a fully urbanized society.

There is, however, evidence of changes with regard to intergenerational relations even among people who grew up in cultures like the Chinese where the notion of filial piety plays a central role. Japan is an obvious example. As an early industrialized country, Japan shows occupational and demographic trends that are very similar to the West, while it shares China's traditional norms for co-residence. As late as in 1980, 69 per cent of all Japanese over the age of 65 were living with their children, and the Japanese family pattern was commonly perceived as an alternative to the European–North American prototype (Harrell 1997: 522–528). The ratio of co-residence has slowly dropped since then, however, and in 2005 it was down to 45 per cent (Ministry of Public Welfare and Labour White Book 2006). This is still much higher than in Western Europe and North America, but it is interesting to note that the mental transformation seems to proceed more rapidly than the changes in actual living arrangements. A 1983 survey showed that 66 per cent of Japanese over 65 preferred to live with their children, but by 2000 this figure had dropped significantly to 38 per cent (Platz 2005). One study of rural Japan actually found that co-residence could be a significant source of stress to the elderly, and it was locally perceived as driving many old people to commit suicide (Traphagati 2004). As for Hong Kong, a recent study found that old people adapted remarkably well to social changes, and that 'living apart from children did not contribute to . . . reduced well-being' (Cheng and Chan 2006).

If we look at urban China, where public social services are much better than in the villages, co-residence is still quite common but far from being an indispensable norm. A 1993 survey in Tianjin and Shanghai showed that 38 per cent of 60–69-year-olds lived alone or with a spouse, while 19 per cent lived with unmarried adult children and 43 per cent with a married child. For the 70+ age group the corresponding figures were 46 per cent, 9 per cent and 45 per cent, so in both age groups fewer than half of the elderly co-resided with married children. The authors reached the conclusion that co-residence might even decline further if housing conditions and social services were improved.[3] John R. Logan and Fuqin Bian summarize previous survey research on attitudes to co-residence in China's urban areas, saying that there seems to be a growing preference for having separate households, and that the '"modern" values in favour of separate households for married children have developed in advance of families' ability to follow them' (Logan and Bian 1999: 1258). Their own survey of actual and preferred living arrangements in nine major cities showed that 'preferences often adjust to circumstance' in the sense that people make practical choices rather than blindly following cultural norms (Logan and Bian 1999: 1274). A survey of more than 2,000 elderly in former rural areas that had been turned into urban districts showed that 45 per cent of the 60+ preferred to live with their married children and 49 per cent did so, while 40 per cent preferred to live alone and 36 per cent did so (Yan and Chi 2001). A 1994 survey of Baoding indicates that co-residence is no longer so important because children will still support their parents even when they live separately. In this way the 'trend toward independent living by the urban elderly need not imply a deterioration of the family support system' (Yan, Chen and Yang 2003: 162). As mentioned above, this conclusion is supported by evidence from the West and other countries in Asia. This all appears to support Logan and Bian's conclusion that 'there is not a single cultural norm [concerning co-residence] in urban China. Instead there are competing strategies of action, among which parents may select' (Logan and Bian 1999: 1278). It seems that while East Asian families are more resistant to change and multigenerational co-residence is a more tenacious phenomenon in Asia than in the West, cultural norms and perceptions in this field *are* undergoing change.

As already mentioned, there are substantial differences between urban and rural areas of China in regard to the material conditions of the elderly, mainly because many people in the cities receive pensions and are better covered by medical insurance. This tends to make rural parents relatively more dependent on their children, and co-residence has traditionally been the norm in the villages. Parish and Whyte found that although the Chinese government attacked particular traditional practices like concubines and child brides it did little to change the core structure of the peasant household, to the effect that during the collective period 'residence remains patrilocal, with virtually all old parents living in the home of a son' (Parish and Whyte 1978: 137). This was confirmed by a 1987 national survey, which found that only 10 per cent of the 60+ in rural areas lived alone or only with their spouse, as compared to 26 per cent in cities and 29 per cent in towns (Wu and Du 1996: 109).

China's rural families, however, are now exposed to many of the changes that triggered the transformation of the family in Western industrialized countries and, to some extent, in the Chinese cities. These changes include lower fertility, longer life expectancy, higher mobility and less dependence on income from agriculture. Ethnographic research shows that there is now also in the villages a growing tendency for the elderly to live independently.[4] Hong Zhang, who did fieldwork in a village in Hubei province in 1993–94, discovered that it had 'not only become more acceptable, but also more and more commonplace' for elderly parents to live alone (Zhang 2004: 85–86). Those informants who lived independently told her that they had much more freedom in this way and, particularly important to them, had regained control over their own budget. She also found, however, that the majority of the villagers still felt that living with a child was the ideal arrangement, while living alone was generally considered disgraceful for the parents and interpreted as a sign of the children's unfilial attitude. More than 80 per cent of those living alone had moved out after 'fierce and constant quarrels with their adult children', which indicates that the individualized lifestyle was often a forced rather than a preferred solution (Zhang 2004: 72, 75).

Eric Miller, who did fieldwork in Zouping, Shandong, likewise observed that many elderly 'preferred the independence and freedom of eating apart from children or in some cases even living apart in separate housing' (Miller 2004: 40). However, he interpreted this trend as an indicator of old people's lack of power in family relations: without power and resources they had to minimize their demands and be grateful for the little support they got. The ethnographic research of Zhang and Miller indicates that the intergenerational contract is being renegotiated also in rural China. The question is how the revisions should be interpreted.

Images of China's Rural Elderly

The Chinese public discourse is dominated by two partly overlapping images of the rural elderly as a *burden* to society and as the *victims* of modernization.[5] They are a burden because the Chinese population, in a much favoured phrase, has become old before it became rich. According to this argument, only more developed countries can actually afford to have a life expectancy rate as high as the one we now see in China, which is said to lack the economic basis for providing public old age care. The elderly are also seen as victims, however, because problematic demographic and economic trends are said to be matched by a moral crisis among the younger generation, who no longer live up the traditional values of filial piety. When old people live independently it is often seen as a sign of their position as victims, as when *Beijing Weekly* in a report on recent survey results wrote that '45 per cent of the old lived separately from their children, 93 per cent did not get a new item of clothing every year, 67 per cent could not afford to buy medicine, and 85 per cent supported themselves by agricultural labour' (Feng 2007). It is obvious that living alone is here listed as one of several problems haunting the elderly.

Influential anthropological research tends to confirm the idea that the rural elderly are victims of the forces unleashed by the post-1978 economic reforms and particularly of recent changes in intergenerational relations. Yunxiang Yan describes the transformation of the emotional relationship between the generations as the 'demystification of parenthood', and argues that 'without the backdrop of a traditional kinship system and religious beliefs and rituals . . . the basis for intergenerational relations became more rational and self-interested' (Yan 2003: 188). Guo Yuhua makes a similar argument when she says that the 'logic of justice' for intergenerational exchange has changed. In traditional China there existed a social contract between parents and their offspring, which obliged children (and particularly sons) to be eternally and unconditionally grateful to their parents who had borne and raised them. At present, however, the young generation sees the relationship more as a contract between individuals with equal rights. They are willing to provide financial support even if their parents behave unreasonably, but they will not allow the old generation to become a nuisance to the life of the young family, so if co-residence leads to domestic trouble the aged parents will have to live by themselves (Guo 2000). Guo's analysis of the emergence of a new logic of justice is very similar to Goode's description of the way 'the terms of the role-bargaining between the generations' were altered by industrialization in the West (Goode 1964: 109).

Both Yan and Guo see the problematic transformation of rural inter-generational relations not just as a general effect of modernization but as a specific consequence of China's post-1949 history. After the revolution the state smashed the existing social structures, primarily the lineage and the patriarchal ideology that underpinned the family system. The rural collectives were to some extent able to take over the care-giving functions performed by the lineage system because they made it possible to allocate the work of caring for the elderly to work team members, particularly daughters-in-law, but after decollectivization the villages were left without any care-giving social institutions, and even without moral standards. As expressed by one of Guo's informants, the present generation of elderly is the most unfortunate. When they were young they had to obey the older generation and put up with their tyrannical behaviour. Now they must obey their own children and live at their mercy. According to Yunxiang Yan: 'The most significant change with regard to elderly support, in my opinion, is the disintegration and ultimate collapse of the notion of filial piety, the backbone of old-age security in Chinese culture' (Yan 2003: 189). To Yan, the collapse of old age support is a prime example of the *negative* aspect of individualism, the rise of what he terms 'the uncivil individual'.

> Precisely because of the state's intrusive influence in everyday life during the collective period, its retreat in the postcollective era has produced an equally strong yet perhaps more negative impact on the private lives of individual villagers – that is, the development of ultra-utilitarian indi-vidualism in a unique context where the survival of traditional culture, the legacy of radical socialism, and global capitalism are competing with each other.
>   (Yan 2003: 233)

While Yan generally portrays the increased autonomy of the individual in rural China as a positive development, he is thus much more sceptical towards its effects on the older generation. In what follows we try to modify this rather pessimistic picture of how the rural elderly have reacted to recent changes. While we fully agree that they constitute a highly vulnerable group and that many elderly lead miserable lives, we argue that a significant proportion of the elderly are actually adapting quickly to more individual-ized lifestyles and no longer see co-residence with a married son as the ideal manifestation of filial piety. Autonomy and individual space have also become crucial to many elderly in China's villages, and living independently is becoming a socially fully accepted option for them.

Old Age and Autonomy in Rural Shandong

The interview data used in the following discussion are part of a larger research project on old age in rural Shandong.[6] In August 2001 we did eight exploratory interviews with people aged 50 to 82 in Z, a village in Boxing county with just over 3,000 inhabitants. In economic terms this used to be a medium-level agricultural village, but its inhabitants have recently become wealthier as they have found employment in enterprises and construction teams in Boxing town and further away. This means that the elderly are exposed to some of the effects of an open and more industrialized economy. Each interview lasted half a day or more. Besides learning about the informant's own situation we also asked their opinion about the general conditions for the elderly in their village. In addition we conducted interviews with people in other age groups, particularly local leaders such as the village Communist Party secretary. One of the things that struck us during the interviews was the flexible and pragmatic attitude of the elderly towards co-residence with married children.

Based on these findings, Ni Anru and graduate students from the sociology department of Shandong University conducted 53 semi-structured interviews in June 2004, May 2005 and May 2006 in C village in Licheng district. C is a mountain village with 960 inhabitants, quite far from the nearest town and with an average yearly per capita income of a modest 3,500 Yuan. The informants were selected to represent different life situations in terms of gender, age, income, family relations and degree of dependency. We did not consider random sampling to be a useful way of selecting informants because we wanted as wide a range of experiences as possible rather than statistical representation. The interviewers asked general questions about the living conditions of the elderly, but particularly in 2006 the focus was on their perception of individuality and family bonds.

We were particularly interested in whether elderly villagers who could still take care of themselves preferred to live alone with their spouse or together with a married son. In contrast to those who are already dependent on the help of others, the healthy old actually have a choice when it comes to living arrangements, and if this group prefers to live alone we believe it can be seen as a sign of their wish for more personal autonomy. In this context we also wanted to learn more about their perceptions of old age and filial piety, which contribute significantly to attitudes towards generational cohabitation.

Perceptions of Old Age and Filial Piety

Our informants offered several different definitions of what it means to be old, which may be summarized in two broad categories reflecting important aspects of old age for Shandong villagers.

The first category concerns the degree of dependency on others and is closely connected to physical health. Yuebin Xu divides the process of increasing dependency into three stages which correspond well to what our interviewees expressed: during the first stage the elderly have their own household and grow their own land, but they need cash from their children for extra expenses; during the second stage they turn their plot over to their son(s) but maintain their separate household and cook their own meals; during the third stage they become dependent on their children for personal care and are forced to move to their children's families (Xu 2001). It is particularly the third stage that is problematic, and many elderly were terrified by the idea of being confined to bed. When asked about what they would do if this situation should occur, most respondents said that they never considered this question because it made them too depressed. Worrying about the future would not change anything, so they might as well wait and see what destiny would bring them.

There was a second category of definitions, however, which looked at old age rather as a time of leisure and retirement after a long working life. As one informant said: 'If your children are rich you get old when you are in your forties. If you are poor you can live to eighty without getting old' (Interview 1/2001). In other words, if you have nobody to support you, you have to go to the fields no matter how old and weak you are, and you will have no chance of enjoying life in the way an old person should. Richer families, however, can let their parents retire from agricultural labour and enjoy 'old age' while they are still quite young. A 60-year-old woman said that you are old when you have 'completed your tasks' (*wanchengle renwu* 完成了任务) by arranging your children's marriages. Then you can relax and know that you have done what is expected of you. You will not have to work so much and can expect your sons to take care of you when you need it (Interview 2/2001). While the first concept of old age is primarily negative and related to physical ailments and dependency, the latter is thus more positive and refers to the gratification you deserve after a long life.

Both these perceptions of old age leave room for ideas of autonomy and individual agency. In the perspective of dependency, living in the household of one's son may certainly become necessary at some stage in the absence of other care providers, but it is not an ideal to be strived for. On the contrary, living alone may be seen as a sign of good health. If, on the other hand, old age equals retirement, your children should, of course, take good care of you, but economic, practical and emotional care may also be provided to parents who prefer to remain in their own homes. Thus none of these perceptions of old age necessarily entails co-residence.

The traditional term 'filial piety' (*xiao* 孝 or *xiaoshun* 孝顺) was generally used to describe the desired attitude of children towards their parents, and the most frequently used definition of what it meant to be filial was that you should 'not upset the old' (*bu rang laode shengqi* 不让老的生气):

> The most important aspect of being filial is not to upset the old. If [your children] just give you money and things to eat and drink but still make you angry, how can that count as being filial?   (Interview 10/2006)

Not to upset the old can mean many different things. Some examples given in the interviews were tokens of love and care such as bringing one's parents small gifts, inviting them over for meals, and covering their medical expenses. But informants also emphasized that old people have their own ideas and habits and prefer other activities and other types of food than the younger generations. Not to upset one's parents also meant that the young should accept and respect such particularities and individual whims. They should not interfere in the old people's lives but let them keep their autonomy.

The right to be left alone and not be bullied may be seen as a sad watering down of the traditional privileges of the elderly, but we may also think of this reinterpretation of *xiao* as a sign of their demand for a more independent life. This would explain what seems to be a contradiction in the literature on rural filial piety. On the one hand many observers, like Yan and Guo cited above, find very little *xiao* in China's villages. To the Zouping informants of Eric Miller, for example, 'the filiality of sons is simply to provide basic support and to not create conflicts' (Miller 2004: 38). On the other hand, a 1995 survey in Shandong showed that 83 per cent of the rural elderly felt that their children and grandchildren were 'very filial' (38 per cent) or 'rather filial' (45 per cent), and in our interviews practically everyone said that unfilial sons were the exception (Cheng and Guo 1995). However, their attitude was somewhat contradictory, indicating that the nature of filiality had changed. The contradiction was most explicitly expressed by an 82-year-old peasant who practically changed his view in the middle of a sentence:

> In the past, a filial son would never make the elders angry, but society has changed now, there is no such thing as a filial son. Well, there are filial sons in the village, they are actually a majority, most people are good, there are not many bad ones. As for those who are not filial, you can't just blame the young, the old are also responsible.
>
> (Interview 10/2006)

One interpretation of this ambiguity is, of course, that the old have simply lowered their expectations, but it is also possible that many accept a new intergenerational equilibrium and actually prefer fewer narrow bonds inside the family. In this way *xiao* – which fundamentally just means making one's parents happy – may have achieved an element of accepting a more autonomous position for the elderly. This interpretation becomes more likely when we look at elderly people's responses to questions about living arrangements.

Attitudes to Living Independently

There were four main types of living arrangements among the elderly we interviewed: (1) living in a separate household with or without a spouse; (2) living permanently with a son's family; (3) rotating between the families of sons (*lunyang* 轮养); and (4) living in an old people's home.

Rotational living meant that those sons who were still in the village took turns in providing their parents with board and lodging. Such arrangements were quite common in both Z and C village and were seen as a practical way of sharing the burden of support and care. The length of each stay became shorter as the burden increased. One old couple, both in very good health, had arranged to live three years with each of their sons. Those who demanded more care would have to move every year, and in one case an old woman who was confined to her bed was moved from house to house every ten days. We were told that in the final stage of an old person's life he or she may be allowed to stay in one room, and the children would take turns in attending to her needs, sometimes down to 24-hour shifts. Rotational living arrangements are only used in some parts of China, while others regard them as degrading to the old person.[7]

Old people's homes are reserved for people with no children, and they are still rare in rural areas. In Z, a former school served as an old people's home. Two sonless couples lived there under the five guarantees system, but their living conditions were evidently very poor. In C village only one old divorced man had moved to an old people's home in the town, and his fellow villagers felt sorry for him.

With a few exceptions, rotational living and old people's homes were thus only relevant for the weakest elderly. The large majority of relatively healthy old couples were living either as a one-generation family or with a married son. Living in a separate household meant cooking one's own meals and maybe also having a separate courtyard. Those elderly who lived in a son's household would normally leave their land to that son in return, but other sons and daughters were still expected to contribute to their care and support.

In the two villages where we did interviews, most informants expressed a wish to live independently as long as possible. A 71-year-old farmer repeatedly stated that he would only live with his children if he became absolutely unable to take care of himself, and he summed up the prevailing attitude in an almost programmatic way:

> Q: Why [do you not want to move to your son's house]?
> A: I wouldn't feel at ease (*zizai* 自在).
> Q: Wouldn't you feel at ease in the house of your own son?
> A: Well, you know, he is he and I am I . . . (*ta shi ta, wo shi wo* 他是他,
> 我是我).
> (Interview 12/2006)

This attitude was not only found among the 'younger old'. An 81-year-old man with three sons said:

> Nowadays each person looks after himself, many [from the young gener-
> ation] leave the village to make money and do not return all year, but we old
> people don't mind . . . It is better to live by yourself, there is more freedom,
> you can take your meals whenever you want.   (Interview 5/2006)

Different eating habits were often seen as a potential conflict area if the
generations stayed together, but the grandchildren's upbringing was also
mentioned several times. A 67-year-old retired school teacher and his
wife lived close to their son and grandson, but they preferred not to share
a courtyard with the young family, because this would involve them too
much in the grandson's education:

> It is a social trend [to live separately]. It is a problem these days that the
> kids are all spoiled. If we tried to give him [i.e. their grandson] good
> manners, would he listen? . . . He makes a lot of trouble . . . If it gets
> really bad the state must take care of him, dial 110 and they will come
> and arrest him, what can old people do about that?   (Interview 8/2006)

One old woman just wanted to have her freedom to sit and gossip with
her mates in the square without having to think about returning for meals.
An old man talked about how he got together with friends to discuss
calligraphy and traditional literature, and felt that he had an independent
life with pleasures and values that had nothing to do with his children. A
middle-aged man put it this way:

> I have five children and they are all doing fine. My three girls often invite
> me to go and stay at their place, but I don't want to go. If I cannot refuse
> I may go, but only for a few days. It is great to live by myself here on the
> hill, it wouldn't be convenient to live with them, it would feel awkward.
> I don't want to live at my son's place either, but if he is going out I can
> watch his house for him.   (Interview 7/2004)

Some informants said that they preferred to live alone because they did not
want to be a burden to their children, but there were also many like this
man, who apparently chose to be on his own because of the freedom and
leisure it gave him. This indicates that the new 'logic of justice' is not always
working in favour of the younger generation. It is tempting to believe that
the new trends are received more easily by the young, and that they will be
the ones to welcome a more contractual relationship disembedded from

the traditional family institutions. However, older people with sufficient economic, mental and physical resources also welcomed the loosening of tight family bonds.

Middle-aged informants made plans that would enable them to maintain their autonomy in old age. A 49-year-old farmer said that his age group had learned their lesson well. Members of the old generation had sometimes been thrown out of their own house after they had divided the family property (*fenjia* 分家) with their sons, and had been left 'without even a place to hide'. To avoid this he had designed a new home for himself and his wife where they could move when his son took over their present house. 'It is better to live separately, it is more convenient for everyone,' he said (Interview 7/2004.). A 59-year-old retired school teacher had also *fenjia* a few months after his son had married. In this way 'they have their freedom, and we have our freedom, we can all do what we want' (Interview 1/2006). A 51-year-old woman said that she and her husband had tried to persuade their son to *fenjia* but he was unwilling to do so. This annoyed them, partly because they preferred to live independently and partly because a separation would reduce their expenses for gift-giving, as part of such family obligations would pass on to their son after *fenjia* (Interview 4/2006). That the younger old expect less from their children than the older cohort is not surprising. Hong Zhang (2007: 866) likewise reports that young parents in the Hubei village where she did her fieldwork found it 'out-dated and out of sync with the changing times' to depend on their own children for old age support.

Our informants' wish for autonomy was apparently not triggered by current family conflicts, but living independently was thought of as a preventive measure to maintain intergenerational harmony by reducing the children's burdens to a minimum. The ideal was to be able to divide the property without breaking up the emotional relationship (*fenjia bu fenxin* 分家不分心). A 75-year-old farmer said that he and his wife were still in good health and perfectly able to take care of themselves: 'You can't just make your children look after you too early. If they have to take care of you for a long time there will be disagreements. That has happened to a lot of people in the village' (Interview 6/2006). He obviously felt that the revised intergenerational contract obliged the elderly to take care of themselves for as long as possible, no matter how old they were. Like the young people interviewed by Hansen and Pang (in this volume), the elderly were coping with changes in family relations while maintaining the family as their principal frame of reference.

Not all informants were equally positive about living alone. Some clearly expressed a wish for co-residence and referred to this as the most 'natural' arrangement. As can be expected, people who had lost their spouse or who were ill often held this view, but it was not the dominant trend.

Could it be that those informants who spoke favourably about living independently would have preferred co-residence but found it embarrassing that their children were not willing to take care of them? The idea that parents bear a substantial part of the blame for their children's unfilial behaviour certainly exists, and few old people talked negatively about their own offspring, while they were more willing to criticize unfilial behaviour in other families. It speaks against this interpretation, however, that new ideas about individual space were most common among high-status groups such as former cadres, teachers, migrant workers and others who had been employed outside agriculture. These people had relatively many resources (savings, pensions, etc.), which it would have been attractive to their children to share, so if they had really wanted to live in their sons' households they could probably have done so. However, they were among the most vocal in their praise of independence.

In conclusion, we found that ideas of autonomy and individual space were widespread among our informants. Old people wanted to be close to their sons and daughters, physically as well as emotionally, and they wanted their grandchildren to come over after school, but much like the younger generation they simultaneously felt a need for an independent social life without the restrictions entailed by generational co-residence. In practical terms, around one third of the families in C village had solved the problem through dividing the courtyard with a wall and opening an extra door to the street for the old couple. This solution meant more privacy for both generations and lived up to the ideal of 'dividing without leaving' (*fen er bu li* 分而不离). While Parish and Whyte (1978) found that co-residence was the norm in the collective period, Hong Zhang (2004) discovered in the early 1990s that many old people enjoyed the freedom of living independently, but that such living arrangements were still not fully accepted by village society. What we saw in Shandong more than a decade later was that living in a separate household was no longer associated with disgrace or failure.[8] Living independently for as long as possible had become a socially fully acceptable choice. Harmonious intergenerational relations were still very important to the elderly and to their reputation in the village, but co-residence was no longer a precondition for being regarded as an ideal family. The elderly we met were not simply the victims of the atomizing trends in a society torn apart by modernization. Many of them had changed their perception of the ideal balance between family and individual, and the idea of autonomy was crucial for the way they now thought about their own lives.

Such mental transformations cannot change the fact that many elderly are extremely vulnerable, and that practically all of them will still have to rely on their family if they become too weak to take care of themselves. However, this dependency on the family is a problem inherent in China's socio-economic structure; it is not caused by the elderly's lack of mental flexibility. The collectives are gone and the traditional family is under strong pressure, but many rural elderly are prepared to change established cultural patterns and organize their lives in new ways. In order to reintegrate the rural elderly in society it will be necessary to develop institutions that can cater to their needs and defend their rights. In the following section we first look at those organizations – or rather, traces of organizations – for the elderly, which we came across in the two Shandong villages, and then turn to examples of collective organizations for the rural elderly in other localities.

Real and Imagined Communities for the Rural Elderly

As family and collective no longer provide stable and reliable frameworks for the rural elderly, they must find alternative ways to defend their interests, and new forms of social organizations that can create a space for them in rural society. However, while urban pensioners actively fight for their rights and often organize social protests (Hurst and O'Brien 2002), the rural elderly are less likely to act collectively because they are scattered, have few resources and rarely think of themselves as members of an interest group. In Z village we interviewed a 79-year-old man who was entitled to a monthly pension of 100 Yuan because he had been a middle-level manager in a township enterprise. He had not received his pension for the last year, however. The township government claimed that the obligation had been transferred to a private contractor, who had taken over the enterprise, but this person simply refused to pay pensions and the old man had no idea how he could collect his money (Interview 1/2001). Old people whose families refused to take care of them had similar problems claiming their rights. In theory they could take legal action against unfilial children, but no old person in the two villages had ever done that. Most of them just silently put up with insults and neglect, or they only grumbled to their confidants (Interview 3/2004.). As is the case with the young people discussed by Hansen and Pang in this volume, state institutions did not have much to offer them, and the family was the only collective unit of direct importance to them.

In principle, the interests of the 60+ should be taken care of by an old people's association (OPA, *laonianren xiehui* 老年人协会). Such an organization existed briefly in Z village in 1991–92. It organized activities for the elderly, such as calligraphy competitions, and was also supposed to mediate in conflicts between the generations. The collective economy of the village withered away, however, and when the two old men who had taken the initiative to establish the OPA died all activities stopped. C village never had an OPA. Old people in both villages were very sceptical about their own ability to cooperate across families and they also feared running into conflicts with the established power structure. Nobody would take the lead in setting up an organization unless the village government encouraged it. One mentioned that village leaders might look at an independent OPA as an attempt at establishing an alternative centre of power. Even attempts in Z village to establish a funeral association and an opera troupe had proved futile because of internal disagreements and lack of initiative.

Also, the younger elderly found it difficult to imagine that old people should relate to each other as members of an interest group. A 58-year-old farmer prided himself on having maintained his full physical and mental capacity, but his reaction to the idea that he should take the lead in establishing an activity centre for old people was completely negative: 'I won't do that, I haven't got the ability. It is fine if we [i.e. he and his wife] can just make our own lives better, we can't manage more than that' (Interview 7/2006).

Although OPAs were not successful in the villages we visited, they play an important role in other parts of China, and they have apparently been successful in reducing poverty in some provinces (HelpAge 2007). In the following we look at two ways of imagining the social function of the OPA, which represents two different visions of how rural China may be socially reconstructed and how groups that have been marginalized by recent social developments can be reintegrated into village society.

The first model has a strong corporatist flavour and sees the OPA primarily as an instrument that can be used by the state in a top-down political process. Mette Halskov Hansen has shown how OPAs are 'obliged to use the traditional authority of older people to promote and support specific policies of the government', and how the traditional prestige and political experience of the old men who head the organizations make them perfect partners for younger officials suffering from a general lack of public respect and confidence (Hansen 2008). This way of utilizing the OPA appears to be particularly efficient in places like Jiangsu and Zhejiang, where lineages have traditionally been strong (Tan 2006), but the party-state's cannibalization of the OPA is a common phenomenon. A Chinese report found that only 37 per cent of village OPAs elected their chairman, while 63 per cent of them automatically appointed either the Party secretary or the village head as chairman. The report complained that the OPAs in many places were turned into administrative organs under the local government, and that members' enthusiasm dropped when they realized that the OPA was not a genuine popular organization (Huang and Yuan 2006).

It is not surprising that the party-state regards the OPA as the old people's equivalent to the Women's Federation, the Youth League or other 'mass organizations' that are primarily instruments of Party control. However, there exists a competing vision of how old people should be organized, which deserves attention as an alternative to the top-down approach. This vision is rooted in the idea of rural reconstruction, which was very popular in the 1920s and 1930s and has recently had a remarkable revival.[9] He Xuefeng is prominent among the scholar-reformers who imagine the way collective organizations may be established by and for old people in rural China. His diagnosis of the present problem is pessimistic and resembles the views of Yunxiang Yan and Guo Yuhua: confronted with a rapidly changing world many old villagers despair and some even commit suicide. The people's communes have collapsed, the market economy has undermined social norms and moral standards, and old people do not know how to operate in an increasingly but still incompletely law- and contract-based society. Once the middle-aged realize that their own children are not likely to care for them in the future, they separate economically from their offspring and try to secure their future by making their own money and saving up. This is one way of solving the problem of how to provide for old people in the villages, but this solution does not satisfy He Xuefeng because it will turn farmers into 'atomized individuals' (*yuanzihua geren* 原子化个人) and destroy the family, which has been the foundation of China's social structure for thousands of years. He sees an alternative to individualization, however: the reconstruction of rural society with economic support from the state, and the establishment of OPAs that will enable old people to defend their own rights and interests (He 2007).

In addition to their theoretical analysis, He Xuefeng and others have also conducted real-life OPA experiments. Inspired by clan-based and economically very successful OPAs in the Wenzhou area, researchers from Central China Normal University in Wuhan, where He worked at the time, stood behind the establishment in 2003 of an OPA in a fishing village in Hubei province. Its 20 board members were democratically elected by all villagers above 60 years of age, and the board elected a former Party secretary as chairman. The OPA first established an activity centre offering the elderly a meeting place with occasional cultural events. This was a big success, according to He, because the old villagers who used to live in isolation now had a chance to meet. Soon the OPA started expanding its range of activities. It helped old people with unfilial children, mediated in domestic conflicts, visited the elderly when they were ill, and appointed ten model 'respect-the-old families' (*jinglaohu* 敬老户). In the following years the experiment was extended to three more villages, apparently also with great success (He 2005).

In the tradition of the rural reconstruction movement He Xuefeng emphasizes the cultural revival generated by the OPAs, the re-emergence of unity, harmony, rich folklore and venerable cultural norms, and the bottom-up nature of the organization's operations. Shen Duanfeng, however, draws attention to the fact that while the OPA established by He certainly managed to organize the old and raised their status in the village, this did not mean that a 'civil society' (*gongmin shehui* 公民社会) had emerged, or that the old had started to think of themselves as 'citizens':

To the contrary, the old people repeatedly expressed their gratitude to the Party and saw the establishment of the OPA as an expression of the higher level Party and government organs' concern for them. When they were up against the official organs of power at the village level they always relied on the support of the higher level Party organization, and they never proceeded from considerations of citizens' rights in an individualistic sense.   (Shen 2004)

Shen concludes that 'the development of a Chinese "society" must depend on external factors, particularly the support of the government, and cannot possibly become a "civil society" in the Western sense'. The difficulties facing organizations for the rural elderly thus clearly reflect the general problems involved in establishing genuine non-state social organizations in China.

Conclusion

The elderly in China's rural areas are exposed to many of the vicissitudes of the reform period. The established patterns that determined their living arrangements have been seriously challenged by socio-economic change. The solid cultural norms that used to guide the relationship between aging parents and their offspring are being replaced by a much broader variety of standards, some of a legal-contractual nature, others influenced by the multitude of 'modern' family patterns reflected in the media and directly experienced by an increasingly mobile rural population. The village, in its capacities both as organ of state power and as community, is an unreliable source of care and support. To describe these new conditions as a happy world of opportunities would be grossly misleading, and we heard enough stories of loneliness, poverty and fear about the future to exclude such an interpretation.

However, in this chapter we have downplayed the problems of old age in order to highlight the fact that the rural old are not just an undifferentiated 'weak group' (*ruoshi qunti* 弱势群体) victimized by aggressive modernity. Their response to recent changes depends on their individual physical, social and economic resources as well as on their mental outlook. A substantial proportion of the healthy old have adjusted their expectations of old age, and not just in the sense that they have lowered their standards for filial behaviour. Their new vision of an ideal life is to stay independent as long as possible, economically as well as with regard to living arrangements, but to maintain close emotional contacts with their children. In this way they gain two things: their own life becomes more pleasant and the period of time when they are a burden to their children is shortened. Miller found that an ideal parent–daughter relationship in Zouping was very similar to the behavioural ideal of parent–child relationships in America (Miller 2004: 52), and although our informants expected more from sons than from daughters, at least with regard to the question of residence, their ideal visions of family life would also be immediately recognizable to old people in the West. The idea that elderly Chinese villagers are trapped in a narrow cage of traditional norms and values does not correspond to what we saw.

It should be kept in mind that the basic problems of old age have not been solved simply through this mental transformation among the elderly. At some stage they will no longer be able to live an independent life. They may become ill and end up immobilized in bed, maybe for several years. It is no coincidence that this last phase of life was surrounded by so much anxiety that it was practically impossible to make people talk about it. At this stage there would be no more individual choice: they would be left to the mercy of their children and could only hope that they had fulfilled their part of the renegotiated contract between the generations well enough for them to get the necessary help.

Reintegrating the elderly into rural society presents the Chinese state with massive difficulties which are typical of one of its classical dilemmas: should it monopolize political power and the right to social organization, or should it allow more grassroots activity? The old people's associations tend to suffer from the general shortcomings of top-down 'mass' organizations and become tools of governance rather than organs of group-based self-help and interest articulation. Are there any alternatives? Judging from our interviews it is difficult to imagine that the rural elderly will organize themselves at grassroots level across family lines, and even if they should try, it is doubtful whether the existing village power structure would accept it. Lineage and religious organizations, although they were not active in the villages where we did our interviews, undoubtedly play an important role for the elderly in some localities and the state may accept that they come to play a larger role in the future. Experiments such as the one carried out by He Xuefeng show that alternative visions of rural organizations are certainly alive among Chinese social reformers and activists. Whether they will succeed in overcoming the challenges of social atomization is still an open question.

Notes

1   For a systematic comparison of rural and urban disparities in support for the elderly, see Xu and Ji 1999.

2   Harrell 1997: 513. See pp. 455–528 for a general discussion of what Harrell calls the 'M-cluster' of modern families.

3   Logan, Bian and Bian 1998. For a discussion of how urban families in Guangzhou coped with intergenerational relations and co-residence around 1990, see Ikels 1993.

4   The definition of living independently/separately (*danguo* 单过) varies in different studies of rural China, but having a separate dwelling, cooking one's own meals and eating at one's own table is a practical and operational definition which appeared to follow local perceptions in Shandong.

5   For an interesting discussion of the public debate on old age, see Boermel 2006: 401–418.

6   The project includes the collection of quantitative data, which we are not able to discuss here because of limits of space.

7   For a discussion of why rotation arrangements are widespread and accepted in some villages but not in others, see Jing 2004.

8   It is interesting to note that Zhang in a footnote mentions that when she came back in 2002, 54 per cent of the 60+ were living separately, compared to 23 per cent during her original fieldwork in 1994. Zhang 2004: 255.

9   The social reformers in the rural reconstruction movement of the early twentieth century represented many different schools of thought: see Hayford 1990. He Xuefeng appears to be inspired mainly by Liang Shuming, a cultural conservative who believed that genuine Chinese culture survived only in the rural areas, and that the revival of rural communities was therefore also the key to national revival.

Bibliography

Asis, Maruja Milagros, Lita Domingo, John E. Knodel and Kalyani Mehta (1995) 'Living arrangements in four Asian countries: a comparative perspective'. *Journal of Cross-Cultural Gerontology*, vol. 10, no. 1–2, pp. 145–162.

Beck, Ulrich and Elisabeth Beck-Gernsheim (2003) *Individualization: Institutionalized Individualism and its Social and Political Consequences.* London: Sage.

Boermel, Anna (2006) '"No wasting" and "empty nesters": "old age" in Beijing'. *Oxford Development Studies*, vol. 34, no. 4, pp. 401–418.

Cheng, Sheung-Tak and Alfred C. M. Chan (2006) 'Filial piety and psychological well-being in well older Chinese'. *Journal of Gerontology: Psychological Sciences*, vol. 61B, no. 5, pp. 262–269.

Cheng Xuechao and Guo Peifang (程学超, 郭培方) (1995) '山东农村老年人社会心理状况的再调查' [A re-investigation of the socio-psychological condition of the elderly in rural Shandong]. *Shandong shifan daxue xuebao (shehui kexue ban)* [Journal of Shandong Normal University (Social Sciences)], no. 1, pp. 66–70.

China Daily (2009) 'More elderly need care as China turns gray', 25.2.09.

China National Committee on Ageing (2008) 'White paper of China's ageing undertakings', http://en.cncaprc.gov.cn/en/iroot10075/4028e47d18edb7d401190901aefd098b.html. Accessed 24 April 2009.

Croll, Elisabeth J. (2006) 'The intergenerational contract in the changing Asian family'. *Oxford Development Studies*, vol. 34, no. 4, pp. 473–491.

Feng Jianhua (冯建华) (2007) '谁来赡养他们? 农村人的养老之忧' [Who will support them? Rural people's worries about old age support]. *Beijing zhoukan* [Beijing Weekly], no. 2.

Goode, William J. (1964) *The Family.* Englewood Cliffs: Prentice-Hall.

Guo Yuhua (郭于华) (2000) '代际关系中的公平逻辑及其变迁. 对河北农村养老事件的分析' [The logic of justice in intergenerational relations and its changes. An analysis of cases of old age support in rural Hebei]. *Zhongguo xueshu* [Chinese Scholarship], no. 4, pp. 221–254.

Hansen, Mette Halskov (2008) 'Organising the old: senior authority and the political significance of a rural Chinese "NGO"'. *Modern Asian Studies*, vol. 42, no. 5, pp. 1057–1078.

Harrell, Stevan (1997) *Human Families.* Boulder: Westview Press.

Hayford, Charles W. (1990) *To the People. James Yen and Village China.* New York: Columbia University Press.

He Xuefeng (贺雪峰) (2005) '老年人协会建设纪事' [A chronicle of the formation of old people's associations], 27.10.05, http://www.snzg.cn/article/show.php?itemid-4471/page-1.html. Accessed 26 Feb 2007.

——(2007) '农村老年人的处境' [The situation of old people in the countryside]. In He Xuefeng (贺雪峰), 乡土的前途. 新农村建设与中国道路 [The future of the rural areas. The construction of a new countryside and the Chinese way]. Jinan: Shandong renmin chubanshe, pp. 213–215.

HelpAge International and CNCA (2007) 'Older people's associations and poverty alleviation in rural areas. The experience in China', http://www.helpage.org/Resources/Researchreports/main_content/gNDX/ChinaOPA_final_13Sep072.pdf. Accessed 24 April 2009.

Huang Qian and Yuan Xin (黄乾，原新) (2006) '构建和谐社会过程中的基层老年群众组织作用研究 – 以老年人协会为例' [Research on the use of basic mass organisations for the old in the construction of a harmonious society – old people's associations as an example]. *Renkou xuekan* [Population Studies], no. 2, pp. 24–28.

Hurst, William and Kevin O'Brien (2002) 'China's contentious pensioners'. *China Quarterly*, no. 170, pp. 345–360.

Ikels, Charlotte (1993) 'Settling accounts: the intergenerational contract in an age of reform'. In Deborah Davis and Stevan Harrell (eds), *Chinese Families in the Post-Mao Era*. Berkeley: University of California Press, pp. 307–333.

—— (ed.) (2004) *Filial Piety. Practice and Discourse in Contemporary East Asia*. Stanford: Stanford University Press

—— (2006) 'Economic reform and intergenerational relationships in China'. *Oxford Development Studies*, vol. 34, no. 4, pp. 387–400.

Information Office of the State Council of the People's Republic of China (2004), 'China's social security and its policy', White Paper, http://english.people.com.cn/200409/07/eng20040907_156193.html. Accessed 26 February 2007.

Jing, Jun (2004) 'Meal rotation and filial piety'. In Charlotte Ikels (ed.), *Filial Piety. Practice and Discourse in Contemporary East Asia*. Stanford: Stanford University Press, pp. 53–62.

Joseph, Alun E. and David R. Phillips (1999) 'Ageing in rural China: impacts of increasing diversity in family and community resources'. *Journal of Cross-Cultural Gerontology*, vol. 14, no. 2, pp. 153–168.

Li Hong and Shan Xueyong (李宏，单学勇) (2004) '农村养老保障: 从"家庭" 到 "社会"' [Old age security in the rural areas: from 'family' to 'society']. *Jingji yu guanli* [Economy and Management], vol. 18, no. 9.

Logan, John R. and Fuqin Bian (1999) 'Family values and co-residence with married children in urban China'. *Social Forces*, vol. 77, no. 4, pp. 1253–1282.

Logan, John R., Fuqin Bian and Yanjie Bian (1998) 'Tradition and change in the urban Chinese family: the case of living arrangements'. *Social Forces*, vol. 76, no. 3, pp. 851–882.

Miller, Eric (2004) 'Filial daughters, filial sons: comparisons from rural north China'. In Charlotte Ikels (ed.), *Filial Piety. Practice and Discourse in Contemporary East Asia*. Stanford: Stanford University Press, pp. 34–52.

Ministry of Public Welfare and Labour White Book, Heisei 18 (2006), p. 24, http://www.mhlw.go.jp/wp/hakusyo/kousei/06/dl/1-1a.pdf. Accessed 12 January 2007.

Parish, William L. and Martin King Whyte (1978) *Village and Family in Contemporary China*. Chicago: University of Chicago Press.

Phillipson, Chris and Graham Allan (2004) 'Aging and the life course'. In Jacqueline Scott, Judith Treas and Martin Richards (eds), *The Blackwell Companion to the Sociology of Families*. Oxford: Blackwell, pp. 126–141.

Platz, Anemone (2005) 'Ochitsukeru basho: Wohn(ungs)wünschen alter Menschen' [A place to settle down: old people's living preferences]. In Roland Domenig, Susanne Formanek and Wolfram Manzenreiter (eds), *Über Japan Denken* [Thoughts on Japan]. Wien: LIT Verlag, pp. 321–344.

Shen Duanfeng (申端锋) (2004) '论农村社区NGO的发育和成长 以洪渔场老年人协会为例' [On the growth and development of rural NGOs. Taking the old people's association of Hongyuchang as an example]. *Shandong keji daxue xuebao (shehui kexue ban)* [Journal of Shandong University of Science and Technology (Social Sciences)], vol. 6, no. 1, pp. 28–31, 42.

Singapore Department of Statistics (2006) 'Key findings of the general household survey 2005. Transport, overseas travels, households and housing characteristics'. Singapore: Government of Singapore, p. 4. http://www.singstat.gov.sg/press/ghs2.pdf. Accessed 2 February 2007.

Tan Tongxue (谭同学) (2006) '老年人协会，村庄生活与民族精神' [Old people's associations, village life and the national spirit]. *Huazhong keji daxue xuebao, shehui kexue ban* [Journal of Huazhong University of Science and Technology, Social Sciences], no. 2, pp. 7–10.

Traphagati, John W. (2004) 'Interpretations of elder suicide, stress, and dependency among rural Japanese'. *Ethnology*, vol. 43, no. 4, pp. 315–329.

Wu Cangping and Du Peng (邬沧萍, 杜鹏) eds. (1996) 人口老龄化过程中的中国老年人 [Elderly Chinese during the process of population aging]. Shanghai: Huadong shifan daxue chubanshe.

Wu, Jiao (2007) 'Nation faces challenges of graying population'. *China Daily*, 18.12.07.

Xu, Xiaohe and Jianjun Ji (1999) 'Supports for the aged in China: a rural-urban comparison'. *Journal of Asian and African Studies*, vol. 34, no. 3, pp. 257–278.

Xu, Yuebin (2001) 'Family support for old people in rural China'. *Social Policy and Administration*, vol. 35, no. 3, pp. 307–320.

Yan, Shengming and Iris Chi (2001) 'Living arrangements and adult children's support for the elderly in the new urban areas of mainland China'. In Iris Chi, Neena L. Chappell and James Lubben (eds), *Elderly Chinese in Pacific Rim Countries*. Hong Kong: Hong Kong University Press, pp. 201–219.

Yan, Shengming, Jieming Chen and Shanhua Yang (2003) 'Living arrangements and old-age support'. In Martin King Whyte (ed.), *China's Revolutions and Intergenerational Relations.* Ann Arbor: Center for Chinese Studies, University of Michigan, pp. 143–166.

Yan, Yunxiang (2003) *Private Life under Socialism: Love, Intimacy, and Family Change in a Chinese Village, 1949–1999.* Stanford: Stanford University Press.

Zhang, Hong (2004) '"Living alone" and the rural elderly: strategy and agency in post-Mao rural China'. In Charlotte Ikels (ed.), *Filial Piety. Practice and Discourse in Contemporary East Asia.* Stanford: Stanford University Press, pp. 63–87.

—— (2007) 'From resisting to "embracing?" the one-child rule: understanding new fertility trends in a central China village'. *China Quarterly*, no. 192, pp. 855–875.

3
Individualization and the Political Agency of Private Business People in China

Jørgen Delman and Yin Xiaoqing

This chapter looks at how the combined forces of globalization, private sector development and individualization contribute to generating individual political agency amongst private business people. It is argued that whereas the formal political participation of private entrepreneurs and the shared interests between the party-state and large segments of private business people are well documented, the dynamics in the state–private business nexus would be difficult to understand if informal political organization and representation are not factored in.

We use Beck and Beck-Gernsheim's notion of 'self politics' (Beck-Gernsheim 2003: 30–53, 184) to explain new types of individual political identity and agency, and Bauman's 'peg community' concept (Bauman 2001: 151–52), understood here as iterative, loose and temporary networks, to explain how processes of individualization, identity-shaping and the re-embedding of individualized business people into new collectivist structures merge in sub-political processes in the state–private business nexus.

Our focus is on a singular yet symbolic case, namely that of Sun Dawu, a private businessman from Hebei who has turned political activist. Sun first tried his political luck as a representative on the local county people's congress. Later, he opted out to pursue his own politics by creating and participating in a sub-political community, a new type of informal political platform that emerged as an alternative to the official channels controlled by the party-state.

We address the factors that contribute to the development of political identity and agency among private business people by, firstly, reviewing why and how private business people exert political influence and what is being contested through their activities. After that, the case of Sun Dawu is analyzed by looking at the history of his business, his business philosophy, his 'self-politics', and finally his role as one originator of a political 'peg' community as a constituent part of the new state–private business nexus.

Private Business and Politics

Sun Dawu's case should be seen against the backdrop of private sector development in China in recent years. First of all, the private business sector has come to play an important role as a dominant driver in China's 'new' capitalist economy. In 2003 it already accounted for 59.3 per cent of China's GDP (OECD 2005: 125).[1] The fast development of the private sector is a result of an increasingly open market that combines with the forces of economic, social and cultural globalization. Against this backdrop, political interests in society have diversified and emerging social groups, such as private business people (*siying qiyejia* 私营企业家) like Sun Dawu, have entered the political scene. The party-state has applied a quasi-corporatist approach to accommodate the need for their political participation, and they are allowed membership of formal political organizations, including the Communist Party, various elected bodies such as village committees and people's congresses, and business associations. Through such political participation, private business people are invited to promote their interests vis-à-vis China's autocratic political system (Dickson 2003; Kennedy 2005; Delman 2005; Ao 2005; Pei 2006: 92–95; Tsui et al. 2006; Li et al. 2006; Dickson 2007).

Private business people seek to address the major institutional un-certainties and constraints in the business environment that affect their business operations. Their main concerns are: (1) the dual economy and market imperfections, (2) excessive regulatory burdens and red tape, (3) heavy formal and informal tax burdens, and (4) the absence of a fully-fledged private property rights regime and a sound legal system (Krug and Mehta 2004; Li et al. 2006). There is a clear correlation between a higher level of formal political participation by private entrepreneurs and the severity of the institutional deficiencies and constraints in certain regions of China as compared to others (Li et al. 2006).

The party-state's acknowledgment of the emerging capitalists as a potentially important social and political group has a double rationale. On the one hand, the Party recognizes the contribution of the private sector to the economy, and on the other, state-corporatist tradition dictates that interest groups should be co-opted to prevent the emergence of independent political groups, movements, or parties (Delman 2005).

The Communist Party's co-optation of private entrepreneurs has been quite successful. There is little difference – at least in the public sphere – between the party-state and business on key policy issues. Private entrepreneurs appear to become increasingly satisfied with the state of affairs, and rather than being potential agents of change working from within, they have become a key resource of support for the official political agenda, and the perception of shared interests tends to preserve the status quo (Dickson 2007).

Beck and Beck-Gernsheim (2003: 1) observe that China's new market economy promotes accelerated individualization and the disembedding of social segments and citizens anchored in the new capitalist economy. Private business people are clearly such a segment, in as far as they have been disembedded from old structures, institutions, positions and affiliations. They are therefore prompted to respond to the party-state's quasi-corporatist approach by defining and redefining their political identity and agency within the framework of the state–private business nexus,[2] i.e. the interface between the party-state and the private business sector. This nexus provides a range of opportunities for formal and informal political representation and negotiations about the disposal of power as well as key material and immaterial resources in society. Sun Dawu's case is highly illustrative of these developments.

The nexus develops in response to the processes of economic reforms as well as of individualization and globalization, two epochal processes that are 'changing the foundations of living together in all spheres of social action' (Beck and Beck-Gernsheim 2003: 169). It provides space for new institutional arrangements as the party-state appears increasingly unable and unwilling to apply its traditional, all-encompassing approach to political and social control to the agents of the new economy. Effectively, in the absence of a 'Western style' democratic political reform in China, there is evidently room to exercise some measure of political freedom (Oi 2004).

However, this must not lead to the assumption that a liberalizing market economy and the emergence of politically articulate new social groupings such as the private capitalists will automatically lead China in a democratic direction (Pei 2006; Dickson 2007). Yet at this stage, private business people have become a new resource for political development, and their political participation may well express a greater ambition than simply to serve the needs of the individual business to mitigate its transaction costs through generating business-focused alliances and networks, as argued by several authors (in Krug 2004). Effectively, private business people are challenged to consider their (objectively induced) role as free-wheeling, disembedded individuals, and are forced to make choices not only about business development but also about their identity and whether and how to exercise political agency. Some may choose to participate politically through formal channels, whereas others may confront the party-state's hegemonic political discourse, either by engaging in 'critical tension'[3] or by creating and re-embedding into sub-politicized communities (Beck and Beck-Gernsheim 2003: 28–29) or other new collectivist structures.

The existence of such informal politics is already officially recognized by the party-state,[4] but due to political sensitivities they have not been well researched. Even though a single case will not allow us to make definitive conclusions, it is argued here that the Sun Dawu case is highly illustrative in its own right as it provides insights into the processes of informal politics as well as the risks associated with moving from formality to informality. The case may thus complement other studies, e.g. those by Li et al. (2006) and Dickson (2007), in regard to the scope and thrust of formal political participation, and it will add new dimensions to important studies on business alliances and networks (Krug 2004; Krug and Mehta 2004).

Individualization and Sub-Political 'Peg' Communities

Like other citizens, China's private business people are prompted to construct a political identity and exert political agency to deal with the challenges they meet in the state–private business nexus which feeds on and breeds individualized political identity and political agency. As Bauman notes:

> . . 'individualization' carries the emancipation of the individual from the ascribed, inherited and inborn determination of his or her social char-

acter: a departure rightly seen as a most conspicuous and seminal feature of the modern condition. To put it in a nutshell, 'individualization'
consists in transforming human 'identity' from a 'given' into a 'task' –
and charging the actors with the responsibility for performing the task
and for the consequences ...   (Bauman 2001: 144)

The challenge is to manage the 'tasks' that are defined by the individual and
not by existing institutions such as – in the Chinese case – the party-state,
the family, the *danwei* (单位), or the village.

In China's socialist past, personal identity (*shenfen* 身份) was assigned
and controlled by the state. 'Identity' signified social position and assignment of power and resources, and it did not encourage consideration of
individual characteristics. The system was hierarchical, and status was
linked to a similar administrative system of organizational identity and rank
(*zuzhi bianzhi* 组织编制), including the ranking of cadres (*jibie* 级别) (Li et
al. 1991; Brødsgaard 2002).[5] The system of officially-assigned, class-based
personal identities is gradually becoming redundant, and private business
people were never part of it in any case, since they were barred from official
recognition. Now, they can be pleased with not being stigmatized any more
and with being able to freely construct their identity.

Beck and Beck-Gernsheim (2003: 39–41) argue that processes of individualization deprive class distinctions of their social identities and dispute
the validity of traditional categories of class. Whereas inequalities do not
disappear, they become redefined as an individualization of social risks
which become increasingly personalized. In attempting to cope with social
problems, people are forced into political and social alliances which do not
have to follow a class model and there is therefore no justification for assigning the modern individual a class tag. In fact, Beck considers 'class' to
be a 'zombie category' (Beck and Beck-Gernsheim 2003: 202–213). The new
capitalists in China are increasingly disembedded from the previous, more
clear-cut collective social contexts and identities and they are re-embedded
in different ways. Therefore, it may easily be argued that private capitalists
in China are not a coherent class either (Tsai 2005). They may in fact share
political interests with other social groupings, as is the case with Sun Dawu
who is an ardent supporter of farmers' rights.

It is argued below that the Sun Dawu case demonstrates that private
business people without the otherwise common party-state alliances can

become agents of new 'self-politics' processes where a political arena or sub-arena can suddenly arise in what appears to be purely private matters of everyday life. Individuals may see themselves as being originators of political interventions and as political subjects crossing institutional boundaries in the political system. Self-politics are not state politics and they are far from identical, although they may seem so to the individual. Self-politics gain ground when system politics fail to suffice in all spheres of life (Beck and Beck-Gernsheim 2003: 44–45). Individuals are therefore looking for opportunities to redefine their social and political identity and relationships (Beck and Beck-Gernsheim 2003: 203), not least importantly their relationship to the party-state. Individuals will opt for re-embedding or reintegration into society, but there are many 'beds', and there are no prospects for final re-embeddedness at the end of the road. Being on the road has become the permanent way of life; the challenge is not how to choose and pursue an identity, but which one to choose at any given time (Bauman 2001: 146–147).

This search for identity divides and separates. The precariousness of the individual, solitary 'identity builder' prompts him or her to seek 'pegs on which they can hang together their individually experienced fears and perform the exorcism rites in the company of others, similarly afraid and anxious individuals. Whether such "peg communities" (understood here as iterative, loose, and temporary networks) provide what they are hoped to offer – a collective insurance against individually confronted risks – is a moot question; but mounting a barricade in the company of others does supply a momentary respite from loneliness' (Bauman 2001: 151–152).

These propositions inform the enquiry below into how relations between political identity and agency and between individuals and collectives in the state–private business nexus may configure themselves. The analytical concepts of 'self-politics' and 'peg communities' are used to probe how processes of individualization, identity-shaping and re-embedding may merge as sub-political processes in the state–private business nexus.

Contesting Master Narratives and Setting the Political Agenda

To understand these processes, it must however be recognized that they interact closely with ideological factors that contribute to the shaping of political identity and political agency that are linked to the formation of a new moral order under which the party-state's ideology can no longer find instant legitimization. First, there are historical roots to consider. In modern times, the dominant national 'master narrative' has focused on marginalization, subordination and exclusion of China as a nation. The idea of national victimhood has been expediently associated with anti-foreignness and nationalism and has been used by China's shifting political elites to consolidate their legitimacy and authority, and to maintain their power (Renwick and Cao 2003: 673). The strength of this master narrative has been its focus on the need for China to emancipate herself and catch up with the West, but it is increasingly being contested by a multiplicity of new master narratives based on new collective or individual identities that are in conflict with each other (Weigelin-Schwiedrzik 2006).

Still, new identities must necessarily relate to the existing official master narratives and, in a wider perspective, to the new moral order. For example, the negative image of capitalism in the past has been replaced by more constructive perceptions. Deng Xiaoping's dictum from the early 1980s that some regions and segments of society could 'get rich first' so that they would bring about prosperity to all later conveniently provided a basis for private capitalism to develop and for the recognition of private business people as such a segment (*zuowei xian fuqilaide yige qunti* 作为先富起来的一个群体, Ao 2005: 61). Simultaneously, the self-perception of private business people regarding their importance as political actors seems to have increased significantly in recent years (Ao 2005: 73).

The focus on 'getting rich first' came at a time of rapid disillusionment with the collective and egalitarian aspirations of the Maoist era, and Wang (2002) argues that China is now experiencing a capitalist revolution without a bourgeois subject that is able to organize its desires and impulses under a new constellation of values. There is no political discourse that can make sense of growing inequalities and general misbehaviour such as corruption, just as there is no political discourse that can help channel resentment against a booming market economy. Since the Communist Party is unwilling, unable, or at least slow to elaborate a workable new ideology, a new meta-type Chinese has emerged with a 'post-communist personality' that is out of tune with the official master narrative.

In this context, the recognition of private business is an important example of how a cornerstone of the original master narrative – a society dominated by working-class rule under the leadership of the Communist Party – is being gradually reworked so that the party-state can incorporate new socio-economic and political perceptions into its legitimizing ideology.

The elite discourse is invariably guided by the elite's need to build consensus (*gongshi* 共识), by its drive for unity (*tuanjie* 团结), and by the perceived need for education in commonly agreed upon ideas (*jiaoyu* 教育) (Renwick and Cao 2003: 72–73). Ideas such as patriotism and socialism as well as the need to reject individualism ('bourgeois liberalism') have been prevalent, and they have been promoted through so-called 'spiritual civilization campaigns' (Wang 2002). The political leadership does not want to be guided by pluralistic debate in its search for a new moral order. The core concept is 'unity' and, by default, there is a need for rejection of dissonant or divergent political ideas. Inappropriate or untimely criticism may receive the harshest punishment. The public political discourse is a game without clear rules where previous mass subjugation has been replaced only by a more cost-efficient and effective approach of selective repression (Pei 2006: 81–83), as experienced by Sun Dawu.

Yet, the national master narrative is being challenged by critical opposition (Oi 2004; Renwick and Cao 2003: 73–78), and the Communist Party seems unable to fully cope with the challenges to its traditional monopoly on public political discourse from the forces that feed on the processes of globalization and individualization. The use of the Internet as a vehicle for dissent is but one example of how these forces operate (Chase and Mulvenon 2002), as also demonstrated by Sun Dawu's case below.

Although the party-state insists on its right to elaborate the national master narrative, the multiplicity of political discourses can be seen as an initial de-politicization of the national level. This can be further exploited by groups and individuals to promote their interests. As far as private business people engage in political discourse or politics, their political identity and the way they exert their political agency in this new space is therefore of principal concern.

Given the autocratic nature of China's political regime, private businesses mostly exert their political agency in relation to constraints in the business environment that are not politically sensitive, i.e. primarily those that directly concern the operation of their businesses. A review of surveys of the business environment across China's regions shows a mixed picture. The overall impression is that China's political leadership is intent on continuing reforms in order to create a more level playing field (OECD 2005: 90–93). However, determination at the central level does not necessarily lead to uniform enforcement at the local level. China's diversity and unevenness in local governance (Saich 2004: 170–179) will – by default – cause both new policy initiatives and laws to take on different shapes locally.

Effectively, the surveys of private business show that there are considerable regional and sector variations and a need for much more consistency in how policies are applied. The situation in the regions depends largely on the institutional arrangements in the nexus between the local party-state and the private business sector. For example, there are particular barriers to private business entry in sectors with a state monopoly, there are severe credit constraints in many regions and sectors, and poor legal protection prompts many private enterprises to seek legal arbitration outside the courts which often leads to unfavourable settlements (China IFC 2000; ADB 2003; WB 2004; Li D. 2006; Li et al. 2006). A recent Chinese survey found that 42.8 per cent of the respondents rank 'corruption' as the most severe problem in society (Ao 2005: 78),[6] but other surveys show that there is considerable disagreement on how constraining corruption is. Finally, there is an institutionalized urban–rural divide that makes it more difficult to run a rural than an urban private business, as we shall see in the case of Sun Dawu below.

The reasons that many entrepreneurs seem to become increasingly satisfied with government are accounted for by Yang Dali, who argues that the Chinese leadership has charted a rather successful course in 'streamlining and downsizing the government, divesting the state institutions of their business operations, and generally remaking the relations between state and business and levelling the economic playing field'. The reforms have reduced the powers of the local party-state and there is an openness and willingness to deal with business people as a distinct social and even political group with legitimate legal and political interests. Yang acknowledges that much remains to be done, but given China's status as a developing country, there has been 'real progress towards making the Chinese state into a regulatory state suited to a functioning market economy' (Yang 2004: 17–18).

Therefore, problems with government are not necessarily seen as a key impediment, and firms are flexible in adapting to the challenges,[7] but the surveys of the regional business environments and the constraints on private business development discussed earlier have demonstrated which factors may prompt the individual business owner to exert political influence to improve the business environment, as also argued by Tsai (2005). The argument here is that this could form the basis for the sub-politicization of business communities as exemplified by Sun Dawu's case below.

Sub-Politicization and Political Agency

Whereas the political views and aspirations of entrepreneurs are normally not touched upon in surveys, a recent World Bank survey did do so and found that entrepreneurs saw 'political freedom' as important (73 per cent of the sample) as compared to 28 per cent of non-entrepreneurs included as a control group (Djankov et al. 2006). This thirst for political freedom may be the reason that China's private business people often act as agents of change without guaranteed sanctions from the state. They act in response to the challenges of globalization and individualization as well as the constraints in the business environment. They act on the basis of new master narratives and they have to make choices when collectives do not or cannot make choices for them anymore, as noted by Beck and Beck-Gernsheim (2003: 1).

In fact, individualization processes increasingly challenge the hegemony of the party-state and new negotiating systems emerge all the time, also within the state–private business nexus. But the processes in the nexus will not easily add up to a 'single all-integrating power of decision' (Beck and Beck-Gernsheim 2003: 28–29) that can challenge the dominance of the party-state.

Being intent on maintaining its power monopoly, China's party-state must deal with the challenge. It has already given up its desire to mobilize the masses and instead it now focuses on political participation by sanctioned groups (Saich 2004: 183–192). As noted by Dickson (2003: 11–13), some have argued that democratization would be a natural outcome of liberalization, free market development and economic growth. With a – presumably – weaker party-state and more pluralism in the political land-scape, such a proposition might be valid. However, there are other scen-arios that contradict such a projection (Dickson 2003:14–15). They range from 'collapse' (Chang 2001), to 'trapped transition' under a dysfunctional developmental autocracy (Pei 2006), to adaptation with space for some political freedom (Oi 2004) and promotion of administrative reform to attain more effective governance (Yang 2004). More specifically, Tsai (2005) has argued that if capitalists are not excluded from the current authoritarian regime and their material interests are not under threat, then it is unlikely that an elite corps of business owners would press for democratic change. Kennedy (2005: 179–182) is in agreement with this, as is Dickson (2003: 135; 2007), who does not find evidence that private entrepreneurs have clear preferences for political change or that they hold progressive or liberal views. In fact, he found that they entertain rather elitist ideas about their own interest in greater political participation and did not endorse wider political participation.

The aim here is not to examine whether China's capitalists would propagate democratic reforms, but rather to analyze how the construction of political identity and agency could influence the configuration and the political agenda of the emerging state–private business nexus, and how the limited space in which to exercise political freedom can be utilized or expanded.

In this context, Beck and Beck-Gernsheim (2003: 28–29) propose that the processes of the sub-politicization of society and the de-politicization of national politics are also valid for China. These processes may be ac-centuated by the emergence of new disembedded social segments, such as private business people who may use the position of their enterprise, their 'brand' name (like Sun Dawu below), their personal qualifications, and the resources at their disposal (including their networks) to engage in public debates and contest the official master narrative or even the politics of the hegemonic party-state. There is already room for them – at the micro- and meso-levels, but not yet at the national level – to establish micro-spaces of power to challenge local authority and the official hegemonic discourse through 'critical tension' (Renwick and Cao 2003: 74).

With the limited official interest in political reform, the quasi-state cor-poratist approach (Pei 2006: 45–95) may, paradoxically, become a window of opportunity for some private business people, since both individualistic and new collectivist arrangements may complement and contest existing attempts by the state to control collective action and, no matter how divergent the background and interests of private business people may be, they will share some concerns that relate to their common pursuit of profit (Tsai 2005).

In 2002, the Chinese communists decided to let private business people become Party members, although many had already been let in through the back door before, as the strategy was to co-opt private business people through joint business ownership and the continuation of Party membership by former state employees (including SOE employees) who had turned entrepreneurs. Private business people were also allowed into people's congresses and village committees, and they were invited to join business organizations controlled by the Party.

However, the 2002 decision definitively opened the doors for the direct political influence of the Party's old arch-enemy. The intention of the Party was and is to maintain control over the articulation of interests and political organization. At the same time, there is also an indisputable interest to create a new, more professional and business-minded political elite based on the conviction that there is a convergence of interests between the party-state and business people. This is demonstrated by the fact that an increasing number of people from the private sector have Party membership (Delman 2005; Dickson 2007) as well as the fact that an increasing number of business people are being (s)elected for other political positions (Ao 2005).[8]

But it is far from clear that private business people see Party membership as an attractive option. For example, in a survey of a sample of 230 private enterprises, only 7.5 per cent of the respondents agreed that joining the Party would be beneficial for raising the social standing of one's enterprise. In fact, 36.4 per cent thought that the best method would be to expand one's own enterprise, since size matters (Ao 2005: 76).

The party-state still keeps private business people at arm's length, however, and acts like the 'dog' wagging the private sector 'tail', and it does not appear to have any immediate intention to relinquish power to other organized interest groups (Delman 2005). But both sides can benefit from their new nexus relationship which allows the business sector to engage the party-state in business environment issues by questioning, redefining, realigning, or even removing areas of governance (*xingzheng zhineng* 行政职能) that have been the traditional preserve of the party-state. Tsai's typology for possible political strategies of private entrepreneurs tells us that to exert political agency, entrepreneurs would have to be 'assertive', i.e. they would need to have both the desire and the ability to confront the party-state, and to do so they must register their business, pay most taxes and fees, organize and participate in associational activities, and confront the party-state with requests and grievances individually or collectively (Tsai 2005). In the subsequent sections we shall see how Sun Dawu exemplifies this 'type'.

The Case of Sun Dawu[9]

Sapere aude! Have the courage to use your own understanding![10] was Immanuel Kant's motif for Enlightenment (Beck and Beck-Gernsheim 2003: 186), and this is exactly what Sun Dawu, a private businessman from Xushui County in Hebei Province, has shown over the last ten or more years. Sun's case is interesting because there are few private business people like him in China with an independent public political stance. The quasi-corporatist tradition and the 'Big Brother' syndrome are so pervasive that most citizens abstain from going public with their political views. Sun's public assertiveness cost him time in jail in 2003. Surprisingly, and in contrast to other entrepreneurs who have befallen political ill-fortunes (Sun 2005b and 2005c), his business survived, and following his release after six months in jail, he continued to develop his business while promoting his political ideas.

Sun's case is suggestive of individualization trends among private entrepreneurs in China and their search for a new identity and re-embeddedment into new types of loose collectives or alliances or 'peg communities'. He is also, if not representative, then emblematic of how private business people can create new alternative political identities and – if they dare – exert political agency by challenging the party-state through critical tension.

Business development

Born in 1954, Sun grew up in a farm family in Langwu Village in Xushui County, Hebei Province, about 150 km southwest of Beijing. Sun was an entrepreneur even as a boy. He started buying and selling small items at the age of nine and continued until he joined the army at 16. Back in Xushui at age 23, he was employed by the local agricultural bank. The salary was quite low and Sun again took up trading on the side (SDW1).

In 1985, Sun's wife and some associates rented a piece of barren land, about 3–4 per cent of the total area owned by Sun's home village (SDW1; VH1; LRH1). Different crop lines were introduced as well as chicken farming and eventually feed processing. Sun helped out, while continuing to do his bank job and his trading. He also set up a small roadside shop. In 1989, he left the bank and established an agro-based company with himself as director and later chairman of the board (SDW1). Effectively, Sun disembedded himself from his state collective and was in a situation where he had to seek opportunities to re-embed. During this period, the original associates left the partnership or were bought out (LRH1). Incidentally, the contract for the land was renewed in 2006, at a price that was much better for the village than the original one (VH1).

Sun's enterprise has grown incrementally and the company now consists of the mother company Dawu Group Company (*Dawu Jituan* 大午集团) which is owned by Sun Dawu, six agro-based daughter companies, a projected hot springs resort with a residential area, and a comprehensive school with 3,000 pupils and more than 200 teachers. As a social project, the school caters to the needs not only of the Dawu Group, but also to society at large. It is not seen as a profit unit (SP1) but it must break even eventually (SDW5). At this stage it is still subsidized by the Dawu Group (SP1). There is also a clinic that caters to employees, pupils and residents in neighbouring villages, each of whom pays one Yuan per month for free treatment that falls within the clinic's areas of expertise. The staff and villagers would otherwise have had no access to medical services in the area. The company has also instituted a pension scheme for all employees, something that is rare in China's rural areas (TU1).

Furthermore, the group has built living quarters for all employees from outside the area. They are provided free of charge as part of the remuneration package. In the eyes of the chairman of the board, the Dawu Group is a conglomerate of small businesses that does not entail much risk, as one of the sub-enterprises can fail without risking the collapse of the entire Group (BC1).

Being rural puts the Dawu Group in a different league compared to its urban counterparts. Government support, services and infrastructure hardly exist and the Dawu Group must for the most part take care of these functions itself. Staff members have a rural *hukou* (户口) which bars them from enjoying the privileges, entitlements and services that their urban counterparts may enjoy, e.g. schooling for children and health services. In that sense, they are secondary citizens (Cheng and Selden 1994).

To make up for this, the company must emulate the state-owned enterprises of the past by providing a range of social services that the government does not deliver. Because of this, the Dawu Group appears to be a socially responsible company; if it were not, however, the Group would be unable to retain out-of-area managers and skilled workers in this relatively secluded place.

The Group employs approximately 1,600–1,700 people (depending on the season) and the turnover of the entire group was about 200 million Yuan in 2006. 70 per cent of the employees are from the local area (CEO1) and 300–400 of these from Sun's home village (VH1). The remainder mainly consist of out-of-area staff with professional or academic qualifications (CEO1). Five years down the line, the goal is to become a large enterprise with an annual turnover of more than 500 million Yuan (CEO1). Currently, the registered assets amount to 170 million Yuan and liquidity to about 60 million Yuan. Salaries are competitive in the local environment and workers seem to get more than reported from other places in China.[11]

One of the stickiest points for a private company in China is to be able to access credit in order to sustain operations and growth, as noted earlier. The Dawu Group faces the same constraint. After being rejected by the local bank, the Dawu Group set up a loan scheme in 1998 to accelerate company investments. The Group took deposits from the staff, initially as shares, and from local farmers, who received a higher interest than the state banks would offer. No tax was paid on the interest on the deposits and the local authorities claimed that the Dawu Group had not been authorized to set up such a scheme by the People's Bank, although Sun Dawu claimed otherwise. In the official indictment against Sun (more below), the procurator accused the Dawu Group of raising – illegally – more than 159 million Yuan from 3,185 individuals or households between 1998 and 2003 (Yan 2006).

During the business development process, Sun's company had to deal with a host of government organizations that constantly harassed and fined the Group (Yan 2006).[12] In Sun's opinion, this was due to the lack of a clear legal framework for running a private business and the government's lack of goodwill towards private enterprises at the time. He also claimed to be reluctant to offer bribes[13] and he refused to display the traditional subservience that is required to deal with officials (SDW2). This was the case also when the Xushui government approached him to make a monetary donation to help their anti-SARS program in 2003. Being wary of potential corruption, Sun offered to make a donation in kind, which the relevant government department refused to accept while expressing their displeasure with Sun's insinuations (SEC1).

Some of the difficulties encountered by the Dawu Group were caused by a former village Party secretary in Laiwu Village who insisted on having a share in the company, officially on behalf of the village. After he was rejected, he asked the local authorities to check on, interfere with and fine the Dawu Group to the greatest possible extent. The Party secretary harassed Sun's family, abused them verbally, and was responsible for arson at the Dawu Group facilities. He even organized a physical attack on Sun Dawu which sent Sun to hospital for three months. Subsequently, the secretary was only detained for two days and not punished otherwise. It is not unfounded to assume that the Party secretary played a role in laying some of the groundwork for the subsequent legal case against Sun Dawu (see below; LRH1).

The legal case

The tension with the local party-state reached its climax when Sun Dawu was arrested on 27 May 2003 at a dinner to which he had been invited by the head of Xushui County (SEC1), presumably to be arrested. Afterwards, more than 20 people from key positions in the Dawu Group were detained as well. Sun's wife managed to escape and stayed in hiding until Sun was released on 1 November 2003 (Yan 2006; LRH1).

The indictment against Sun listed three charges: (1) the Dawu Group took illegal deposits from ordinary citizens (see above); (2) illegal possession of ammunition; (3) harming the public image of the government. A work group of about 60 people from a variety of local government departments took possession of the company immediately after the arrests and started checking the company's documents, transactions and accounts. The Dawu Group was allowed to continue business, but the work group controlled the finances, to the extent that workers were not paid salaries, which lead to a strike (SEC1; TU1).

Sun's family did not hire local lawyers to defend them, but they subsequently managed to put together a group of well-known, out-of-province defence lawyers who specialized in citizens' rights. These lawyers offered their services free of charge. Local people, business associates and other private business people actively spoke out for Sun Dawu, consistently in support of his business practices and his individual rights. A group of intellectuals/academics, particularly from Beijing, some of them quite well known, also spoke out in public and through connections, and a few of them became personal advisers to the family.

Even local farmers made appeals to the local government on Sun's behalf (VH1). In fact, during Sun's time in jail, more than 150 media and 200 journalists reported on the case in China. In addition, the case was reported by at least 32 foreign media (Yan 2006). Finally, some central leaders appear to have taken an interest in the case.

The activities of all of these players put heavy pressure on the local leadership, which (according to the website of the Dawu Group) was criticized locally for having created an 'evil and corrupt business environment'. This, combined with the fact that no records of other criminal offences than the running of an informal deposit and loan scheme were revealed during the large-scale investigation, may explain why Sun Dawu was treated rather leniently. He received a three-year sentence for illegal banking with immediate release and a probation period of four years. Furthermore, he had to pay a fine of 100,000 Yuan (Yan 2006, various interviews).

It may be argued that by refusing to make an alliance with the local party-state, Sun had to resort to a form of financing, i.e. lending from staff and villagers, which cost his business more than government credits would have done. At the outset, he had been a local People's Congress representative, which meant that he was a kind of 'government entrepreneur'. He seems to have used the position to tap the funding from the local residents with implicit consent from the local government. But as soon as he had resigned as a people's delegate, he was arrested for illegally taking loans from the public (Financial 2006). Eventually, Sun was only convicted for having lent 1.4 million Yuan from 523 households, i.e. ten times less than the charge in the original indictment (Yan 2006).

This settlement involved a compromise between Sun and the local government: he was only to be released when he admitted to having committed an economic crime of limited scale and agreed not to appeal the case. The accusation about harming the government's image was handled administratively during his detention. The procurator referred to three specific articles on his website which were then deleted. In addition, he was fined 15,000 Yuan for this offence (Yan 2006). The last point of the indictment relating to possession of explosives was dropped.

The company was saved not least due to younger family members taking charge while the top managers were in jail. The current general manager, a young woman now in her early 30s, and Sun Dawu's eldest son were the key figures (CEO1). Furthermore, most employees decided to stay on despite the problems (SDW5).

Although Sun Dawu was found guilty, he was released from jail after only six months. Furthermore, the government decided to support him directly and indirectly from then on. He was invited for a new dinner by the head of Xushui County with the heads of the departments that had investigated him during the case, and all agreed that the case was now over and that both sides would have to move on. The purpose was also to advise Sun to focus on his business and not make appearances in the media (SEC1).

Relations with government

Relations with the local party-state improved considerably after the settlement, but Sun still claims not to be willing to budge on key principles in terms of relationships with officials such as the local county Party secretary (SDW2). Key members of the executive team at the Dawu Group did the same (CEO1; BC1; BM1; BM2; LRH1). However, some executives modified Sun's – in the local context – rather fundamentalist approach to the handling of *guanxi* (关系) by agreeing to host modest dinners for local officials. This practice, while legal, had rarely occurred earlier (BM1; BM2).[14] They now have rather close ties with the local authorities through professional and personal relations as well as through memberships in professional and business associations (BC1; CEO1; BM2).

Even though relations are better, Sun Dawu was of the opinion that there has been no major improvement in the local business environment in the last few years. He also noted significant local variations (as discussed above) and provided evidence documenting the difference between the ease of doing business in Beijing as compared to Hebei Province (SDW2).[15]

Despite the problems with the local government, the Dawu Group has received a number of official awards over the years as being among the 'biggest' or 'best' private enterprises in various contexts. In 2005 for example, the Dawu Group was number 66 on a national list elaborated by the China Association for Industry and Commerce of China's 100 most vibrant companies.[16] The listings show that the Dawu Group is most unusual and that there are few private enterprises like it in China's more secluded rural areas. The interviewees also noted that there are no similar companies in Xushui County.

The Dawu Group is like a small town, and the name 'Dawu Town' (*Dawucheng* 大午城) is in common use. It is Sun's ambition that the Group should be given the status of an administrative unit with all the rights and obligations that that entails in terms of collective ownership of land, tax collection, social services, government-financed infrastructure and management of household registration (SDW1; SDW2; SEC 1). The implications are that the Dawu Group will continue down the road of the state-owned enterprises of the past. Sun argued that in the future the government would have to deliver social services, but that for the time being the Dawu Group had no choice but to provide them instead. The associated costs had to be covered through the development of new products with a higher value-added content. The current profit margin is too narrow to continue as is (SDW5).

Sun Dawu's experience as a rural entrepreneur is typical (Odgaard 1992; Yep 2003) and it shows that if entrepreneurs decide to act independently of the party-state in rural areas they are often forced to enter into alliances with and/or to bribe representatives of the local party-state. If not, they may be harassed, as in the case of the Dawu Group.

In recent years, Sun Dawu has stepped down from managing the day-to-day affairs of the Dawu Group. This has allowed him to devote more attention to his social and political activities. In fact, what distinguishes him from other private business people in rural areas is not necessarily his business career and the ability of his business to survive for such a long time, but rather the way he disembedded himself from the party-state to create a new dynamic between his business and political activities. Effectively, he has been prompted by individualization processes to develop a new platform to tackle the challenges that his business encountered and this has developed into a wider political platform.

Political ideas

Since the beginning, Sun Dawu has been articulate in public on issues relating to rural development, defined officially as 'the three problems of agriculture, farmers, and rural development' (*sannong wenti* 三农问题), as well as the public bias against private business. Most of his ideas and propositions are formulated on the basis of problems encountered when developing and running his business in a rural area, against which there is considerable party-state and urban bias. Furthermore, China's market economy was emerging and struggling with the lack of proper legislation regarding private enterprise development (Pei 2006: 67–72). Indeed, Sun Dawu has spoken on many occasions about the need for legal reform to protect private business (Sun 2004).

These factors, combined with Sun's personal background as a villager coming from a home with strong Daoist and Buddhist beliefs, prompted him to search for answers to the challenges that he, his company, the local farmers, China's rural areas, and China encounter. He explained that his inspirational sources are manifold: Chinese and Western philosophy, religion, and political and economic studies. He is a syncretic thinker, with a strong preference for Confucianism. He is also interested in modern legal discourse and deliberations on how to develop a socialist welfare society (Sun 2004). To some extent, he is preoccupied with constructing the moral basis for a 'post-communist personality' as discussed earlier.

Sun claims to be a Marxist and a believer in communism, not as an outcome of class struggle but rather as the highest form of capitalism, which should ensure prosperity for all. He sees the market economy as a moral economic system where businessmen are the moral actors (Sun 2005c). He views China's governance as predatory. The party-state has built a 'licensing society' (*xukezheng shehui* 许可证社会) with numerous, superfluous bureaucratic functions that have rent-seeking as their primary goal (SDW1).[17] Even more, the new economic system is dominated by bureaucratic capitalism,[18] and he argues that the pattern of state monopolies being controlled by the party-state must be changed (SDW5). In commenting on other private business people who have been arrested for various criminal activities, Sun argues that they are not necessarily law-breakers. Rather, with strong encouragement from their local party-state, they have surrendered to their own ambition and then have been made scapegoats for misperceptions and wrong decisions, and have even been persecuted by the same local governments when their ventures went astray (Sun 2005b and 2005c).

The assumption underlying Sun's analysis is that the main contradiction in human society is between officials and the people. He quotes former US President Ronald Reagan as saying: 'Government cannot solve problems, only create them.' China needs a small government and a strong legal and regulatory framework (in his words a 'cage': *longzi* 笼子), i.e. a system with checks and balances, both at the enterprise level, like the management system implemented at Dawu Group (see below), and at the societal level through a proper constitutional and legal system. Such a system should guarantee necessary constitutional and human rights. Democracy is a means to reach that stage, not the end goal. The Constitution should protect both good and bad people, and, if it does not, China could end up with a fascist political system. Sun sees the US system with elections every fourth year as a possible inspiration, since the system provides the mechanisms for organizing legal opposition to the government. Essentially, ordinary people should be allowed to make the big decisions in society and this would overcome the contradiction between officials and the people (SDW5).

In Sun's view, the problems in rural areas have to be solved by liberating the peasants from their social and political stigma. Rural areas should enjoy democracy and self-development, and the government should show restraint and self-discipline and stop exploiting the peasants. There should be a non-biased framework for economic and social development where farmers are free to sell their land and their labour, and where their fundamental rights are protected. Farmers should be liberated from their state-assigned identities associated with their household status (*hukou* 户口), put on an equal footing with urban residents, and able to make their own choices in life. In fact, China needs to start trusting its farmers, argues Sun (Sun 2004).

Sun's key political vision is to create a 'republican' (*gonghe* 共和) society which should be a community with space for conflicting viewpoints and interests. Special privileges for interest groups should be abandoned. It should have checks and balances and be in harmony with itself. Although people would have diverging rights – e.g. property rights, the right to free-dom of speech, and political rights – a republican society would still have a high degree of tolerance. It should be able to comprise and simultaneously cater to the differences between races, beliefs, the sexes, and age groups. Republicanism should create the basis for a 'normal' state of affairs (SDW2; SDW4). Evidently, Sun uses the concept to challenge the current consti-tutional system in China which is a 'People's Republic' (*Renmin Gongheguo* 人民共和国), and it exemplifies how Sun is far from shy from engaging in 'critical tension' with established concepts and perceptions, although he has become more cautious in recent years.

At this stage, Sun has identified three main types of problems in society: (1) radical problems that can only be solved through dramatic shifts or transformations; (2) sensitive issues that can only be solved by helping the government, i.e. issues like land property rights, and legal rights; (3) issues that can be solved by adopting a cooperative and constructive approach towards the government. With the current regime, it is only possible to work politically with what Sun defines as 'mainstream' (*zhuliu* 主流) issues. They do not entail criticism of or create problems for the government. Still, assistance to the government in addressing such issues could entail the suspicion of currying favours. Therefore, independent researchers and organizations should act as representatives of civil society and only propose how to deal with such 'mainstream' issues; they should not work directly under the government's tutelage (SDW5).

Sun sees no alternative but to stay away from sensitive political issues that irritate government officials and, within that constraint, he would then only work with concerns that can enjoy support from ordinary people. The groups in society that care for and represent 'mainstream' issues should only concern themselves with the happiness of ordinary people in their daily lives. Such groups may deal with issues such as the organization of popular festivals, research on popular education, and care for the elderly. Even if they are concerned with hotter political issues, they should not point their fingers at any particular department, but rather focus constructively on developing new ideas and frameworks (SDW2).

The term 'governmentalization of the individual' (*geren zhengfuhua* 个人政府化) came up as a basic tenet in Sun's political philosophy during the interviews. The party-state must accept, he argued, that as citizens each individual must have equal rights and responsibilities. Government must dispose of some of its functions (*zhengfu zhineng* 政府职能) and leave society to deal with them. The key is the 'cage', i.e. the framework that will make governance more accountable and transparent. The idea of 'governmentalization of the individual' is an exemplary way of describing what the potential political role of individuals in an individualizing society entails, i.e. a new type 'self-politics' (as discussed above) where individual citizenship is institutionalized as the basis for political agency and new processes of governance.

Whereas Sun maintains a certain political vigilance, he has recognized that he cannot change society single-handedly and that 'critical tension' is the only way forward. It seems that he has accepted the hegemony of the Communist Party, which is linked to its historical role as custodian of China's emancipatory efforts to leave 'victimhood' behind her. Yet, he is still trying to construct a new master narrative.

Business philosophy and organization

Sun's business philosophy is integrated with his political ideas and it is written into the mission statement of the Dawu Group, which reads: 'Not with profit as a target, but with development as a goal. The ultimate end goal is common prosperity' (*bu yi yingli wei mudi, er yi fazhan wei mubiao, yi gongtong fuyu wei guisu* 不以盈利为目的, 而以发展为目标, 以共同富裕为归宿). Sun's explanation was that profit-making must be combined with social responsibility. This vision establishes a clear link between his business philosophy and his political ideas about a republican society with common prosperity as its goal.

In concrete terms, the staff members of the Dawu Group and the local community are the first to benefit since the Group must continuously bear in mind the common social good in the local context (SDW1). The representative of the trade union at the Dawu Group interpreted this to mean that the Group must cater to the needs of employees before thinking of earning profits. 'Without staff', she said, 'there would be no money' (TU1). The interviewees were well aware of the basic principles of the business philosophy, and one of the managers was attracted to the company for exactly that reason (BM1). Still, the top managers had divergent views about its interpretation. The Chairman of the Board and the CEO endorsed the motto strongly, but they also argued that there had to be an appropriate balance between profit and social obligation (BC1; CEO1). The vision and the practical measures that the philosophy entails have become part of the brand of the Dawu Group (BC1) as well as part of Sun Dawu's political brand. Additionally, the provision of high-quality products and services is another core principle of the Group that helps to brand both the business and Sun himself (SDW5; BM2).

Sun Dawu retains sole ownership of the Dawu Group, but a new organizational system has emerged in recent years. Sun does not hesitate to call this the beginnings of a major organizational innovation: 'Constitutional monarchy at the enterprise level' (*qiye junxian zhidu* 企业君宪制度, SDW2). The system combines democratic elections for management positions with shared responsibilities, a 'division of three powers' (*sanquan fenli* 三权分立) between a board (*dongshihui* 董事会), an executive management council (*lishihui* 理事会) and an internal auditing committee (*jianshihui* 监事会). Sun designed the system with inspiration from the British and American constitutional systems to solve the issue of control and transparency in managing the business (SDW2). In addition to being owner, Sun is chairman of the internal auditing committee only, but it gives him a veto-right over major company policies and investment projects. The responsibility for developing the business and its day-to-day running has been delegated to the board, the executive committee, and the elected managers.

In principle, staff in all categories can participate in elections for the board and the executive positions in the Dawu Group, and they are keen to do so (SDW2; BM1; BM2). Eligibility is determined by duration of employment, which can vary for different types of positions. But all staff members have a voice in proposing candidates initially; each candidate needs at least five colleagues from within specified areas of the Dawu Group as supporters. This is to ensure that all aspects of operations are represented on the board. Candidates must have shown results in their work, they must be able to express themselves clearly, and possess 'people skills' (BM1).

The chairman of the board, the CEO, and the leaders of the sub-units are elected from amongst the board members. There are provisions for rotation, but also a possibility for re-election. Board members are elected every two years while the chairman of the board, the CEO, and the managers of the sub-units are elected only every four years. The positions have associated privileges in terms of apartments, access to company cars, free schooling for children, and so forth (Dawu Group 2006). More than 30 per cent of top managers are members of Sun's family, including the three top leaders in the new system, whereas family members constitute one sixth of mid-level managers (SEC1).

The system is under development. The first election was held in 2004, where Sun Dawu proposed the names of candidates. The second election was held in December 2006 when the current version of the system was put in place. The rules applying to the elections and the regulations concerning benefits to the elected managers are public knowledge within the Dawu Group (SEC1) and journalists were invited to observe and report on the election in 2006 (BM2; Muji Dawu 2006). It is but one example of how Sun Dawu's views on business and politics have become part of the branding of the Dawu Group.

The new organizational structure came about through a discussion between Sun and his wife on how to ensure a smooth transition of ownership and leadership without the risk that their two sons would eventually split up the Group (*fenjia* 分家) when it became time to inherit their parents' assets (LRH1). Once again, we note how practical problems encountered by the business can lead to solutions that draw on and inspire Sun Dawu's wider societal and political considerations.

The organizational structure is unique and the system has helped the Dawu Group stabilize its management group and operational systems. It also has a strong motivational effect on board members, managers and staff (BM1; BM2; TU1; SEC1). One of the managers of the company was not completely convinced about the approach, however, since it does not necessarily ensure that all elected leaders possess adequate qualifications (CEO1). At the same time, the Chairman of the Board was not opposed to the idea that a merger with or an acquisition of another company could be considered at some future point (BC1), a situation where the system could conceivably be challenged.

Sun's business philosophy and the new management system incorporate some of his key philosophical and political ideas and contribute to the branding of both himself and the Group. If successful, it may also contribute to improving his standing in society as it combines basic ideas of collectivism, representative democracy, common prosperity and social responsibility.

Status and political identity

During the interviews, Sun was hesitant about defining his identity (*shenfen* 身份), but he has clearly had shifting sub-identities relating to either his professional, social, or political work. Before 2003, he thought of himself as a businessman (*qiyejia* 企业家), which other interviewees agreed with (CEO1; BM1). In fact, he used to be a so-called 'government entrepreneur' when he was a member of the local county people's congress (Financial 2006). The current village leader saw Sun as a trustworthy private entrepreneur who never cheated anybody (VH1). Sun also ventured – with hesitation – to consider himself a Confucian businessman (*rushang* 儒商) and a social practitioner, an opinion also voiced by others (SEC1; SP1). But he also claimed to be much more than just a Confucian (*rujia* 儒家), as exemplified by his political ideas.

Sun argued that he is 'everything and nothing' (*shenme dou shi, shenme dou bu shi* 什么都是,什么都不是) and that he 'does not need society, nor does society need me' (*wo bu xuyao shehui, shehui bu xuyao wo* 我不需要社会,社会不需要我), which are both perfect responses for an individual engulfed by the process of individualization. He did not see himself as a politician (*zhengzhijia* 政治家) as he has neither the political resources nor the personal strength to assume that role. He argued that it is 'dangerous' to operate outside the established political system, and he criticized the West for being obsessed with assigning status to everyone, since it is only meant to obtain or display special privileges (SDW5).

Sun is clearly a political thinker (SDW5) and he did concede that he could be a powerful resource for other people, for society, and also at a political level, although his influence is not strong (SDW2). One of the interviewees stated that Sun does not understand politics, as shown by his inability to handle relations with the local government in the past, and by the fact that he is not a real politician (CEO1). His wife argued that he does not have political ambition, he is only reflecting on social issues (LRH1).

Sun's identity was seen as having even more dimensions. Some regarded him as a philosopher (CEO1) or a reform thinker who loves to study (SEC1). One interviewee stated that as a philosopher, he is only a 'small thinker', not a 'big one' (BM2). He is an idealist (Yan 2006), and he is clearly acknowledged for his strong sense of social responsibility: 'He has a bottom line for taking social responsibility' (SEC1; VH1) and he insists on equality in his relationships with others (SEC1). Finally, he is an eminent local person and widely respected in local society (BM2).

These are subjective assessments only, but they show that identities can shift and be adapted to different life projects, tasks and roles. His palette of identities indicates that Sun is a person who does not easily re-embed after having disembedded himself from his original status and identity as a government employee. He symbolizes the modern individual who is constantly on the road without a definite end goal.

Political agency: a sub-political community at work?

While Sun claims to have no political resources or ambition, he exerts a certain measure of influence through his political agency, which is embodied in a network developed incrementally over the years. Despite the setback in 2003, he has increasingly become known in society as an outspoken private businessman. He has participated in countless conferences and official meetings organized by academic, government and business organizations, and he has given numerous lectures. One of them – a lecture at Beijing University during the spring of 2003 – drew particular attention due to his unusual frankness about social and political problems in rural areas (Sun 2004).

In 2003, views expressed at a conference in Zhongnanhai on rural development, at which State Counsellor Wu Yi presided, strained his relationship with the provincial government in Hebei. Sun criticized China's official statistics as he had done in other talks at Beijing University and China Agricultural University, and Wu Yi was reportedly unreceptive to his views. After the meeting, an accompanying official from Hebei told him: 'This was your first as well as your last meeting at Zhongnanhai!' (SDW4; SEC1).

Through the years, Sun has created a network of contacts comprised of representatives from many walks of life. First of all, people from the family and the local community, including local farmers and leaders, then media people, intellectuals of various convictions (from left, right and centre, claims Sun), academic institutions, government officials, the legal profession, publishers,[19] resident foreign organizations and a few other businessmen. Many of the Chinese dialogue partners are pondering social and political issues just like Sun, and he is eager to be challenged by as many viewpoints as possible. He does not, however, subscribe to any specific political inclination (SDW2). A Confucian quote we saw at the Dawu School reflects this approach: 'Reading makes a full man, meditation a profound man, discourse a clear man.'

Sun also draws the attention and support of people with significant influence. Two examples from the legal case against him will serve to illustrate the point. On 31 October 2003, when Sun was about to be released from jail, Liu Chuanzhi, the Chairman of the Board of Lianxiang (now Lenovo), one of China's major private corporations, wrote to Sun through the Dawu Group website. He stated that it was natural that entrepreneurs would meet all kinds of problems during the transition to a market economy. He advised Sun to stay calm and not to waiver. He expressed the conviction that China's private enterprises would be fully recognized and treated more fairly in the future (Yan 2006). Such a public display of sympathy from a leading high-tech tycoon would not go unnoticed at the highest political level.

The second example relates to an intervention on Sun's behalf by a retired professor from Beijing. The professor wrote a letter in July 2003 to approximately one hundred of China's top leaders to inform them that the foreign media had reported negatively on the case against Sun, and that they had asked whether China's reforms had stopped and whether China did not support private enterprise. The letter referred to the importance of China's entry into the WTO and the need for a level playing-field. According to the professor, one retired central leader instructed a Vice Premier to follow up on the case.[20] Yan (2006) speculates that Professor Yao's letter could have played a crucial part in securing the early settlement of the lawsuit against Sun, but such speculations defy verification.

Sun claims not to be an active network organizer, since he does not have the strength to do so, nor is it possible at this stage of development in China (SDW2; LRH1). However, judging by his activities, he appears to be a modern networker. His network is loose and spontaneous,[21] people move in and out, he selects and discards, but the network expands incrementally and appears to be somewhat coherent. Modern means of communication enable him to stay in touch and to disseminate his ideas. Interestingly, during his suspended sentence, he has no restrictions on his movements or actions, except that he cannot travel abroad (SDW4).

The network provides opportunities for re-embedding that fit his individual project to continuously be 'on the road' in search of ideas and proposals for solutions to the challenges faced by his company as well as by China's rural areas. While having a strong sense of social responsibility, he is also focused on his own needs, and his approach could be seen as an expression of 'self-politics' as discussed by Beck and Beck-Gernsheim (2003: 184). He is supported efficiently by a small secretariat that organizes all his activities, drafts all his speeches and documents, organizes his meetings and contacts, and manages the comprehensive and highly informative website of the Dawu Group (SEC1), which includes both business-related information and considerable documentation of Sun's political activities and views. It has been one of the platforms for Sun's 'critical tension' with the party-state.

Sun also makes appearances in the media and he often publishes in publications with national-level VIPs (e.g. Tian 2005). Some interviewees agreed that he has a certain influence in society, but one family member was not so keen on his political activities as they might negatively influence the company (SP1).

Sun is not dependent on any particular organization. He has remained a Communist Party member throughout, but not a 'staunch' one. He is rather pessimistic about the possibility of establishing a new political party in the current climate in China, even if it would help the government, and he has no intention to do so (SDW2). He does, however, consider establishing an independent think tank that could advise government on the 'mainstream' issues discussed earlier (SDW5). He does not believe that the current government-organized NGOs (GONGO) in China have a role to play and he is not a member of any such organization (SDW2). He claims not to be politically ambitious and says: 'I do not choose history, history must choose me' (*wo bu xuan lishi, lishi xuan wo* 我不选历史，历史选我, SDW2), indicating that he must 'obey' history (SDW5; SEC1). The authors' interpretation of this is that if 'history' decides that he should stay in Xushui, he will do so, and if he should be 'chosen' for a higher-level cause he would not decline.

It may be argued that Sun's self-politics, i.e. his political agency, is anchored in a sub-politicized community with him as a hub. This type of community is difficult for the party-state to control, since it is fluid and supported by modern means of communication as well as by the media.

Participants in the community may be jailed, as happened with Sun, but the support from the media, local people, VIPs of various sorts and the legal profession helped solve the case without ruining either Sun Dawu or the Dawu Group (SDW2; LRH1).

Sun has proved himself to be a fairly assertive businessman who fits into Tsai's typology discussed earlier (Tsai 2005), and the party-state has been far from able to control the activities of his 'community' because of its wide-spread connections and the willingness of its 'members' to invest their resources, reputation and influence in the network. The network is an illustration of how a sub-political community, what we could term a 'peg political community', may construct itself and operate in China.

Conclusion

This chapter has discussed how private business people are prompted by China's market reforms and by the twin processes of globalization and individualization to develop a new political identity and to exert political agency. The Sun Dawu case has been used to show how an individual engulfed by the process of individualization has constructed shifting identities and developed his life tasks and projects. His goal was to develop an enterprise to secure the livelihoods of himself and his family. This led to deliberations about social and political issues, moving from the local to the national, which eventually prompted him to articulate increasingly mature political viewpoints in public.

Sun's political philosophy is not a system of thought. Rather, his ideas have emerged organically as his life unfolded. He became better versed in different schools of thought, and wiser. His point of departure was the problems that he and his business encountered over the years. This led him to make rather unspecific proposals for improvements of the business environment in rural areas. He gradually developed political ideas that address issues of social injustice and the biases and weaknesses in the economic and social structures and institutions that constitute the basis for conducting private business, and for allowing citizens, especially those in rural areas, to decide their own destinies.

Sun has become more cautious after the lawsuit in 2003. He is now propagating a less confrontational and more accommodating approach to

Table 3.1. Interviews 9–16.1.2007

	Identifier	Date	Interviewee
1	SDW1	10.1.07	Sun Dawu, Chairman of the Internal Auditing Committee and owner of Dawu Group
2	SDW2	10.1.07	Sun Dawu
3	CEO1	11.1.07	General Manager, Dawu Group
4	SEC1	11.1.07	Head of Secretariat and Assistant to the Head of the Internal Auditing Committee, Dawu Group
5	BC1	12.1.07	Chairman of the Board, Dawu Group
6	SP1	12.1.07	Deputy School Principal, Dawu Group School
7	BM1	13.1.07	Board Member and General Manager, Dawu Group
8	BM2	13.1.07	Board Member, Dawu Group and General Manager, Dawu Group
9	VH1	13.1.07	Chairman of Village Committee, Langwuzhuang Village
10	SEC2	13.1.07	Head of Secretariat, Dawu Group
11	SDW3	14.1.07	Sun Dawu
12	LRH1	14.1.07	Former Chief Accountant of Dawu Group, now Financial Adviser (Supervisor). Married to Sun Dawu.
13	SDW4		Various informal conversations with Sun Dawu. Notes only taken after the conversation.
14	TU1	15.1.07	Former head of trade union at Dawu Group, now Head of Office of Feedstuff Company and member of the Board of Dawu Group
15	SDW5	15.1.07	Sun Dawu

Dawu Group = Hebei Province Dawu Agricultural and Livestock Group Co. (Ltd.)/ Hebei Sheng Dawu Nongmu Jituan Youxian Gongsi 河北省大午农牧集团有限公司.

The interviews were conducted separately (except for the interview with BM1 and BM2). During all interviews, at least one of Sun Dawu's secretaries was present.

dealing with challenges in society while arguing in favour of a more rules-based society with less direct government involvement. He propagates freedom and responsibility, even democracy, but he does not argue for a multi-party system or the removal of the current party-state system. He is developing his own master narrative of a social-liberal nature. But he still claims to be a Marxist and he treads the political minefield extremely cautiously. He does not agree with the autocratic developmental approach, and like others in his 'community' he engages in considerable critical tension with the party-state from the grassroots level.

One of the main findings of this study is that Sun's loose 'community' has helped promote his political life project and protects him from the vagaries of the party-state. His 'self-politics' have contributed to creating a sub-political or 'peg' community where he and others can create their master narrative collectively and exert a certain measure of political agency vis-à-vis the party-state. Sun Dawu has thus shown that individualization does not at all conflict with new forms of political action, as also argued by Beck and Beck-Gernsheim (2003: 184).

This sub-political community is but one example of the dynamics of the new state–private business nexus in China. It shows how the nexus can be exploited informally by assertive private business people even as the rules of the game in the nexus continue to change. The strength of the community is its subtle coherence amidst its fluidity. It may embrace a variety of life projects by many individuals that change and adapt over time, and it represents one way of seeking to re-embed in a new type of collectivist structure outside the control of the party-state. But under China's current system of party-state autocracy, it is still doubtful whether it will make a significant impact and make Sun's political philosophy more realistic and influential in the future. 'History' has not 'chosen' him as yet.

Notes

1   The China OECD survey distinguishes firms on the basis of their controlling shareholder, i.e. whether it is the state (directly or indirectly), a collective (local government), or a private entity (individuals, domestic legal persons, or foreign companies) (OECD 2005: 81). However, the demarcation lines between SOEs, hybrid enterprises, and true private enterprises are blurred and 'private enter-

prise' is as yet an imprecise concept statistically, see Li D. 2006: 128. However, for the sake of our argument, the OECD definition of a private firm has been accepted without reservations.

2   Concept adapted from Yang 2004: 8–13 who speaks of a 'state-enterprise nexus'.

3   See Renwick and Cao 2003.

4   As an indication, the existence of one million informal NGOs has been recognized officially, Huang 2007.

5   The system of state-assigned identities did, of course, not prevent other 'identities' from existing, but people with such identities did not enjoy the benefits of the state's distribution of power, privilege and resources.

6   Subtly, Ao's question focused on corruption as a social problem, not as a problem faced by the individual enterprise. The survey was conducted in Guangzhou and Wenzhou in late 2003/early 2004. Information was gathered from 400 enterprises, 230 of which by questionnaire. The sampling procedure is not described. The author is employed by the Party School under the Guangzhou Party Committee, Ao 2005.

7   Tsui et al. 2006, various pages.

8   Some top CEOs from China's SOEs have already reached top positions in China's Communist Party. At the 16th National Congress of the CPC in 2002, 24 top CEOs became full or alternate members of the 356-member Central Committee (Li 2005). In the future, CEO's of private companies will most probably join them. However, few private firms are as big as the SOEs now represented in the CPC CC and they are still not considered politically reliable.

9   This section relies on three different sources: (1) interviews undertaken from 9–16.1.2007 (see Table 3.1); (2) published sources; (3) information at the website of the Dawu Group, www.dawu.com.cn, that was accessed during weeks 50–51 of 2006 and weeks 1–4 of 2007. The latter source has not been referenced directly, and whenever information is given without reference, it has been taken from the website. The case is presented from the point of view of the Dawu Group, as it was not possible to organize interviews with local government departments. This is defensible as the attempt here is not to establish the facts of the legal case, but rather to discuss how Sun Dawu has developed his business, his political identity and agency.

10 Original source: Immanuel Kant, 'Beantwortung der Frage: Was ist Aufklärung?', *Berlinische Monatsschrift, Dec. 1784.*

11 The lowest salary at the Dawu Group was about 700 Yuan per month in the feed company (about 90.5 USD on 21.2.2007). Company managers are paid 1,500–2,500 Yuan per month, and an additional maximum bonus of 10,000 Yuan

annually (BC1). The official minimum salaries set by local governments across China range from 45 USD to 101 USD a month. Cheating with payroll records to conceal lower than reported wages is widely reported (BusinessWeek 2006).

12 On the web site of the Dawu Group (www.dawu.com.cn), a series of confrontations with land, industry and commerce, tax, health, and technical supervision departments are listed. These happened before Sun's arrest. They often led to fines and incurred significant losses to the company.

13 In 2000, some friends advised Sun Dawu to provide a 10,000 Yuan 'gift' to the head of the local credit cooperative to obtain a credit of six million Yuan to develop a vineyard. Apparently, the bribe was not big enough, no loan was forthcoming, and Sun demanded his money back. He received only 6,000 Yuan (Yan 2006).

14 It was not possible to meet government officials during the stay in Hebei. Reportedly, many of those involved with the case against SDW had already left their jobs (LRH1).

15 A business licence from Beijing allowing a company to deal with anything that is legal. In Hebei, this is not possible. The line of business must be registered and it confines the scope of new development.

16 *Zhongguo zui you shengmingli baiqiang qiye* 中国最有生命力百强企业

17 The use of the term 'rent' is the authors' interpretation of Sun Dawu's statements. Sun Dawu's writings are full of examples of rent-seeking behaviour by local officials, see for example Lei and Hong 2004: 119–142.

18 Sun used the term: *liyi bumenhua* 利益部门化, i.e. [own] interests have become the priority of [government] departments.

19 A representative of a high-level academic government publisher visited Sun, when the present authors were there, to get an agreement to publish a book on Sun's experiences and views as a private businessman.

20 Personal information from Professor Yao Jianfu 18.1.07. A copy of the letter is to hand.

21 The interviews with Sun Dawu were arranged on the spur of the moment through a phone call to Sun from Denmark. He immediately agreed to receive the authors.

Bibliography

ADB (2003) 'The Development of Private Enterprise in the People's Republic of China'. Manila: Asian Development Bank, March 2003.

Ao Daiya (敖带芽) (2005) '私营企业主政治参与研究报告' [Research report on the political participation of private business people]. 中国私营企业发展报告 [A report on the development of China's private enterprises]. Beijing: Social Sciences Academic Press, no. 6, pp. 61–83.

Bauman, Zygmunt (2001) *The Individualized Society*. Oxford: Polity.

Beck, Ulrich and Elisabeth Beck-Gernsheim (2003) *Individualization: Institutionalized Individualism and its Social and Political Consequences*. London: Sage.

Brødsgaard, Kjeld Erik (2002) 'Institutional reform and the *Bianzhi* system'. *The China Quarterly*, no. 170 (June 2002), pp. 361–386.

BusinessWeek (2006) 'Secrets lies and sweatshops', 27.11.06, http://www.businessweek.com/magazine/content/06_48/b4011001.htm. Accessed 21 April 2007.

Chang, Gordon G. (2001) *The Coming Collapse of China*. New York: Random House.

Chase, Michael S. and James C. Mulvenon (2002) *You've Got Dissent! Chinese Dissident Use of the Internet and Beijing's Counter-Strategies*. Arlington: Rand Corporation.

Cheng, Tiejun and Mark Selden (1994) 'The origins and social consequences of China's hukou system'. *The China Quarterly*, no. 139 (September 1994), pp. 644–668.

China IFC (2000) 'China's emerging private enterprise – prospects for the new century'. Washington D.C.: International Finance Corporation.

Dawu Group (2006) '大午集团第二届董事会成员选举办法' [Election procedures for the members of the second board of the Dawu Group]. *Mimeo*, Dawu Group: December 2006.

Dawu Group website www.dawu.com.cn. Accessed during weeks 50–51 of 2006 and weeks 1–4 of 2007.

Delman, Jørgen (2005) 'China's Party State and the private business sector: "Dog wags tail" or "tail wags dog"?'. *Norwegian Journal of Geography*, vol. 59, no. 3, pp. 207–216.

Dickson, Bruce J. (2003) *Red Capitalists in China. The Party, Private Entrepreneurs, and Prospects for Political Change*. Cambridge: Cambridge University Press.

—— (2007) 'Integrating wealth and power in China: The Communist Party's embrace of the private sector'. *The China Quarterly*, no. 192 (December 2007), pp. 827–854.

Djankov, Simeon, Yingyi Qian, Gérard Roland and Ekaterina Zhuravskaya (2006) 'Who are China's entrepreneurs? ' (World Bank) http://www.doingbusiness.org/documents/china_entrepreneurs.pdf. Accessed 22 March 2006.

'Financial discrimination, corruption and the rise of China's private enterprises: observations on China's economic transition' (2006) Knowledge@Wharton

Finance and Investment, 14.3.2006. www.knowledgeatwharton.com.cn/index.cf m?fa=viewArticle&articleID=1338&languageid=1. Accessed 21 February 2007.

Huang, H.M. (2007) 'China's NGO sector' (London: BOND – British Overseas NGOs for Development, 2007) http://www.bond.org.uk/networker/2007/september/chinas-ngos.htm. Accessed 1 April 2008.

Kennedy, Scott (2005) *The Business of Lobbying in China*. Cambridge: Harvard University Press.

Kirby, William C. (ed.) (2004) *Realms of Freedom in Modern China*. Stanford: Stanford University Press.

Krug, Barbara (ed.) (2004) *China's Rational Entrepreneurs: The Development of the New Private Business Sector*. London: RoutledgeCurzon.

Krug, Barbara and Judith Mehta (2004) 'Entrepreneurship by alliance'. In Barbara Krug (ed.), *China's Rational Entrepreneurs, The Development of the New Private Business Sector*. London: RoutledgeCurzon, pp. 50–71.

Lei Dian and Hong Chen (雷霣,洪尘) (eds.) (2004) 孙大悟为农民而生.一个农民企业家的努力与发展 [Sun Dawu – born for the peasants. The efforts and development of a rural entrepreneur]. Beijing: Zhongguo shehui kexue chubanshe.

Li, Cheng (2005) 'The rise of China's yuppie corps: top CEOs to watch', *China Leadership Monitor*, No. 14, http://www.hoover.org/publications/clm/issues/2903791.html. Accessed 28 March 2006.

Li, David D.K. (2006) 'A survey of the economics literature on China's non-state enterprise's. In Anne S. Tsui, Yanjie Bian and Leonard K. Cheng (eds.), *China's Domestic Private Firms. Multidisciplinary Perspectives on Management and Performance*. Armonk: M.E. Sharpe, pp. 128–145.

Li, Hongbin, Lingsheng Meng and Junsen Zhang (2006) 'Why do entrepreneurs enter politics? Evidence from China'. *Economic Enquiry*, vol. 44, no. 3 (July 2006), pp. 559–578.

Li, Lulu, Yang Xiao and Wang Fengyu (1991) 'The structure of social stratification and the modernization process in contemporary China'. *International Sociology*, vol. 6, no.1 (March 1991), pp. 25–36.

Muji Dawu 目击大午 (2006) "私企立宪法选举" ' [Witnessing Dawu's "constitutional elections in a private company"]. *Gongshang shibao*, 19.12.

Odgaard, Ole (1992) *Private Enterprises in Rural China. Impact on Agriculture and Social Stratification*. Aldershot: Avebury.

OECD Organization for Economic Cooperation and Development (2005) 'OECD economic survey of China'. Organization for Economic Cooperation and Development, vol. 2005, no. 13.

Oi, Jean C. (2004) 'Realms of political freedom in Post-Mao China'. In William C. Kirby (ed.), *Realms of Freedom in Modern China*. Stanford: Stanford University Press, pp. 264–284.

Pei, Minxin (2006) *China's Trapped Transition. The Limits of Developmental Autocracy*. Cambridge: Harvard University Press.

Rawnsley, Gary D. and Ming-Yeh T. Rawnsley (eds.) (2003) *Political Communications in Greater China. The Construction and Reflection of Identity*. London: RoutledgeCurzon.

Renwick, Neil and Qing Cao (2003) 'Modern political communication in China'. In Gary D. Rawnsley and Ming-Yeh T. Rawnsley (eds.), *Political Communications in Greater China. The Construction and Reflection of Identity*. London: RoutledgeCurzon, pp. 62–82.

Saich, Tony (2004) *Governance and Politics of China* (2nd ed). New York: Palgrave Macmillan.

Sun Dawu (孙大午) (2004) '解读三农问题.孙大午在北京大学中国农业大学的演讲摘要, 2003.03.13–14' [Deconstructing the three problems in agriculture and rural affairs. Excerpts from Sun Dawu's speeches at Beijing University and China Agricultural University, 2003.03.13–14]. In Lei Dian and Hong Chen (雷瑱, 洪尘) (eds.), 孙大悟为农民而生.一个农民企业家的努力与发展 [Sun Dawu – born for the peasants. The efforts and development of a rural entrepreneur]. Beijing: Zhongguo shehui kexue chubanshe., pp. 222–243.

—— (2005a) 孙大午行思录 *2005.7–2006.5* [Records of Sun Dawu's train of thoughts 2005.7–2006.5]. Dawu jituan mishuchu 大午集团秘书处 (eds.), Xushui: Dawu jituan.

—— (2005b) '孙大午大企业家的大教训' [A big lesson for big entrepreneur Sun Dawu]. In Sun Dawu (孙大午) (2005a) 孙大午行思录 *2005.7–2006.5* [Records of Sun Dawu's train of thoughts 2005.7–2006.5]. Dawu jituan mishuchu 大午集团秘书处 (eds.), Xushui: Dawu jituan, pp. 13–15.

—— (2005c) '孙大午目标正义与程序正义' [Sun Dawu – just goals and just procedures]. In Sun, D.W. (孙大午) (2005a) 孙大午行思录 *2005.7–2006.5* [Records of Sun Dawu's train of thoughts 2005.7–2006.5]. Dawu jituan mishuchu 大午集团秘书处 (eds.), Xushui: Dawu jituan, pp. 15–19.

Tian Yongsheng (田永胜) (ed.) (2005) 中国之重 – 32位权威人士解读三农问题 [Where China is heavy – 32 authoritative people deconstruct the three problems in agriculture and rural affairs]. Beijing: Guangming ribao chubanshe.

Tsai, Kelle S. (2005) 'Capitalists without a class: political diversity among private entrepreneurs in China'. *Comparative Political Studies*, vol. 38, no. 9 (November 2005), pp. 1130–1158.

Tsui, Anne S., Yanjie Bian and Leonard K. Cheng (eds.) (2006) *China's Domestic Private Firms. Multidisciplinary Perspectives on Management and Performance*. Armonk: M.E. Sharpe.

Wang, Xiaoying (2002) 'The post-communist personality: the spectre of China's capitalist reforms'. *The China Journal*, no. 47 (January 2002), pp. 1–17.

WB (2004) 'Investment climate for small and medium sized enterprises (SMEs) in Southwest China'. Beijing: World Bank (WB), 28.10.04.

Weigelin-Schwiedrzik, Susanne (2006) 'In search for a master narrative for 20th-century Chinese history'. *The China Quarterly*, no. 188 (December 2006), pp. 1070–1091.

Yan Yu (阎雨) (2006) '企业发展和公权社会' [Enterprise development and civil rights society]. *Mimeo*, Dawu Group Secretariat.

Yang, Dali L. (2004) *Remaking the Chinese Leviathan. Market Transition and the Politics of Governance in China*. Stanford: Stanford University Press.

Yep, Ray (2003) *Manager Empowerment in China – Political implications of rural industrialization in the reform era*. London: RoutledgeCurzon.

4. A Collective of Their Own: Young Volunteers at the Fringes of the Party Realm[1]

Unn Målfrid H. Rolandsen

Scholars both in China and abroad have called attention to what they describe as a growing self-centredness and even egotism in contemporary Chinese society. One example is the argument, made by Yunxiang Yan, that the violent experiences from the Mao period combined with the social changes of the reform era have given rise to what he characterizes as an ultra-utilitarian individualism in Chinese society (Yan 2003: 233). With this in mind, it is interesting to bring to the fore the young people who choose to spend some of their time and money to provide services for others: China's young volunteers. In the recent past, Chinese volunteer work was a duty forced on individuals through the system of Party branches and work units. Today, volunteers in China are individuals who choose to give of their time for their own reasons. This chapter analyzes the significance of the organization China Youth Volunteers (*Qingnian Zhiyuanzhe Xiehui* 青年志愿者协会) in the lives of a group of young volunteers, and the way participation in volunteer social work provides the urban middle class with an opportunity to re-embed in a modified version of the old mass organizations.

Recent Chinese research on organized volunteering in China has paid much attention to how young volunteers can benefit from volunteering as a source of experience, knowledge and self-development.[2] In doing so, these articles serve to strengthen the image of contemporary Chinese youth as self-serving individuals. It is a fact that the life choices of young white-collar workers in China are strongly influenced by the increased competition for desirable jobs in the state and private sector. Moreover, to an increasing degree, the responsibility for success or failure in education and in work life is placed at the level of the individual, rather than at the level of society or even the state. As Lisa Hoffman's study of Chinese graduates entering the labour market shows, the importance of personal success in the educational system influences young people's sense of values: the rationale that 'hard work and ability justified (. . .) social stratification' was widespread among graduates as early as the 1990s (Hoffman 2001: 58). Some Chinese studies suggest that participation in volunteer work provides individuals with skills and knowledge that increase their ability to compete in the labour market (Ran et al. 2005: 33; Tan 2001: 53). This study shows that the type of 'capital' young people gain through volunteering is, however, of little significance outside the immediate realm of the Communist Party. The article concludes that what attracts youth to the volunteer movement is the opportunity to be part of a collective where they can contribute to society, while at the same time being recognized as individuals.

The role of China Youth Volunteers as a relevant collective in the lives of young people demonstrates the complexity of the gradual process of individualization taking place in contemporary Chinese society. In *Individualization*, Beck and Beck-Gernsheim propose that the social categories which have been regarded as a source of structure in the lives of individuals, such as family, class, gender and community, are withering (Beck and Beck-Gernsheim 2003). In the Chinese context, some social categories have been weakened by the process, while others have been strengthened. First, the individual has become disembedded from social categories which were forced on the populace during high socialism. One example of this is the partial dismantling of the work units and the system of rural and urban residence permits; the gradual irrelevance of class background as an indicator of social and political status is another. Second, the Party-state's gradual withdrawal from its domination of the private sphere has given new relevance to the family as a collective and to new kinds of networks and associations in the lives of Chinese individuals.[3] Third, existing state-organized collectives have become transformed through the process of individualization, a process which is, importantly, promoted by the Party-state itself. As demonstrated by Li Minghuan in her case study of overseas Chinese farms,[4] the changing governmental policies towards the farms have caused the residents to reinterpret the meaning of the overseas Chinese farm as a collective. In recent years, farm residents have sought new ways to profit from their collective identity as 'others'.[5] This chapter focuses on the similar process whereby young volunteers reinterpret the meaning of the Party-dominated mass organization to fit their own sense of what volunteering should be.

Empirical data for this study was collected through informal interviews and participant observation in a local branch of the China Youth Volunteers in Quanzhou, Fujian Province, during the springs of 2006 and 2007. I contacted the local branch of the organization after reading an article about their work in a local newspaper. Subsequently, I conducted informal group interviews with three of the most enthusiastic, long-term members, and was also invited to join them on a house call. Later, I accompanied a group from one of the organization's sub-branches, consisting of vocational school students, on one of their weekly visits to a local home for the elderly. In 2007 I had the opportunity to join a new volunteer at the introduction meeting where she and other newcomers – most of them young low-level employees in local enterprises – were introduced to the organization's principles and goals. Here, the data from interviews and participant observation are supplemented with written materials from the organization itself, Chinese sociological literature on volunteering, and articles from the local media, as well as data from numerous formal and informal interviews which I undertook during this period as part of a broader study of leisure practices in the Quanzhou area.

In this chapter I analyze and discuss the ambiguous portrayal of young Chinese volunteers as these are (re)presented in the local media, in scholarly articles, in publications from the local volunteers' organization, and – importantly – through the actions and words of the volunteers themselves. If we look at China Volunteers solely from the point of view of the Chinese Party-state and the (GO)NGOs it governs, it is best described as being part of the Communist Party system. If we take the volunteers themselves as a point of departure, however, it becomes clear that China Volunteers is not merely a satellite in the Party universe, but an association with its own gravitational pull. Therefore, taking individual volunteers as a starting point for analysis is a conscious choice in this study. As pointed out by Robert LeVine, standard ethnography 'produces a cultural description analogous to a map or aerial photograph of a community', whereas a more person-centred ethnography 'tells us what it is like to live there – what features are salient to its inhabitants' (LeVine 1982: 293, cited in Hollan 1997: 220). The challenges involved in studying the changing forms of organized volunteering from the point of view of the participants are that this approach does not lead us to one unequivocal answer to the question of what volunteering 'is', nor does it provide a clear-cut description of the nature of the relationship between the volunteer's organization and the Communist Party. The data from Quanzhou shows that while the prospect of qualifying for party membership has made China Volunteers an attractive and relevant collective to some, it is the benefits of social experience and an increased social network that makes it a collective of relevance in the lives of other volunteers.

Bauman describes the piecing together of one's life choices and their outcomes into a consistent narrative as the mandatory exercise of 'life politics' or 'self politics' brought about by the process of individualization (Bauman 2001: 9; Beck and Beck-Gernsheim 2003: 44–46). In this chapter I argue that the act of volunteering is imbued with different meanings in different people's lives, depending on their personal outlook and the life course they are attempting to piece together for themselves. Beck and Beck-Gernsheim stress that 'the individualization and fragmentation of growing inequalities into separate biographies' is very much a 'collective experience' (Beck and Beck-Gernsheim 2003: xxiii–xxiv). This means that the reaction to the process of individualization does not necessarily take the form of increased self-centredness and the atomisation of the individual. Another equally plausible reaction is a strengthening of the awareness among individuals of existing and increasing social inequalities, and an urge to do something about it. This tendency, I argue, may explain why, since the middle 1990s, an increasing number of young middle-class Chinese have chosen to spend their spare time and energy in the kind of social work organized by China Youth Volunteers. By examining volunteer social work from the point of view of volunteers as individual agents, this chapter focuses on the features of contemporary Chinese volunteering that are – to borrow LeVine's terms – salient to its participants, i.e. the individual's personal commitment to volunteering and the role of the volunteer's organization as a significant collective.

The New Face of Volunteering: From Forced Duty to Individual Choice

As a result of the policy of 'letting parts of the population become rich first', Chinese society faces the challenge of an increasing gap between rich and poor, and between developed and underdeveloped regions. During the process of development and reforms the Chinese government has abandoned many of its social responsibilities, and relies increasingly on 'popular' or community-based welfare providers to assist the weaker groups in society (Xu 2005: 6, 19). Some of these tasks are carried out by the increasing number of Chinese volunteers. Volunteer activities in China include neighbourhood watch programmes, tutoring students in poor families, assistance for the elderly and disabled, and the solicitation of donations for disaster relief (Xu 2005: 24; Ran et al. 2005: 29; QZSQNZYZXH 2006: 1). Since the mid-1990s, volunteer efforts have been organized mainly through China Youth Volunteers, one of the 'popular organizations' (*minjian shetuan* 民间社团)[6] under the umbrella of the Communist Youth League. According to unofficial statistics, young volunteers in China contributed 5.5 billion volunteer hours in 2004 (Ran et al. 2005: 29).

The Quanzhou China Youth Volunteers was founded in 1994 and had a total of 4,300 registered volunteers in 2006 (Liu 2006: A6). Volunteers in Quanzhou were students, teachers and office clerks, as well as low-level employees in state and private enterprises. Only a few were factory workers or self-employed. Joseph Fewsmith writes that in the Chinese context 'middle-class' usually refers to the combination of college education, urban residence and white-collar job (Fewsmith 2007: 7). The volunteers I interviewed and observed were not among the wealthy in Quanzhou, but they had stabile incomes or parents who could afford the cost of supporting a child through college. Based on factors of vocational background and educational level, only a few of the Quanzhou volunteers can be said to belong to the emergent Chinese middle classes. However, as argued by Zhou Xiaohong and also Joseph Fewsmith, when defining the Chinese middle class(es), people's attitudes and aspirations must also be taken into consideration (Zhou 2005: 1–8). As I argue in the following, the willingness of volunteers to spend their time, and also some of their money on the welfare of people outside the immediate family constitutes a break with the 'family-first' values which have come to be associated with Chinese societies. Moreover, in the case of China Volunteers, the act of volunteering is also closely linked to narratives of a Western way of life, and of similar associations in Hong Kong and the US in particular. I argue that the discourse employed by the local volunteers in their descriptions of their own volunteer participation is characteristic of the middle-class tastes and values (i.e. a Western lifestyle, individual choice and flexibility) to which an increasing number of urban Chinese aspire. I therefore regard the actions and values of the volunteers as distinctively 'middle-class'.

The majority of the Quanzhou volunteers were in their 20s, which is an age when most urban Chinese are without responsibility for children or elderly members of their own families. When in their 20s, urban Chinese therefore enjoy an abundance of spare time compared to individuals in other social strata and age groups (Wang 2003: 76). These young people's own material needs were met, and in addition they had the time and money needed to enjoy leisure. This combination of assets (time and money) may explain why volunteering is most widespread in the areas of China that have benefited from economic development during the last decades, namely the urban areas and metropolises along the south-eastern coastline (Tan 2001: 55). Chinese researchers and volunteers alike regard the rise of volunteering in the PRC as a direct consequence of the increased living standards brought about by the reform policies of the last two decades. As an example, Tan Jianguang states that having their basic needs met is a prerequisite for people's participation in volunteering (Tan 2001: 55). The importance of a certain level of affluence for the emergence of volunteering was also made clear by one of the long-term members of China Volunteers in Quanzhou. His analysis, however, also included the importance of time as a resource. He held that only when material needs are met do people have the time and money to think about the needs of others. 'Otherwise,' he said, 'people will spend their time trying to make extra money for themselves by doing some extra work on the side.' Tony Saich expects that new donations laws will cause philanthropic contributions from affluent business people in China to increase (Saich 2000: 240). I argue, however, that the emergence of new economic elites and a growing middle class cannot alone explain the existence of philanthropy[7] – or more specifically the growing interest in volunteer work – in present-day China. Contemporary volunteering has historical roots both in philanthropic practices in early modern China and, importantly, in the Communist tradition of forced labour contribution.

Philanthropy – defined by Ilchman as 'activities of voluntary giving and serving to others beyond one's family' (Ilchman et al.1998: x) – has been practised at various points in Chinese history. Studies by Vivienne Shue demonstrate that philanthropic activity was widespread among the elite in late-imperial China (Shue 2006b: 411–452; Shue 1998: 334).[8] Moreover, it has long been common practice among wealthy overseas Chinese to donate money for education and for the reconstruction of temples in their native communities. This practice is most common in the areas where overseas migration has a long history, i.e. the rapidly developing south-eastern coastal region of China. In the area surrounding Quanzhou, successful local entrepreneurs have already taken up the donation practices of their overseas counterparts. In recent years they have contributed not only to the construction of school buildings but also by setting up scholarships and funds for promising students from underprivileged families. A thorough discussion of donation practices and volunteer social work in Chinese religious associations is beyond the scope of this chapter.[9] Here, it is sufficient to acknowledge that religious organizations, both foreign and Chinese, have played an important role in the history and revitalization of Chinese volunteering. In order to increase our understanding of the activities of the contemporary volunteer associations, however, a closer scrutiny of the legacy of volunteering organized by the Chinese Party-state and its system of work units is indispensable.

There is a continuous history of Party-initiated 'voluntary labour' (*yiwu laodong* 义务劳动) in the People's Republic. The Mandarin term *yiwu* (义务) means 'obligation' or 'duty' in both the moral and the legal sense. But used as an adjective the term refers to an action carried out without thought for reward or remuneration (*baochou* 报酬). In the politicized jargon of the Chinese Party-state, 'voluntary labour' has not referred to work done voluntarily in the sense that individuals take part in an activity on their own initiative; more often than not, volunteering has meant a forced contribution for the collective good at the expense of the individual. During the Mao era, local authorities demanded that each village contribute a certain amount of their labour force for communal projects. Many construction projects in rural China were built by just such 'voluntary labour', as in Fujian Province (Friedman 2006: 44). Similarly, local Communist Party branches initiated 'voluntary work' (*yiwu gongzuo* 义务工作)[10] activities in urban areas through the system of work units. Party representatives in the work units would dispatch the unit's employees to an appointed place to contribute in a given way in celebration of Elderly People's Day, Spring Festival and other public holidays. These employees' participation was not voluntary but compulsory, and according to the volunteers I interviewed in Quanzhou this practice was widespread as late as the 1990s.

Starting from the mid-1990s, volunteer social work has increasingly been organized by China Youth Volunteers, a 'popular' organization that is a part of the Communist Youth League. According to an article in the *Journal of Guangdong College of Young Cadres*, this reorganization of volunteer work means that volunteering has become something that people 'participate in on account of their personal wishes and aspirations (*zhiyuan canyude* 志愿参与的)' (Yu et al.1999: 32). This indicates a shift in the Chinese discourse of volunteering: the term *yiwu*, with its connotations of duty and selfless sacrifice, has now been replaced by *zhiyuan* (志愿), which implies something that is 'not forced' but springs out of the 'wishes' and 'aspirations' of the individual. Volunteers are increasingly referred to as *zhiyuanzhe* (志愿者, lit. 'one who volunteers') and they are no longer engaged in volunteer 'work' or 'labour', but in 'volunteer services' (*zhiyuan fuwu* 志愿服务). Commenting on the PRC tradition of volunteering, one of the most active volunteers in Quanzhou argued that 'although it used to be called "volunteer work" it was not really voluntary [at that time]. What we do now, however, is real volunteering; it is not a passive act (*bu shi beidongde* 不是被动的).' This new focus on the element of individual choice in volunteering is also evident in the way the membership criteria were presented to me by a group of student volunteers. They stressed that to become a volunteer you must be willing to participate: you should not be forced by anybody else. As one of the instructors in a training class for new volunteers put it: 'We will not come knocking on your door and drag you here. It's up to you (*ziyoude* 自由的) whether or not you choose to participate in our activities.' Newcomers to China Volunteers were also told that a member can leave the organization at any time, and if a person is busy during a certain period of time – for instance when getting married or having a baby – it would also be possible to take a temporary break from volunteer work. It is not only the individual volunteers who are brought into focus in this new volunteer discourse; significantly, those who receive assistance from volunteers are also regarded as individuals. In a short article entitled 'The volunteers' help-the-elderly school', volunteers are advised that 'each client is an independent individual (*duli zhi geti* 独立之个体) with special qualities and needs' (QZSQNZYZXH 2006: 2). The elements of choice and flexibility were also present in the organization's regulations: anyone over the age of 16 can become a volunteer, and a mere 48 hours of volunteer work is all that is required of each member in the course of a year.

Although it is still the case that Chinese university students are required to participate in social activities of the kind that the Youth League and also China Youth Volunteers organize, this does not mean that individuals are still coerced into volunteering in a manner similar to the Party-led social work as described above. First of all, even if the majority of volunteers in China are young, not all members of China Volunteers are students. In Quanzhou, the organization had established branches in one of the local colleges, but their membership base consisted of a range of white-collar workers from both official departments and private enterprises. Furthermore, it is important to note that the reinterpretation of volunteering is a discourse which is primarily communicated by and among the volunteers themselves. The members' own narratives of customized service and participation based on choice signals a break with the glorification of self-sacrifice, which Madsen has described as emblematic of Maoist ethics (Madsen 1984: Chapters 4 and 5 especially). This discourse also serves to establish China Volunteers as a distinct collective where volunteers and their social work – rather than the demands of the Party organization – occupy centre-stage. This insistence on the importance of willingness on the part of the individual, and also on practical accommodation to the life situation of the individual volunteer, is significant in a historical perspective as it goes against the general trend in Chinese political and philosophical thinking. As both Svarverud and Yan demonstrate in their contributions to this volume, Chinese intellectuals have envisioned the rise of the Chinese individual primarily as a means of strengthening the greater collective, i.e. the Chinese nation state.[11]

In informal conversations with members and in written materials intended for prospective members, it is evident that the volunteers themselves have a new perspective on volunteering, namely that the collective effort of social work is and should be based on the principle of individual motivation and choice. However, if we look at how China Volunteers and its activities are presented in the local Party-dominated media and in the official publications issued by the organization itself, the rhetoric is still strongly influenced by the old CCP discourse of selfless contribution by model citizens. In a 2006 publication from the Quanzhou branch of China Volunteers, the volunteers are presented as a group of unselfish enthusiasts; they contribute selflessly to society (*wusi fengxian, fengxian shehui* 无私奉献, 奉献社会) and they do so without seeking anything in return (*bu qiu huibao* 不求回报) (QZSQNZYZXH 2006: 1). The rhetoric employed here is reminiscent of the calls to 'serve the people' that characterized the Maoist ethics of the 1960s. The language is formulaic and repetitive, and the frequency of politicized buzzwords is typical of the Youth League and its propagation of the 'Lei Feng spirit'. According to one of the anecdotes, originally printed in a Quanzhou newspaper, a young man with an excessively introverted personality became sociable through his participation in volunteer work, and a friendless young person became a very popular member of China Volunteers. The same paper reported that a boy who used to sleep late in the mornings became 'diligent and conscientious' once he became a member of the organization, and began to spend his weekends helping those in need (Zhuang 2003). These anecdotes present volunteer activities as a means for young people to mould their characters and as a vehicle for self-cultivation.

The text brings to mind the widespread use of hero narratives and models for emulation in Chinese schools and ideological propagation, as analyzed by Børge Bakken (Bakken 2000: Chapter 4 especially). In effect, China Volunteers is portrayed as a successful means of social engineering: volunteering causes a positive transformation at the level of the individual, but the benefit of this transformation is directed towards the greater collective, i.e. a society of socially well-functioning and selfless people. Volunteering as it is discussed among the members of China Volunteers is also directed towards the greater good in the sense of increased welfare for weaker social groups. It is, however, important to note that in the new discourse of volunteering based on individual initiative, the contribution to society is no longer expected to be made at the individual's expense.

The new rhetoric of personal choice and flexibility may be gaining ground among the volunteers themselves and among scholars who study the current trends in volunteering (see Tan 2004 especially), but as we shall see in the following, the actual activities of the local branch of China Volunteers in Quanzhou rely heavily on support from the Youth League. Moreover, in exchange for logistic support, the organization is utilized as a mouthpiece for Party propaganda directed towards a group of young, well-educated people who might otherwise be out of the reach of the Party apparatus.

Volunteering at the Fringes of the Party Realm

In the article 'Negotiating the state: the development of social organizations in China', Tony Saich writes that social theorists often describe the relationship between the Chinese state and social organizations as that of a patron and clients, focusing mainly on the Chinese Party-state's control and repression of social organizations (Saich 2000). In an attempt to break with this tendency, Saich analyzes these relationships in terms of a symbiosis where state and social organizations are mutually dependent. According to Saich, the state uses this opportunity to transfer parts of its responsibility for social security and welfare provision over to social organizations. For their part, the social organizations position themselves close to the state bureaucracy at different levels in order to win influence on behalf of their members (Saich 2000: 125). The relationship between the Party-state and the growing volunteer movement in China is special because the movement has its roots within the Communist Party organization itself, and is still nurtured by (and in some cases actually under the direct management of) the Communist Youth League (Tan et al. 2002: 39). In her work on philanthropy in China, Vivienne Shue found that the central personages in local campaigns and charity drives were usually Party members or people who had retired from government posts (Shue 2006a: 14). I did not find a similar overlap in my material, but as in Shue's case, the existent ties between the volunteers and the Party-state are significant. This relationship necessitates not only a scrutiny of the extent to which China Volunteers depend upon the Youth League for practical support, but also an analysis of how the volunteers' organization is used by the Party apparatus as a propaganda tool.

The Quanzhou branch of China Youth Volunteers relies on support from the local branch of the Youth League for its practical organization. One example is the fact that the organization's office is situated in the Youth and Children's Palace (*Qingshaoniangong* 青少年宫), an activity centre administrated by the Youth League. This is also where prospective volunteers go to sign up, and where they receive their basic training from long-term members of the group. According to the Quanzhou Youth Volunteers' own publications, the district branch of the Youth League also assists the volunteers in organizing a range of activities for various disadvantaged social groups, including a 'volunteer station' that offers tutoring for students from poor families.[12]

The Party apparatus also plays an important role in recruiting new volunteers. Starting in 2001, China Volunteers opened up for 'public recruitment' (*gongkai zhaomu* 公开招募). This meant that people from outside the Party and Youth League circles could also become members. Quanzhou Youth Volunteers regards this as a turning point on their way to becoming a 'popular' (*minjian* 民间) organization. Even so, the leadership of the local branch acknowledged that recruiting still largely depends on information disseminated through the Party organization and the Party-dominated press. The problem of reaching prospective volunteers outside Party circles is also evident in a 1999 case study of the development of volunteer activities in a small town in Guangdong (Yu et al. 1999: 34).

Information about China Volunteers and the social work in which the organization is engaged seldom reaches people who are not in some way connected either to the Party or to local administrative units. During my fieldwork in Quanzhou I brought up the topic of volunteering in discussions and interviews with a variety of people. The few people who knew of Quanzhou Youth Volunteers were either Party members or employed in the state sector, and they regarded the organization primarily as an outgrowth of the Youth League. This image of China Volunteers as an appendix to the Party became evident when one of my local acquaintances considered joining. One of her old classmates informed her that China Volunteers is quite Party-oriented, and that members must attend all kinds of time-consuming [political] 'activities' (*huodong* 活动). Because of this new information my friend decided against becoming a volunteer. She had no interest in becoming associated with the Party apparatus, she said, so volunteering did not sound like a suitable activity for her.

The challenge facing China Volunteers is that the group remains nearly invisible to the world outside the Party realm, and if or when it is portrayed in the media, its members are (re)presented as self-sacrificing model youth. Consequently, the most noticeable aspect of the movement – to the outside world – is its link to the Party apparatus, not its social work or importance as a collective of social relevance in the lives of the volunteers.

When talking about being a volunteer and about the organization as a social unit, volunteers never made any reference to the Youth League or the kinds of support that China Volunteers receives from the Party apparatus. From the actual activities I observed, however, it became clear that the Party not only supports but makes active use of the organization, mainly in large-scale propaganda campaigns. The local volunteers organize activities on 5 March as a joint celebration of Youth Volunteers' Service Day (*Qingnian Zhiyuan Fuwuri* 青年志愿服务日) and the annual Study Lei Feng Day, for example. Lei Feng was a model hero of the Mao era and is still commemorated, especially by the Youth League, for his spirit of selfless actions for the common good. The Civilized Traffic (*Wenming Jiaotong* 文明交通) campaign in March 2007 is another example of the role played by China Volunteers in Party-initiated propaganda. This campaign saw several hundred members of the organization assisting the Quanzhou traffic police in monitoring the afternoon rush hour and handing out leaflets calling on townspeople to travel in a civilized and healthy manner, and 'to be civilized people' (*zuo wenmingren* 做文明人). This campaign is part of the preparation for Quanzhou's hosting of the eighth National Peasant Games (*Nongmin Yundonghui* 农民运动会) in 2008 (Pan 2007: A12). The local administration regards the Games as a prestigious event, and planning from the local steering committee mimics the Beijing Olympics, even down to the concern for the behaviour and conduct of the host city populace.[13] And, as in Beijing, China Volunteers will play a key role in propagating the desired image of 'civilized games'.[14] The agendas of the local government are also present in the group's official publications. A newsletter published by the Quanzhou branch of China Volunteers in January 2006 has numerous references to the drive for a 'harmonious Quanzhou' (QZSQNZYZXH 2006: 1). This is a local campaign moulded on the concept of a 'harmonious socialist society' which was introduced by the central level of the Communist Party in 2004. These are only a few examples of the Party-initiated campaigns in which the local branch of China Youth Volunteers has taken part.

During my field research in Quanzhou I also observed how the local China Volunteers branch actively instructs its own members in Communist Party ideology. One Sunday in April 2006 I accompanied a group of young volunteers on one of their regular visits to an old people's home run by a local neighbourhood committee. During the few morning hours we spent there, some volunteers cleaned the private and common rooms while others sat down to have a chat with the elderly. The organization had also invited a retired teacher to give a short lecture for the elderly about health and old age. Nevertheless, most of the morning was spent on a plenum discussion of the application of the 'Eight Dos and Don'ts' (*Barong Bachi* 八荣八耻), a part of the Socialist Honour and Disgrace (*Shehuizhuyi Rongruguan* 社会主义荣辱观) campaign launched by the Chinese Communist Party to strengthen public morality. The head of the organization gave an improvised speech in which he stressed that the volunteers should study these moral guidelines 'just as it is done at all other levels of the Party organization'. Thereupon, the volunteers were asked one after another to expound and comment on the practical application of these principles in their daily lives. The volunteers present were all vocational school students organized by an on-campus branch of Quanzhou Youth Volunteers. Since the session was conducted in Mandarin, a language which is largely incomprehensible to the inhabitants in the old people's home, the study session was undoubtedly directed at the young volunteers. The head of the local branch of China Volunteers, who also chaired the study session, told me that this kind of ideological study session is quite common in the organization.

According to Tan Jianguang, an abundance of Party-initiated activities is characteristic of the workings of China Youth Volunteers (Tan 2004: 54). The above examples indicate that the activities of the local branch were all in the hands of the Communist Party apparatus. But, as stated above, when I discussed the activities of the organization with its members, their focus was always on their engagement in social work, i.e. on visiting and assisting the elderly and the handicapped in their local community. When I asked one of the senior members of the organization about activities in his local group and the practical assistance they received from the Party, he held that the support was meagre. He explained that at present they did not have sufficient funds to organize any activities other than regular visits to the elderly and handicapped. And when I asked another long-term member whether or not it would be possible to approach the Youth League or the local government to get funding for more visible, large-scale activities, he answered that the local Youth League and the government would seldom provide money for activities initiated by the volunteers themselves. He added that 'when activities are initiated by "them" [referring to the relevant authorities in the Party system], there might be money though (. . .)'. The experience that economic support is only available when the administration orchestrates the activities was also shared by other 'popular' associations in Quanzhou, such as the municipal choir and the local photo association. The choir and the photo association, for example, only received support when their activities could fill the dual purpose of artistic display and promotion of the Quanzhou 'brand-name' to prospective investors (Rolandsen 2008: 113–117). This indicates that the symbiotic relationships between 'popular' associations and the local Party apparatus is one of mutual exploitation. In this case, the volunteers' organization depends on the Communist Party apparatus as a facilitator for their activities[15] and the Party in turn uses the volunteers as a substitute welfare provider and a vehicle for the propagation of Party ideology.

As stated by Feng Xu, 'Chinese civil society cannot be said to be separate from the state, rather it depends on the state for its survival to a degree unknown in the West. On the other hand, the state needs civil society in its effort to combat social problems' (Xu 2005: 6). Vivienne Shue also stresses the use of charitable individuals and social organizations for the legitimacy of the Chinese government. Shue argues that Chinese authorities seek to 'borrow some of the social prestige that attends upon those who have earned themselves a genuinely good reputation' in the 'charitable arena' (Shue 2006a). The significance of volunteers' social work for the image of local authorities is also confirmed in Tan Jianguang's 2004 case study from the Pearl River Delta (Tan 2004: 51–53). Here, Tan analyzed the conditions of a successful volunteers' organization which did not have its origin within the Party apparatus, but which was founded by people who were inspired and backed by volunteers in Hong Kong. The popularity of this organization among the local populace made it opportune for the local government not only to tolerate the existence of the organization, but even to make a public display of the Party's support of their social work. While the local Party attempted to prey on the efforts of this community of volunteers, the independent volunteers' federation utilized this position to direct attention to their cause, which was the social welfare of migrant labourers in the region. Tan's case of the independent volunteer federation epitomizes the symbiotic relationships between the state and social organizations in China as described by Tony Saich. The federation in Shenzhen succeeded in devising 'strategies to negotiate with the state a relationship that maximizes their members' interests or that circumvents or deflects state intrusion' (Saich 2000: 125). The Quanzhou branch of China Volunteers, however, with its roots within the realm of the Party-state, has no place from which to launch a similar bargaining strategy vis-à-vis the Party apparatus.

When looking at Chinese volunteering from 'above', i.e. from the perspective of organization and Party affiliation, our attention is inevitably drawn towards questions of domination, propagation and the Communist Party's struggle for legitimacy. By shifting our perspective to the point of view of the individual volunteers, other aspects of contemporary Chinese volunteering are brought into focus. To the volunteers themselves, what matters more than a connection to the Party is the social work itself, and the benefits of being part of the social community that the volunteer organization represents.

China Volunteers as Experienced by Individual Volunteers

Volunteering may serve different purposes depending on the individual participant, as demonstrated by a closer scrutiny of the varied roles of volunteering in the lives of Mr Dai, Miss Gong and Mr Lin.[16] Dai, a computer technician in his late 20s, stressed that becoming a volunteer was a great opportunity to make friends with new people. In Quanzhou it was customary among the local volunteers to help each other out with practical matters in daily life, in much the same way as family members and old classmates do in China. Fellow volunteers would often approach Dai and ask for his advice in computer-related questions, and by helping others Dai expanded his network of friends and contacts. This exemplifies how participating in volunteer work may add new links in a person's social network, providing him or her with a new group of people on whom to rely for favours and exchanges as well as companionship. In Quanzhou, all volunteers were organized in smaller groups according to their main activity (the environmental-protection group, the visiting-the-elderly group, the assisting-the-handicapped group, etc.). Members of each small group were encouraged to gather at a designated place each week, often a café or fast food restaurant, to socialize with fellow volunteers. The small-group members also kept in touch and exchanged information about upcoming activities via Internet chat and SMS. For the most active among the volunteers, the organization and fellow volunteers became their main peer group, a collective outside of the family, workplace or college to which they related in their daily lives.

The importance of the volunteer organization as an arena for social-izing was confirmed during the aforementioned Sunday morning visit to a government-sponsored home for the elderly. The volunteers cleaned dormitories and chatted with the elderly, and also underwent propaganda education. However, the fact that close to 30 volunteers were gathered to assist a total of five elderly meant that many of the participants never exchanged a single word with any of the residents, nor did they participate directly in any kind of assistance. Moreover, the lively chatting, friendly teasing and general inattentiveness during the ideology session indicated that the break from campus life and the chance to hang out with friends was just as important to the participants as the actual volunteer effort – or, indeed, the ideological training.

Even if the visit to the elderly people's home left me with the impression that most volunteers did not pay much attention during the ideological training session, some volunteers took this aspect of the organization's activities very seriously. One evening I joined four volunteers for their weekly visit to old Auntie Wang in their neighbourhood. At one point during the evening, Miss Gong, a student of accounting responsible for mustering the volunteers at her vocational college, told me that she was under assessment for Party membership. Party membership is still a prerequisite for many coveted jobs in China, and the other volunteers as well as the woman we visited commended Gong on her ambition. The close relationship between China Youth Volunteers and the Youth League indicates that being a volunteer may indeed be a valuable asset for poten-tial Party members. During the aforementioned study session on the 'Eight Dos and Don'ts', it was evident that the leaders of the volunteers' organization treated Gong as a prospective Party member. She was clearly expected to take the lead and expound upon the teachings with extra vigour. The energy with which she participated in the study session, and her frequent use of slogans and set phrases – typical of China Volunteers' publications and the Youth League and Communist Party jargon – made Miss Gong stand out among the volunteers as particularly Party-oriented.

Judging from our conversations and my observations in the organization, I have no reason to doubt the authenticity of Miss Gong's commitment to the volunteer cause. But her actions and manner of speaking showed that she regarded the organization chiefly as part of the Party realm. Gong's commitment was to the larger collective – the Party-state – as much as to the organization itself.

Lin, one of the central personages in the local branch, acknowledged that their organization was a part of the Party universe, but he did not aim to be a Party member himself. He was a low-level employee in a public company and spent most of his leisure time doing volunteer social work. In addition to taking responsibility for administrative tasks in the organization, Lin had committed to visiting a lonely elderly woman twice a week, and also to keeping in touch with her via mobile phone at least once a day. During the last five years Lin had contributed more than 500 hours of volunteer work, and it is fair to say that Quanzhou Youth Volunteers was a nodal point in his life. Lin was pragmatic in his approach to the cooperation between the volunteers and the Party apparatus, and valued the Youth League and the Party chiefly as providers of logistic support. He was personally in charge of teaching Party ideology in the organization, but at the same time he stated that he was personally more inspired by Buddhist teachings, and he expressed disillusionment with the emptiness of Party rhetoric. The fact that he kept relying on this very rhetoric in order to secure recruitment and support for the organization indicates his level of commitment to the group, and to the various weak social groups they seek to assist.

Seen from the perspective of the volunteers themselves, China Volunteers functions in several ways. It offers an arena wherein one can extend one's social network, it may provide a chance to realize one's potential as organizer or leader, and it is an opportunity to spend one's spare time in a meaningful way. It may even mean a step towards becoming a Party member. Still, a volunteers' organization should not be reduced to any of these diverse functions; it is not simply a welfare provider, nor a social club or a nursery for budding cadres. While a growing number of young people take an interest in China Volunteers and the companionship they become part of through participating in its activities, volunteering is not equally appreciated by the parent generation.

Collectives in Conflict: The Concern for Volunteers' Families

In a society where many urban families have only one child, the capability and competence of the young is all-important for the future sustenance of the family (Croll 2006: 188). As a consequence, the way young people distribute their time between studies and other activities becomes a topic of importance for the family as a collective. In the training classes for new volunteers, instructors stressed that volunteering is an educational activity; through volunteering, the individual can increase his or her sense of responsibility (*tigao zijide zerengan* 提高自己的责任感) and knowledge of society (*tigao dui shehuide lijie* 提高对社会的理解) while gaining a distinctive kind of experience (*bu yiyangde yizhong tiyan* 不一样的一种体验).[17] It seems, however, that this experience and knowledge is not cherished by Chinese parents in the same way as the type of education provided in a regular classroom.

In a survey from Beijing and Guangdong, young people under the age of 25 were asked about volunteer participation and also about hindrances to their participation in such activities. Among those who participated in volunteering quite often, 21.4 per cent answered that the greatest hindrance to their participation was the disapproval of their family (*jiaren bu zhichi* 家人不支持) (Ran et al. 2005: 35). Because 88 per cent of the respondents in this survey were university students, all below the age of 25, 'family' as a general rule referred to students' parents. Although university students have more time for leisure and may also control their own time to a larger degree than do younger pupils, their parents will often have strong opinions on how they put their time to use. After all, the school fees and living expenses provided by the parents, or in some cases by the extended family, serve as an investment in the future of the individual student as well as in the family as a whole. Judging from the Beijing survey, parents do not regard volunteering as sufficiently beneficial to their children – hence the tendency to advise students against 'wasting' time on philanthropic activities.

This brings us back to Ilchman et al. and their definition of philanthropy as 'giving and serving to others beyond the family' (Ilchman et al. 1998: x). There is an historical tradition in China for charitable contributions within the clan and the family: wealthy clan members had a certain responsibility for assisting kinsmen in need (Spence 1990: 10). In modern China, the importance of providing for one's family prevailed even during the collective era,[18] when families tended private vegetable plots in their spare time (however scarce) in order to raise money for expenses within the family (Unger 2002: 15; Huang 1990: 203). When Chinese youth choose to spend their time and resources to improve the life conditions of people outside the family, this may be considered a break with the kind of 'familism' which has been attributed to Chinese society for centuries. Still, volunteers in Quanzhou apparently did not regard spending time and money on the welfare of strangers and being attentive towards one's own family as a conflict of interests. On the contrary, according to their own publications, the local branch of China Volunteers considers their assistance to the elderly as acts of 'filial devotion' (*xiaoxin xian laoren* 孝心献老人) (QZSQNZYZXH 2006: 2), a virtue of long historical standing in Chinese society. As part of their preliminary instructions, volunteers were asked not to call attention to the possibly unfilial behaviour of sons or daughters of the elderly clients they assist. In addition, the volunteers were encouraged to take responsibility for chores at home, to 'ensure that their own families would not suffer from the fact that they had become volunteers'.[19]

As stated above, I consider China Volunteers to be a new form of collective which provides its participants with an opportunity to be members of a meaningful social group. In a society where social categories are withering, participation in the volunteer movement can function as a form of re-embeddedness for the individual. This does not necessarily imply, however, that the organization replaces the family as a collective of relevance for the individual. Rather than challenging conventional family values, it seems that China Volunteers strives to make room for the family within the world of volunteering. As mentioned above, volunteers can take leave of their duties in case of pregnancy, marriage preparations or other important family activities. Moreover, some young parents had started taking their children along to volunteer activities. This was applauded by other volunteers as an ideal arrangement. Volunteers also told anecdotes about how people in Hong Kong supposedly take their entire families to sing and dance and talk with the elderly in retirement homes. I also heard volunteers claim that people in Hong Kong regard volunteering as a good way of relieving tension and stress after a busy week at work, and that in Hong Kong helping others is regarded as a kind of recreation (*yule* 娱乐).

Anecdotes describing volunteer practices in Hong Kong and the US were often provided by volunteers as examples of how volunteering should work and be perceived. Tan Jianguang writes that when volunteer organizations were first established in Shenzhen in the 1990s, the concept of volunteer social work was poorly understood by people in general (Tan 2001: 54). In Quanzhou, volunteers have encountered similar challenges. Local townspeople have approached Quanzhou Youth Volunteers in the hope that volunteers could take care of their housework or help their children pass examinations. The following anecdote from an interview with one of the volunteers in a local Quanzhou newspaper shows that, at times, volunteer social work is not merely misunderstood but may even be disapproved of:

> Miss Zhang and some of her volunteer friends used to visit an elderly woman in their local community. Since the younger members in the household had taken up jobs elsewhere, the old woman spent most days alone, and so the volunteers decided to visit her and thereby try to ease her feelings of loneliness. Then one day when they knocked on the old woman's door, they were met by a furious woman who shouted at them, 'We are filial descendants! We take care of our ageing parents ourselves, so there's nothing here for you to worry about!' It turned out that the younger family members worried that the neighbours would wrongfully accuse them of being unfilial [and that this] was what the woman was angry about.   (Zhuang 2003)

This episode illustrates the extent to which the image of good family relations is pursued by contemporary Chinese.[20] The anecdote also shows that volunteer social work remains a poorly understood practice in a medium-sized city like Quanzhou. This calls for a closer scrutiny of the motivations of those young people who nevertheless choose to engage in volunteering.

Volunteers' Motivations and Volunteering as Capital

Among social scientists in both China and North America, self-interest and self-realization are central concepts in studies of volunteering as a leisure activity.[21] These concepts go hand in hand with the new Chinese rhetoric of volunteering as based on individual choice and beneficial for the individual in terms of self-development. The volunteers in Quanzhou did not underplay the ways they themselves benefited from being part of the volunteer movement. But while some individuals may regard volunteering as a means to personal gain, a general tendency of self-centredness on the part of the Chinese individual can hardly explain why an increasing number of young people in Quanzhou and elsewhere take part in volunteering.

A survey among youth in Beijing suggests that the factors motivating youth to spend time on volunteer work are their interest in the public good, the chance to make life more meaningful, the chance to increase their knowledge and skills and the chance to acquire work experience and social experience (Ran et al. 2005: 33).[22] Tan's case study from Shenzhen provides a similar list of motivating factors among volunteers: the urge to show compassion, to pay something back to society, to replenish one's own spirit, to display one's talents and to fulfil one's duties (Tan 2001: 54). Although concerns for the public good are listed among the motivating factors in these studies, the factors that are given most attention in the analyses are the gains involved for the individual. As an example, Tan Jianguang writes that 'those who benefit the most from volunteer work are actually the volunteers themselves' (Tan 2001: 54). The general tendency in these surveys is to present volunteers' pursuit of personal benefit as something positive. Tan acknowledges that there may be a very few cases where individuals seek to 'increase their fame' or 'accumulate social capital' by way of volunteering, but holds that their ulterior motives will always be moulded by their experiences within the volunteers' environment (Tan 2001: 55). Here, Tan combines the 'old' discourse of volunteering as a means for the successful socialization of model youth with the novel discourse of volunteering based on the needs and interests of the individual participant. A similar amalgamation can be found in statistics from the Youth League in Beijing, which indicate that the primary reasons young people take part in volunteering are the chances to 'contribute to community and residents' and 'to accumulate experience through social practice' (Yu 2003: 31).[23] A recent study by Feng Xu shows that even local government agencies now rely on the individual-centred discourse in their attempts at mobilising people to contribute towards their local community through volunteering or charitable donations. Xu writes:

Under Mao, Chinese people were also mobilized to participate in public causes, but in a Maoist participation style that inherently disavows the self; one had to give up one's self interest totally for the public interest [. . .]. In today's call for citizens' participation, participation is considered good for the public, but also for self-realization: hence the motto or slogan 'I help others; others help me' (*renren wei wo, wo wei renren* 人人为我，我为人人).
                                                        (Xu 2005: 22–23)

An increasing proportion of the Chinese populace organize their work lives and leisure outside the system of government units, and as Feng Xu points out, this reorganization of society makes it impossible for the Party apparatus to marshal and rally people by way of old Mao-style mass mobilization (Xu 2005: 22–23). As a consequence, government units increasingly promote community service and volunteering through a discourse which blends concepts of cultural competence (*suzhi* 素质, lit. 'quality') and self-realization with a concern for the common good.

Much Chinese writing on volunteering relies on the tacit premise that philanthropic contribution is prestigious; it belongs to the sphere of big-city China and to a modern lifestyle, mainly represented by anecdotes from Hong Kong and the US (Ma 2004, Chapter 3 especially; Tan et al. 2002: 37). Moreover, in their eagerness to promote volunteering, the above-mentioned survey studies – as well as the government's new mobilization rhetoric – tend to overestimate the instrumental value of volunteering for the individual. The survey studies in particular describe volunteering as an attractive asset in terms of cultural capital (i.e. self-development, acknowledged skills and knowledge) as defined by Bourdieu.[24] But, as is indicated by the above examples from Quanzhou and the above-mentioned survey from Beijing and Guangdong, volunteering as a practice is often poorly understood, and the potential value of volunteering has yet to be recognized among the general citizenry. This means that as long as volunteering is not regarded as an actual asset, young Chinese people's participation in volunteering cannot be explained with reference to the selfish pursuit of personal benefits.

Turning now to the ways young volunteers in Quanzhou talk about volunteering, we shall see that the logic of reciprocity that governs Chinese gift-giving practices can contribute towards explaining how self-interest and personal gain go hand in hand with philanthropic sentiments in contemporary China.

Volunteering as a Form of Reciprocity

Vivienne Shue suggests that philanthropy in China is governed by the same norms as those associated with the exchange of gifts, namely the element of reciprocity (Shue 1998: 348). The giver always expects to gain something from the exchange, as does the philanthropist who contributes money or time for the benefit of others. Reciprocity is a keyword to understanding what makes young people in a city like Quanzhou choose volunteering as a leisure activity. The kind of personal gain that volunteers in Quanzhou talked about the most was the opportunity to be part of the volunteers' organization itself. To the volunteers, the organization was valuable both as a social milieu and as a network of contacts on which to rely for the exchange of favours. As we have seen, the value of volunteering as cultural capital in contemporary China is rather limited. However, at the level of the individual volunteer, the reciprocal networks and relationships which the organization provides are considered desirable assets. As the examples of Mr Dai, Miss Gong and Mr Lin showed, the young volunteers themselves clearly acknowledge the value of this kind of social capital in their lives.

When talking about their involvement in Quanzhou Youth Volunteers, the young volunteers in Quanzhou relied on a combination of the 'old' and the 'new' volunteer discourse. By defining the organization as a social space and as part of the Party system, Mr Dai and Miss Gong both drew attention to the personal benefits which drew them to the group. Some volunteers expressed their motivations in more naïve terms, such as a recent member who wanted to help the elderly and orphans because she hoped 'to make somebody else's life happier'. Other volunteers spoke of their social work in terms of 'contributing to society' (*fengxian shehui* 奉献社会) or promoting 'spiritual civilization' (*jingshen wenming* 精神文明). It is tempting to regard the latter utterances as examples of how social organizations in China and their members must pay lip service to the slogans of the central and local Party authorities. But by observing the actual practices in which the volunteers engaged, it became clear that the difference in rhetoric among the members did not indicate a varying degree of commitment to the volunteer cause. As demonstrated by the case of Miss Gong, there were those who successfully combined a display of enthusiasm for Party teachings with sincere involvement in the volunteer effort.

Most of the volunteers I met in Quanzhou were born in the late 1970s, which means that they are too young to be directly affected by the disillusionment with social activism which followed from the experiences of idealism gone astray during the Cultural Revolution, or the demise of the students' movement of 1989. This also means that young Chinese volunteers' claims to altruism should not be rendered as 'empty rhetoric' by default. Their claims must be met with a level of scepticism equal to that one would demand in analyses of volunteers' motivations in Western countries, where volunteering is regarded as a philanthropic act while at the same time being considered important additions to a young person's CV (Day and Devlin 1998: 1180; Thoits and Hewitt 2001: 128). Thus, in the context of the Chinese volunteer organizations, both the concern for 'spiritual civilization' and the happiness of one's fellow townspeople are valid expressions of the kind of social consciousness and concern which motivates contemporary young Chinese to devote their spare time and energy for the benefit of others.

In its teaching materials, Quanzhou Youth Volunteers encourages its members to seek good and lasting relationships with the individual who is in need (QZSQNZYZXH 2006: 2). It is difficult to measure the effect of the volunteers' efforts on the lives of those they aim to help, but one of my experiences in Quanzhou testifies to the significance of the relationship of reciprocity that can develop between those who give generously of their time and those who receive their attentiveness. While Lin kept his mobile phone on at all times in order to ease the loneliness of old Auntie Wang, she – having no one else to care for – served him cup after cup of hot steaming herb medicine to ease his recurring coughs and colds.

Conclusion

Seen from the perspective of the Party apparatus, the intended function of China Volunteers is twofold: on the one hand, the organization takes on some of the social responsibilities that were once provided by the state; on the other hand, the organization aims to socialize youth into active support of the values and policies of the Party-state. For the volunteers as individuals, however, China Volunteers serves as a relevant collective outside the family, neighbourhood, college or workplace; it provides a space where people can make new friends while at the same time getting the chance to give and share something in real and concrete ways.

The recent changes in the social structure has made it necessary for Chinese individuals to rely increasingly on family and kinship networks in order to carve out a predictable future. But, as this study demonstrates, the process of individualization has also given relevance to new kinds of collectives. Individuals belong to multiple social groups; they are family members and employees, and they may identify with a certain ethnic or cultural community. These multiple group memberships, however, cause tensions over group loyalties at the level of the individual. The negotiation of these tensions is part of the individual's struggle with the individualized 'project of the self' (Hoggett et al. 2007: 100). And, as argued by Hoggett et al., in order to make informed and skilled manoeuvres between the demands of the greater society, family and peer groups (as well as the demands the individual makes on him or herself), the individual must take on the position of author in his or her own life (Hoggett et al. 2007: 105). In other words, the successful negotiation of loyalties rests on an exercise of moral authority on the part of the individual. The data from Quanzhou shows that while volunteering may be praised by the political authorities, the same activity is often questioned or even misunderstood by family and community. This means that the individual's commitment to the volunteer cause is not an effortless choice. The volunteers' negotiations of loyalty towards their families, the volunteers' organization and – to a certain extent – also the Communist Party illustrates that volunteers must make active choices where factors other than personal rewards and dividends are given serious consideration. Even if China Volunteers has its roots within the Party realm, the focus of the volunteers in general is on reaching out, rather than on nurturing their Party connections or career opportunities.

We have seen that the Chinese discourse of volunteering increasingly accommodates new notions of individual choice and flexibility, both for the volunteers and for the recipients of their services. But even if the politicized rhetoric of selfless contribution is losing ground, the establishing and continuation of popular associations is still governed by the Party-state. As demonstrated by Thøgersen and Ni in this volume, organized activity which is not vouched for by any branch of the party apparatus is sometimes avoided by ordinary people for fear of raising suspicion with local authorities.[25]

Vivienne Shue has focused attention on the few independent charity workers who have established small-scale social welfare institutions outside the system of government-sponsored 'popular' organizations. Some of these do consider their own activities in terms of political activism and a critique of government policies, and the Party-state tends to regard the activities of such activists as challenges to the existing social order (Shue 1998: 349–350).[26] The young volunteers in Quanzhou expressed a growing concern for the welfare of the weaker groups in their local community; their criticism was, however, never articulated in terms of opposition towards existing social policies or power structures. Nevertheless, if we look at volunteer social work from the angle of social discontent, the renewed interest in volunteer social work in China may be regarded as an unintended consequence of the reforms in PRC social policy: the down-sizing of the Chinese state sector has led to the disintegration of the so-called 'iron rice bowl'. This system of pensions, living subsidies and food allocation was reserved for people employed by the state, and as a rule these people were also city-dwellers. In China the loss of state-sponsored social security has predominantly been an urban experience, as is the loss of the above-mentioned privileges. To borrow the terms used by Beck and Beck-Gernsheim, the withering of social categories is in some instances very much a 'collective experience' (Beck and Beck-Gernsheim 2003: xxiii–iv). In this context the increased participation in volunteer social work in big-city China can be interpreted as a reaction to a shared experience of loss of economic privileges and stable employment. Summing up, the re-emergence of philanthropic practices in China has been fuelled partly by the growth in personal wealth, partly by individuals' pursuit of personal benefit, and also by the collective experience of social fragmentation and increasing social inequality.

Notes

1   I would like to thank Vivienne Shue and Feng Xu for their generosity in letting me read and quote unpublished material.

2   Many of the articles on volunteering published in China are written in co-operation with the Youth League at different levels. The articles discussed in this study were chosen primarily because of the extensive survey material they provide. For examples, see Ran et al. 2005; Tan 2001; Tan 2004, Tan et al. 2002; Yu 2003 and Yu et al. 1999.

3   For examples, see Delman's chapter in this volume, and Hansen 2008.

4   Farming collectives set up by the PRC government to house overseas Chinese returnees, starting from the 1950s.

5   See Li Minghuan's chapter in this volume.

6   The expression 'popular organizations' (*minjian shetuan* 民间社团) suggests that the organization in question has risen from among the people. In the Chinese case, popular organizations are mass organizations initiated by the political elite. I will therefore retain the inverted commas when referring to such 'popular' organizations.

7   Ilchman et al., 1998: x–xi, argue that the distinction between 'philanthropy' and 'charity' is 'a recent invention' related to ideas of the Enlightenment such as rationality and progress. In her study of philanthropy in China, Vivienne Shue uses the two terms interchangeably, as do I in the following. See Shue 1998: 332–354.

8   For a review of sources on charity in late-imperial China, see Shue 1998: 354.

9   On religious societies as a coveted source of revenue for the modernizers of the early Republic, see Duara 1991: 75, 78; on donations for the building of clan temples, see Hsu 1971: 126–127; for an analysis of the rising importance of Buddhist women's charity in Taiwan since the 1960s, see Huang and Weller 1998 and Huang (forthcoming); on the role of Hong Kong religious organizations in the establishing of volunteer social work in the Pearl River Delta, see Tan 2004.

10 Tan et al. state that in the context of volunteering the term *yiwu* translates as 'volunteer' in English. Both *yiwu gongzuo* (义务工作) and the short form *yigong* (义工) are still used by some organizations in the Pearl River Delta. This was the term used by the first volunteer organizations in the area, established with assistance from volunteer organizations in Hong Kong in the late 1980s. See Tan et al. 2002: 51–52.

11 See the chapters by Svarverud and Yan in this volume.

12 Articles from Quanzhou wanbao (2004) and Dongnan zaobao (2005) quoted in QZSQNZYZXH 2006: 2–3.

13 Interview with the Peasant Games preparation committee, 7 March 2007.

14 In the spring of 2008, the China Volunteers' web pages posted 'Civilized Olympics' (*Wenming Aoyun* 文明奥运) as the main theme for their activities. See http://www.zgzyz.org.cn/volunteer/index.html (accessed 21 April 2008).

15 This is also evident in studies such as Yu et al. 1999:33; Tan et al. 2002: 39 and Tan 2004.

16 All names have been altered to protect the anonymity of the interviewees.

17 Quotes from training session in Quanzhou, 4 February 2007.

18 The exceptions being the Great Leap and other all-encompassing campaigns, such as the Three Loyalties campaign in 1968. See Huang 1990: 203; and Madsen 1984: 183, respectively.

19 Quote from training session in Quanzhou, 4 February 2007.

20 See also Hansen and Pang in this volume.

21 See, for example, Sun 2004: 78, 81; Wang 2003: 51; Kleiber 1999: 148; Day and Devlin 1998; Thoits and Hewitt 2001.

22 Interviewees for the survey in question were chosen among youth in general.

23 All interviewees in the survey in question were active volunteers.

24 For definitions of social and cultural capital, see Bourdieu 2006 [1983] and 1984, Chapter 2, and p. 133 especially.

25 See chapter by Thøgersen and Ni in this volume.

26 A similar point is made in Xu 2005: 24 and Wang 1995: 169.

Bibliography

Bakken, Børge (2000) *The Exemplary Society: Human Improvement, Social Control and the Dangers of Modernity in China.* New York: Oxford University Press.

Bauman, Zygmunt (2001) *The Individualized Society.* Cambridge: Polity Press.

Beck, Ulrich and Elisabeth Beck-Gernsheim (2003) *Individualization: Institutionalized Individualism and its Social and Political Consequences.* London: Sage.

Bourdieu, Pierre (1984) *Distinction. A Social Critique of the Judgement of Taste.* Translated by Richard Nice. London: Routledge & Kegan Paul.

—— (2006) [1983] 'Kapitalens former'. *Agora: Journal for Metafysisk Spekulasjon,* vol. 24, no. 1–2, pp. 5–26.

China Volunteers net 中国志愿者网, http://www.zgzyz.org.cn/volunteer/index.html. Accessed 21 April 2008.

Croll, Elizabeth (2006) *China's New Consumers: Social Development and Domestic Demand.* New York: Routledge.

Day, Kathleen M. and Rose Anne Devlin (1998) 'The payoff to work without pay: volunteer work as an investment in human capital'. *The Canadian Journal of Economics/Revue canadienne d'Economique,* vol. 31, no. 5, pp. 1179–1191.

Duara, Prasenjit (1991) 'Knowledge and power in the discourse of modernity: the campaigns against popular religion in early twentieth-century China'. *The Journal of Asian Studies,* vol. 50, no. 1, pp. 67–83.

Fewsmith, Joseph (2007) 'The political implications of China's growing middle class'. *China Leadership Monitor*, no. 21, pp. 1–8.

Friedman, Sara L. (2006) *Intimate Politics: Marriage, the Market, and State Power in Southeastern China*. Cambridge: Harvard University Asia Center, Harvard University Press.

Hansen, Mette Halskov (2008) 'Organising the old: senior authority and the political significance of a rural Chinese "NGO" '. *Modern Asian Studies*, vol. 2, no 5, pp. 1057–1078.

Hoffman, Lisa (2001) 'Guiding college graduates to work: social constructions of labor markets in Dalian'. In Nancy N. Chen et al. (eds), *China Urban: Ethnographies of Contemporary Culture*. Durham: Duke University Press, pp. 43–66.

Hoggett, Paul, Marj Mayo and Chris Miller (2007) 'Individualization and ethical agency'. In Cosmo Howard (ed.), *Contested Individualization. Debates about Contemporary Personhood*. New York: Palgrave Macmillan, pp. 99–116.

Hollan, Douglas (1997) 'The relevance of person-centered ethnography to cross-cultural psychiatry'. *Transcultural Psychiatry*, vol. 34, no. 2, pp. 219–233.

Hsu, Francis L. K. (1971) [1967/1948] *Under the Ancestors' Shadow: Kinship, Personality and Social Mobility in China*. Stanford: Stanford University Press.

Huang, Chien-Yu Julia (2009) (forthcoming) 'Genealogies of NGO-ness: the cultural politics of a global Buddhist movement in contemporary Taiwan'. *Positions: East Asia Cultures Critique*, vol.18, No. 1.

Huang, Chien-Yu Julia and Robert P. Weller (1998) 'Merit and mothering: women and social welfare in Taiwanese Buddhism'. *The Journal of Asian Studies*, vol. 57, no. 2, pp. 379–396.

Huang, Philip C. C. (1990) *The Peasant Family and Rural Development in the Yangzi Delta, 1350–1988*. Stanford: Stanford University Press.

Ilchman, Warren F., Stanley Katz and Edward L. Queen (1998) 'Introduction'. In Warren Ilchman et al. (eds), *Philanthropy in the World's Traditions*, Indianapolis: Indiana University Press, pp. ix–xv.

Kleiber, Douglas (1999) *Leisure Experience and Human Development: A dialectical Interpretation*. New York: Basic Books.

Liu Bo (刘波) (2006) '志愿者爱心接力12载' Zhiyuanzhe aixin jieli 12 zai [A record of 12 years of compassionate relay]. *Dongnan zaobao* 5.3.06, A6.

Ma Huidi (马惠娣) (ed.) (2004) 走向人文关怀的休闲经济 *Zouxiang renwen guanhuai de xiuxian jingji* [Toward a leisure economy with humanistic concerns]. Beijing: Zhongguo jingji chubanshe.

Madsen, Richard (1984) *Morality and Power in a Chinese Village*. Berkeley: University of California Press.

Pan Deng (潘登) (2007) '数百名志愿者冒雨倡导文明交通' Shubai ming zhiyuanzhe mao-yu changdao wenming jiaotong [Several hundred volunteers braving the rain to initiate civilized traffic]. *Dongnan zaobao,* 6.3.07, A12.

QZSQNZYZXH 泉州市青年志愿者协会 Quanzhou shi qingnian zhiyuanzhe xie-hui [Quanzhou Youth Volunteers' Association] (2006) '五月花志愿者, 活动回顾' Wuyue hua zhiyuanzhe: Huidong huigu [Mayflower Volunteers: Activities in Retrospect].

Ran Lüqi, Yu Yiqun, Ji Qiufa and Mu Qing (染绿琦, 余逸群, 纪秋发, 穆青) (2005) '北京青年志愿者行动调查报告' Beijing qingnian zhiyuanzhe xingdong diaocha baogao [Survey report on the operations of Beijing youth volunteers]. *Qingnian yanjiu* [Youth Research), no.7, pp. 27–35.

Rolandsen, Unn Målfrid H. (2008) 'Leisure in urban China: popular practices and official discourse in a contemporary Chinese city'. PhD thesis submitted spring 2008, University of Oslo.

Saich, Tony (2000) 'Negotiating the state: the development of social organisations in China'. *The China Quarterly*, no. 161, pp. 124–141.

Shue, Vivienne (1998) 'State power and the philanthropic impulse in China today'. In Warren Ilchman et al. (eds), *Philanthropy in the World's Traditions.* Indianapolis: Indiana University Press, pp. 332–354.

—— (2006a) *Agonistic Authority: Striving for Legitimation with Chinese Characteristics.* First Annual Distinguished Lecture, Asianettverket, Oslo, March 2006.

—— (2006b) 'The quality of mercy: Confucian charity and the mixed metaphors of modernity in Tianjin'. *Modern China*, vol. 32, no. 10, pp. 411–452.

Spence, Jonathan D. (1990) *The Search for Modern China.* New York: W. W. Norton & Co.

Sun Xiaoli (孙小礼) (2004) '建立科学,健康, 文明的生活方式' Jianshe kexue, jiankang, wen-ming de shenghuo fangshi [Establishing a scientific, healthy and civilized life style]. In Ma Huidi and Zhang Jing'an (马惠娣、张景安) (eds) 中国公众休闲状况调查 *Zhongghuo gongzhong xiuxian zhuangkuang diaocha* [Survey studies of leisure life among the Chinese public]. Beijing: Zhongguo jingji chubanshe, pp.73–90.

Tan Jianguang (谭建光) (2001) '深圳年轻志愿者 的个案研究' Shenzhen nianqing zhi-yuanzhe de gean yanjiu [A case study of some young volunteers in Shenzhen]. *Zhongguo qingnian zhengzhi xueyuan xuebao,* vol. 20, no. 6, pp. 52–55.

—— (2004) '志愿服务与义务工作:两种观念影响下的行为模式 — 以广东省珠江三角洲为个案的研究' Zhiyuan fuwu yu yiwu gongzuo: liang zhong guannian yingxiang xia de xingwei moshi – yi Guangdong sheng Zhujiang sanjiaozhou wei ge'an de yanjiu [Voluntary service and obligatory work: the behaviour pattern influenced by two kinds of concepts – a case study from the Pearl River Delta in Guangdong province]. *Zhongguo qingnian zhengzhi xueyuan xuebao*, no. 5, pp. 50–56.

Tan Jianguang, He Guosen and Liu Shan (谭建光, 何国森, 刘册) (2002) '中小城镇青年志愿服务发展模式初探' Zhong xiao chengzhen qingnian zhiyuan fuwu fazhan moshi chutan [Development modes of youth voluntary service in small–medium towns]. *Guangdong qingnian ganbu xueyuan xuebao,* vol. 48, no. 2, pp. 36–41.

Thoits, Peggy A. and Lyndi N. Hewitt (2001) 'Volunteer work and well-being'. *Journal of Health and Social Behavior*, vol. 42, no. 2, pp. 115–131.

Unger, Jonathan (2002) *The Transformation of Rural China*. London. M.E. Sharpe.

Wang Yalin (王雅林) ed. (2003) 城市休闲——上海，天津，哈尔滨城市居民时间分配的考察 *Chengshi xiuxian: Shanghai, Tianjin, Haerbin chengshi jumin shijian fenpei de kaocha* [Urban leisure: Time distribution study among the inhabitants of Shanghai, Tianjin and Haerbin cities]. Beijing: Shehui kexue wenxian chubanshe.

Wang, Shaoguang (1995) 'The politics of private time: changing leisure patterns in urban China'. In Deborah Davis et al. (eds), *Urban Spaces in Contemporary China: The Potential for Autonomy and Community in post-Mao China*. Cambridge: Cambridge University Press, pp. 149–172.

Xu, Feng (2005) 'Building community in post-socialist China: towards local democratic governance?' Paper presented at The Annual Meeting of CPSA, University of Western Ontario, June 2005. *Quoted with author's permission.*

Yan, Yunxiang (2003) *Private Life under Socialism: Love, Intimacy, and Family Change in a Chinese Village*. Stanford: Stanford University Press.

Yu Bing, Ceng Xiongwei and Lin Yuewang (余冰, 曾雄伟, 林悦旺) (1999) '小城市地区志愿服务发展探讨—对广东省新会市青年志愿者行动个案研究' Xiao chengshi diqu zhiyuanzhe fuwu fazhan tantao; Dui Guangdong sheng Xinhui shi Qingnian zhiyuanzhe xingdong ge'an yanjiu [An enquiry into the development of volunteers' services in small city China; A case study of volunteers' activities in Xinhui, Guangdong]. *Guangdong qingnian ganbu xueyuan xuebao* [Journal of Guangdong College of Young Cadres], vol. 38, no 4: 31–37.

Yu Yiqun (余逸群) (2003) '论青年志愿者行动与精神' Lun qingnian zhiyuanzhe xingdong yu jingshen [About the activities and spirit of Youth Volunteers]. *Qingnian tansuo*, no 1, pp. 31–33.

Zhou Xiaohong (周晓虹) (2005) '导言:中国中产阶层的历史与现状' Daoyan: Zhongguo zhongchan jieceng de lishi yu xianzhuang [Introduction: history and current situation of the Chinese middle class]. In Zhou Xiaohong (周晓虹) (ed.), 中国中产阶层调查 *Zhongguo zhongchan jieceng diaocha* [Survey of the Chinese Middle Stratum]. Beijing: Social Sciences Academic Press, pp. 1–28.

Zhuang Lihong (庄黎虹) (2003) '记志愿者 "五月花" 助老组:送人玫瑰手有余香' Ji zhiyuanzhe 'wuyuehua' zhu lao zu: Song ren meigui shou you yu xiang [The Mayflower help the elderly group: The scent lingers on their hands after giving out roses]. *Quanzhou wanbao* 25.12.03 (*facsimile* in QZSQNZYZXH 2006, pp. 4).

5 Between Self and Community: The Individual in Contemporary Chinese Literature

Anne Wedell-Wedellsborg

Concerns and questions about the individual are probably the most conspicuous aspects of Chinese literature from the beginning of the reform period up to the present. If one were to mention one continuing trend transcending the multitude of developments, schools and isms that have pervaded the literary scene from late 1970s into the new millennium, it would have to be the investigation from various angles of the role and place of the individual person, whether in relation to history, nation, family, sexuality or just the daily world of mundane matters. While it could be argued that all literature in one way or the other is, and has always been, about individuals, the case of Chinese literature during the last thirty-five years stands out, not only on the stark background of the immediately preceding Maoist–socialist rejection of individual vision, but also as a special version, or special versions, of the focus on the individual person that characterizes what we term the modern condition or simply modernity.[1] As Steven Lukes puts it:

> [Central to our western notion of modernity] is a distinctive picture of the individual in relation to his roles and to his aims and purposes. To the former he exhibits role distance: confronting all possible roles, he may in principle adopt, perform or abandon any at will (though not all, and probably not even many, at once). Over the latter he exercises choice: as sovereign chooser, he decides between actions, conceptions of the good, plans of life, indeed what sort of person to be. The will, choice, decision, evaluation and calculation are central to this picture; and the individual to whom these features are essential thinks and acts as an autonomous, self-directing, independent agent who relates to others as no less autonomous agents . . . (Lukes 1985: 298)

This picture of the archetypical individual person constitutive of western modernity contrasts with another one,

> . . . in which the individual is largely identified with and by his roles (though these may conflict) and who relates to his ends and purposes less by choice than through knowledge and discovery. This second picture is one in which self-discovery, mutual understanding, authority, tradition and the virtues are central. Conceptions of the good are not seen as subject to individual choice, let alone invention, but rather as internal practices within which individuals are involved by reason of their roles and social positions. Reason, innovation, criticism, argument can all be part of this picture, but are differently understood within it, as operating within an accepted social framework. And, most important, that framework is seen as constitutive of the identity of the persons within it: who I am is answered both for me and for others by the history I inherit, the social positions I occupy, and the "moral career" on which I am embarked. (Lukes 1985: 299)

So, the question one could ask is which of those descriptions, if any, fit with the pictures of individuals and their condition that we find in Chinese literature of the post-Mao era? Or rather where in between those two would we place representative literary characters? And further, which are the choices and evaluations, or roles and social positions available to the individual person? Finally, which are the real or imagined communities to which those fictional individuals in various literary texts relate?

In discussing these questions I find that Jonathan Friedman's notion of modernity as an *identity space* offers a useful perspective. To Friedman modernity is not bound to any specific time or place but is rather 'a kind of identity space or field of alternative identities that is structured by certain parameters such as individualization and developmentalism, which are themselves generated by the rise of a hegemonic power or zone in a system based on commercial reproduction'.[2] Friedman sets up modernism[3] (culture and nature are to be overcome), traditionalism (valuing culture), primitivism (valuing nature) and postmodernism (culture and nature have relative value) as the four poles of potential identification that define a space of identity variation, i.e. ways of orientation available for the single individual according to the given situation. In periods of rising hegemonic status of a particular place in the global system, the pole of modernism tends to be the dominating one, while the three other poles tend to be activated in periods of crisis. Foundational for this notion of modernity is what he terms the principle of *alterity*. This refers to a situation where the self is never quite defined, where there are always other possibilities of identity or existence. With the separation of the subject from his or her social expression as a result of the breakdown of holistic structures, the individual may experience the possibility of creating his or her own status, which may be experienced more as a chosen role rather than essential identity. The search for 'the real me' in turn becomes essential (Friedman 1994: 241 ff). I find these notions, the concept of identity space and the principle of alterity, to be implicitly or explicitly at work in most of the literary examples discussed below, as an as yet undeveloped, underlying potential, as an openly confronted problematique or as a frame of reference that may help to explain phenomena.

Reading some Chinese literary works from the last three decades with Friedman's framework in mind does not imply any evaluation of the 'quality' or level of Chinese modernity, for example as compared to a Western one. What I am investigating is not objective reality but how the subjective individual consciousness as represented in literature experiences its situation and how it chooses to negotiate within the four poles of this identity space.

The Literary Individual in Post-Mao China

When analyzing the role and representation of the individual in Chinese literature during last thirty-five years it is important to remember that this period spans some deep changes in the discursive conditions and in the role of literature in Chinese society. While in the 1980s discussions on single works, writers or issues could attract a focused intellectual attention that spilled out to a wider audience, the situation became much more blurred and diversified from the mid 1990s onwards, and it became definitely no longer, if it ever was, meaningful to refer to Chinese literature as a – however loosely – unified body of work. What I want to do in this chapter is nevertheless to show a certain line of development, to point to some tendencies in the literary and discursive treatment of the relationship between the individual and its collectives, as they emerge from selected examples of interesting texts (interesting in terms of popularity, media/intellectual focus or artistic quality) and their critical reception. I wish to illustrate that much of the most talked about literature in the 1980s, the first decade of reform, can be discussed in terms of one overall concern, namely the (re)establishment of the individual as within or against history or nation.[4] Thus in the still centralized discourse of the 1980s, literature and literary debate were still largely concerned with asserting or probing the individual self versus its social role and repressive structures of 'old' social or cultural norms or institutions. The stories or poems which focused especially on the problems of the individual – and were read as such by critics – would rarely seem detached from the theme of the state of Chinese society or nation.

Then, in the course of the 1990s, there is a change of priority as the literary representation of the individual splits out into many directions but most often tending towards the private and personal, away from the grand narratives of nation and politics (this simultaneously with a distinctly nationalist upsurge in the popular cultural climate of the day). If we should summarize a general tendency with regard to individual/collective, many works would now focus on either unrestrained individual agency or human solitude, on the problems created by both, and by the loss of ethical values linked to the common good. The many novel titles including words like private (*siren* 私人), alone (*yige ren* 一个人), individual (*geren* 个人) testify to this. By the turn of the millennium this tendency was further enhanced and diversified, along with remarkable counter currents as for example what looks like the return with a vengeance of the national character syndrome.[5]

All this of course happens in the context of – and is not to be separated from – the increasing commercialization of both the literary market and the general social spheres and, especially for the most recent period, under the impact of globalization.[6] Here I want to focus my attention on the texts themselves and on the unique kind of subjective evidence they offer for the investigation of the Chinese individual in the reform period.[7] I do this from a subjective bird's eye view, looking down on three decades of literary activity, and selecting works that to me seem to epitomize the above-mentioned trends in the presentation of the individual. I argue that in the 1980s the individual is mainly posited in or against the grand forces of history/culture/nation, often with very limited agency; by the 1990s the dominating theme is that of individuals searching to negotiate their places vis-à-vis the collectives of family or friends; while by the late 1990s and after the turn of the millennium the impact of globalization seems to generate an increasing focus on individual orientation in the private sphere along with renewed concern with nation and culture.

The Individual versus History and Culture

Looking back from the point of view of the new millennium towards the early years of the reform period, the intellectual and literary activities of the 1980s may indeed look almost like a shared project aiming at (re)establishing the individual as the central concept through which history, culture and nation could be understood. By shifting attention to individual experience as a recognized mark of authenticity, new space was created allowing for reinterpretation of anything from marriage customs to alienation or the Cultural Revolution – political restrictions notwithstanding. A strong subjective awareness emerged in literature, an awareness also reflected in theoretical discourse, with Liu Zaifu's ideas about the subjectivity (*zhuti-xing* 主体性) of writer-person, literary characters and reading experience as the most prominent expression.[8] The appearance of outsider-characters, the use of the limited point of view, the techniques of multiple narrators, stream-of-consciousness and interior monologue, all well-worn techniques of western modernist writing, to Chinese writers and readers appeared new and calling for attention to the self. Of course, an interest in the individual and its condition does not necessarily mean a focus in literature on individuality as such or on personal psychology. Indeed many texts, especially from the late 1980s, instead turned their main attention towards the deep cultural or social forces the individual interacts with or is up against. Behind this general outline lie such diverse trends as the early unofficial writing of the *Jintian*-group, the stereotyped writing of scars, the literature of self-reflection, reportage literature of individual versus system, the modernists, the root-searchers, the experimentalists or whatever epithets were put on the successive new phases of literary developments through that period.[9]

In her study of the literary subject 1976–89, Rong Cai sees two parallel discourses: one aims to present the individual as an autonomous humanist self, the other reveals a problematic subject suffering from mental or physical deformity (Cai 2004). However, the autonomous humanist self, such as the integrated and autonomous person theoretically expounded in the writings of Liu Zaifu, did not, in my view, gain prominence in actual literature. But it hovers above many works as the longed for, yet unattainable, ideal. Ba Jin's personal reflections in *Random Thoughts* (*Suixiang lu* 随想录) on that great national trauma, the Cultural Revolution, as seen from the point of view of the weak single individual and probing his/her treble role as victim, persecutor and accomplice, represents at least a search for and a plea for a human autonomy hitherto absent (Ba 1979). The introspection that characterizes Ba Jin's essays was also reflected in numerous works written in a more fictionalized form, such as novels by Dai Houying (on university intellectuals in crisis with their Marxist faith), Zhang Xianliang (labour camps), and Bai Hua (the Cultural Revolution). With individual feelings as the focal point, these stories were all closely linked to the grander national narratives of recent history as the emotional, ethical and political space in which the individual seeks to come to terms with his/her predicament. At the same time a wave of critical realist and reportage literature focused on the rights of the individual as opposed to the system, all within the ever so gradually widening limits of political censorship.

One of the earliest works to feature a subjective vision of history through the technique of multiple narrators was Bei Dao's novel *Waves* (*Bodong* 波动).[10] The novel's main theme is emblematic of the problems of individual existence situated somewhere between the two descriptions offered by Lukes above. The characters in the novel, which takes place sometime during the late Cultural Revolution, all feel that they can no longer identify with their social roles. But the possibility of alternative identities – what Friedman terms the principle of alterity – does not exist except as a lack, a void, which functions as a kind of unrealizable vision activating the search for 'the real me'. Thus the characters are caught in the conflict between genuine self and social role, pinched between loyalty to the self and compliance for reasons of social acceptance, but without the option of shifting between roles that we meet in later fiction. It is symbolic that the heroine of the story (who hides an illegitimate child), the most autonomous and self-loyal of all the characters, dies in an accident as a result of this predicament.

The existentialist attitude and the conflict between role and self was a conspicuous theme in the early to mid 1980s, taken up by writers of various generations and social positions, from the establishment writers Wang Meng and Zhang Jie to the young so-called modernists Xu Xing and

Liu Suola. The dilemma for the protagonist and first person narrator in Liu Suola's 'In Search of the King of Singers' (*Xunzhao gewang* 寻找歌王) is shown to be between on the one hand a perceived authenticity to be found in traditional primitive culture and on the other hand a semi-artificial modern urban lifestyle (Liu 1986). The I in this story, a singer of pop-songs, experiences herself as living in the maelstrom of modernity, in western-ized city surroundings, presenting her with numerous superficial choices, which only makes her confused and indecisive. In contrast to this are her recollections of following her boyfriend, a composer, into the wild regions of a primeval forest where he searches for the mysterious *King of Singers* amidst shamanistic rituals beyond civilization. Although she feels this search as more genuine and true to nature than her empty urban lifestyle she is unable to give up the latter. Here the crisis of the vacillating narrator is played out as a dichotomy between modernism and authenticity, with primitivism – the third pole in Friedman's identity space – mobilized to represent authentic values.

In Liu Suola's story the search for identity is linked to an alternative source of original Chinese culture which differs from the Confucian or Taoist versions of traditional high Han-culture. Her text can thus be read as part of the search for roots, the most prominent literary trend in the mid 1980s. Certainly the *xungen* (寻根) movement was an investigation into Chinese culture, especially its more marginalized and local aspects, marked by diversity and a wide range of narrative methods, but it was also, as Yi-tsi Mei Feuerwerker has pointed out, marked by 'its self-conscious, self-exploratory processes' (Feuerwerker 1998: 251). Taken as a whole the literature of roots (*xungen wenxue* 寻根文学) broadly including such different writers as Ah Cheng, Mo Yan, Wang Anyi, Han Shaogong, Gao Xingjian and many others was concerned with the construction of a new collective or national memory – or rather a number of alternative collective memories – as a means of understanding or explaining the predicament of the individual in China's recent history and, by extension, in contemporary society.

Both traditionalism associated with culture and primitivism associated with nature (in Friedman's identity space) were brought into play by the majority of these writers who simultaneously addressed the immediate crisis of what they saw as an overly Westernized literary scene, and the deeper one of Chinese culture and civilization in the aftermath of the Maoist era. With the possible exception of Ah Cheng's famous *King of Chess* (*Qiwang* 棋王) (Ah 1984), where the two poles of traditionalism and primitivism combine in celebration of natural life and Chinese core culture among sent-down youth during the Cultural Revolution, these notions are fraught with ambiguity and ambivalence in most *xungen* texts. This ambivalence, and its implications for questions of individual identity and self, is almost emblematically expressed in Han Shaogong's story 'Going Home' (*Guiqulai* 归去来) (Han 1985). A young man from the city enters a remote mountain village, and although he does not seem to have been there before the villagers recognize him as having been sent there during the Cultural Revolution. As the story progresses and he gets deeper and deeper into the primitive, almost primeval lifestyle of the local inhabitants, he begins to doubt his identity. This local 'culture' is presented as frightening, violent and strange as well as natural, original and sensual. The first-person narrator is thus offered a choice between two roles or two identities, one rooted in modern city life (only sketched in glimpses in the text) and one rooted in a primitive original culture, far from the traditional high culture of central China. Unable to actually confront the dilemma, he flees the village in deep crisis. The story is clearly an allegorical representation of the loss of a fixed identity in a national culture that has forgotten or repressed the more 'uncivilized', natural or primordial aspects which are uncontaminated not only by modernity but also by the rhetoric of official high culture: Confucianism and Socialism: an official culture that no longer provides the individual with the framework within which to establish his/her personal moral identity.

If the fictional individuals in much of the literature of the early and mid 1980s seemed weak and vacillating as they strove to establish themselves as focal points in society, history and culture, Yu Hua in his stories from 1987 on presents the individual as almost crushed by those forces. The characters in stories like *Nineteen Eighty-six* (*Yi jiu ba liu nian* 一九八六年) (Yu 1989a) and *One Kind of Reality* (*Xianshi yizhong* 现实一种) (Yu 1989b) are devoid of psychological traits but endowed with a kind of negative subjectivity, emanating from somewhere deep in the darkness of Chinese history.[11] The school-teacher in *Nineteen Eighty-six*, who was persecuted and who disappeared during the Cultural Revolution, now returns to his hometown as a madman, totally obsessed with ancient barbaric methods of punishment. The self here is nothing but congealed past, with the recent and the remote past merged, bound to return as the suppressed spectre of memory, unrecognized by people living in the present consumerist society, only affecting a vague sense of unease among them. In *One Kind of Reality*, a story of killing and revenge between two brothers, the actions seem to be generated by some pre-existing pattern that simply *is* there, thus flaunting the lack of psychological explanation or even emotional motivation on the part of the individual characters. Yu Hua's stories of the late 1980s are not about identity or roles, or possible recourse to nature or culture when the modernist sense of progress promoted politically appears inadequate, as with the 'roots' and earlier literature. We may say that Yu Hua's strong focus on the individual in these stories is created paradoxically by pointing to its absence, and by demonstrating the impossibility of individual agency in the grip of predetermined structures inherent in the dominating culture.

Yu Hua and other late 1980s elite writers (dubbed avant-garde, new wave, experimental, post-modern) perhaps mark the temporary end of the concern with the individual as in or against the grand forces of history, nation and culture which characterized that decade. However, simultaneously with this a very different perspective on the individual burst through in the novels of best-selling author Wang Shuo. With their quick-witted descriptions of new individualized urban youth in contemporary society, Wang's early novels in many ways seem to belong more to the literary scene in the 1990s. Scorned by many critics for their irreverent attitude to authorities and positive portrayals of petty criminals and loafers, these stories soon won a huge readership, and Wang Shuo became the first independent or individualized (*gerenhua* 个人化) author, able to live off his royalties alone. Wang's so-called hooligan fiction has a lot to do with roles, games, identities, literally so in 'Masters of Mischief' (*Wanzhu* 顽主) (Wang 1987) where the protagonists run a bureau where they sell their services as surrogates/ substitutes for people in unpleasant situations. *Playing for Thrills* (*Wan-de jiu shi xintiao* 玩得就是心跳) (Wang 1989) revolves around a fictitious murder, a play with identities and memories made up by a group of friends. The principle of alterity, the popping in and out of roles and identities, is here played out in an ironic meta-fictional game, where the search for 'the real me' which runs through the text as a sub-current, is sabotaged by the intervention of the implied author at the end. Typically Wang's characters keep outside established institutionalized communities, but are strongly attached to their community of friends (*gemenr* 哥们儿) with their own code of honour.[12]

Individual versus Self

It is generally acknowledged that the 1980s–1990s juncture marks a rather fundamental change on the literary scene in China, both in terms of the material conditions of production and distribution of literature, and in literature itself (Kong 2005). Although some of these changes were already under way in the late 1980s, rapidly increasing commercialization, together with post-Tiananmen de-politicization and the privatization of a still larger part of social life, all contributed to pushing the trend towards individualization and diversification, and to an explosive growth in the field of popular literature. Altogether the focus on the personal vision continued though with a slightly different accent. Words like privacy (*yinsi*), privatization (*sirenhua* 私人化), individualization (*gerenhua* 个人化), individuality (*gexinghua* 个性化) are the keywords relating to the most conspicuous literature of the era.[13] Another way of summing this up is: individuality (*gerenxing* 个人性), subjectivity (*zhuguanxing* 主观性) and interiority (*neizaixing* 内在性) (Han 2005).

But how does this specific concentration on the individual person differ from what we saw in the previous decade? First, the exploration of the world through the eyes of the individual continues but now with more attention to the repercussions on the immediate circle of family and friends, and second, a wave of literature emerges, mostly written by women, exploring the inner world of the individual with a focus on sexuality and psychological conflict.

Yu Hua is a good example of the former. Yu, famous for showing the obliteration of an individual self by major forces of history and national culture in his fiction of the late 1980s, returned to the literary forefront with three novels strongly affirming the value of the individual person. *Cries in the Drizzle* (*Zai xiyu zhong huhan* 在细雨中呼喊*)* (Yu 1991) is a sensitive portrait of a solitary soul, a boy who is mentally and physically rejected by his own family. This was followed by his two best-selling novels, *To Live* (*Huozhe* 活着*)* (Yu 1992) and *Chronicle of a Bloodseller* (*Xu sanguan mai xue* *ji* 许三观卖血记*) (Yu 1996), both of which are historical narratives seen from the point of view of an ordinary Chinese person. Both relate the turbulence and tragedies of individual human life, but also show the resilience, vitality and will to live generated most of all by attaching importance to the family as the community that gives meaning to existence. Historical events such as revolution and political movements are not there for the individual to step into and establish himself within. On the contrary, their arbitrariness, absurdity and irrelevance to what really matters is an underlying theme in both novels. Reinstating individual agency, Yu Hua shows people not as grand players or innocent victims in history, but as autonomous units of meaning in the defining collective of significant others made up of members of the close family.[14]

However, it is the second trend, the semi-autobiographical or even confessional stories by (mostly) women that in the eyes of most critics epitomize the individualized writing (*gerenhua xiezuo* 个人化写作) of the 1990s and early 2000s.[15] This term covers a wide range of epithets such as body-writing (*shenti xiezuo* 身体写作), privacy writing (*sirenhua xiezuo* 私人化写作), alternative writing (*linglei xiezuo* 另类写作) and babe-fiction (*baobei xiaoshuo* 宝贝小说). This literature is vast and includes writers of three generations. Those born in the 1960s like Lin Bai and Chen Ran are regarded as controversial but serious writers and path-breakers, while male writers like Qiu Huadong, Zhu Wen and Han Dong are seen to display a more cynical attitude. The 1970s generation is represented by, for example, the notorious Shanghai women Wei Hui and Mian Mian and the lesser known Wei Wei and Zhu Wenying. The youngest, born in the 1980s, include Chun Shu, Zhang Yueran, Sha Qing and the media celebrities Han Han and Guo Jingming. Despite considerable differences in style, outlook and the degree of intimacy revealed, the writers of the two youngest generations are often referred to collectively by the paradoxical expression: individualist writing group (*gerenhua xiezuo qunti* 个人化写作群体) (Xie 2005).

It is tempting to see these autobiographically oriented works in the light of what sociologists Beck and Beck-Gernsheim have described as the 'self-thematization of people's biographies' that follows upon the break-up of the traditional rhythm of life. Of course Beck and Beck-Gernsheim are discussing western societies in what they term 'the second modernity' and referring to biography as a sociological term, not as a literary text. But the experience of individualization and instability reflected in stories by Chinese writers has much in common with Beck and Beck-Gernsheim's description of the situation where people find themselves 'bereft of unquestionable assumptions, beliefs or values', but nevertheless 'faced with the tangle of institutional controls and constraints which make up the fibre of modern life'.[16] Novels and stories by the above-mentioned writers, and many others, very often read like attempts to change chaos into some kind of order by turning it into text. Creating your own biography and incorporating hitherto suppressed or marginalized areas of psychology and sexuality is one way of coming to terms with a changing world.

Here I want to take a closer look at one particular novel, which in many ways could be said to epitomize the individualist writing of the 1990s, Chen Ran's *A Private Life* (*Siren shenghuo* 私人生活) (Chen 1996). Chen Ran is a well-known, talented and prolific author, she was among the first to proclaim herself an independent or individualized writer (*gerenhua zuojia* 个人化作家) and she has expounded her ideas about individualized writing in essays and articles, pronouncing her intention to 'dissolve the public, grand and collective model of literary representation endorsed in earlier periods' (Wang 2005: 173). To her the single individual (*geti* 个体) is characterized by marginalization and separation from the group, and represents quality as opposed to quantity. The individual is authentic as opposed to the average; the keywords are independent attitude, complexity and ambiguity, as opposed to standardization and unification, which relate to abstract concepts like society, the times, etc. Individualized writing means to return to the innermost, deepest and most intimate parts of life for exploration and reflection.[17] *A Private Life* is the artistic and semi-autobiographical reflection of these views, written with a narrative technique that in itself seems to illustrate the predicament of the solitary individual.

It is a story of loneliness, of feeling different – all the words for solitude (*gudu* 孤独, *jimo* 寂寞, *gudugan* 孤独感, *yige ren* 一个人) keep recurring throughout the book – and scene after scene depicts the protagonist`s sense of being an outsider, especially mentally but also physically. The novel is told in the first person narration of Ni Niuniu, a strongly limited point of view, with the I constantly watching itself in a narcissistic manner. In one long monologue, or dialogue within the self, she looks back on her life, from age eleven up to the present where she is recovering from a mental breakdown. The characters in the book are all single: her mother, a young widow she attaches herself to erotically and emotionally, her teacher, and a school-mate whose parents died during the Cultural Revolution. All of these solitary individuals in one way or the other reflect the break-up of former communities of family, neighbours and work-place. As the narrator moves into a high-rise flat and mother and widow-friend both die, her solitary existence is even more pronounced. When her short time boyfriend disappears in the crowds of Tiananmen in June 1989 and then flees to the West, she practically moves into her bathroom, in fact into her womb-like bathtub: the smallest and most private space at all imaginable.

So the narrator is from the beginning existentially and psychologically alone, a solitude which gradually turns into a physical one, here presented as a deliberate subjective choice and not the result of being rejected by the community. Even time has become individualized ('time is created by the flow of my thoughts' *shijian shi you wode sixu de liudong er goucheng de* 时间是由我的思绪的流动而构成的), separated from the objective time of external reality to which other people relate. The text reads as a classical study of typical modernist solitude, with a self-reflective, almost obsessively self-centred, I-narrator, haunted by the paradox of on the one hand having no sense of self (she calls herself Miss Nothing, Ling Nüshi, and 'a fragment in a fragmented age'), and on the other hand being obsessed with self and identity. Her attitude to her body shows the same duality: she is alienated from it, talks to her arms as 'misses Do and Don't', at the same time as being intensely focused on it, and erotically attracted to it. The whole text is permeated with ambiguity, sexually as she tends towards lesbianism and socially as she fears the crowds in the street at the same time as wishing to be one of the unknowns among them. A weak individual, caught in the dichotomy of fighting to maintain individual authenticity without interference from others, while facing the loss of an integrated self that comes from lack of contact. In the terminology of Richard Jenkins we may say that this is the result of stepping back from the interaction order and attempting to retreat altogether from the institutional order, while desperately striving to negotiate her identity by confining herself to the individual order (Jenkins 1996). We may also interpret the seclusion of the protagonist as a longing for a different kind of community from that available to her, and her subsequent breakdown as that of a self without embedding in some sort of collective. Her self falls apart as the small female community she has invested in, mentally, physically and sexually, is dissolved. What is left is the imagined community to which the text repeatedly, implicitly as well as explicitly, refers: that of writing.

The main character in Chen Ran's story is clearly in the middle of an identity crisis caused by several factors: the dissolution of the collectives of family (her parents divorced) and neighbourhood (the courtyard in which she grew up), her reluctance to mentally join other social communities (at school or university) and her ambiguous sexuality. But the point is that her problems are predominantly shown to be caused by herself, simply by the recognition of the possibility of choice, rather than being the result of suppression, confinement or rigid structures, such as we saw in much of the literature of the 1980s. The individual senses, as Friedman notes, the opportunity of choosing a role, of creating a socially acceptable identity, which in turn generates a strong urge to find 'the real me'. But in this case the two are so much in conflict that the search for 'the real me' ends up being sabotaged by the I itself, which consequently – whether or not we are to believe the ironic ending in which she promises her doctors to join the masses – fails to become a truly autonomous self.

The fragility of the individualized person, predicated on the separation of self from social identity, is acutely described in Chen Ran's novel about a mental collapse. Other writers related the general sense of floating identities and confusion of roles from different perspectives. The roaming narrator in Zhu Wen's prose, observing a moral decline and a hedonistic search for instant gratification while cynically aware of his own lack of real identity, represents one end of the spectrum, Wei Hui's narcissistic dependency on the presentation of the self via the commodity construction of identity the other.[18]

The Individual as Wolf

Semi-autobiographical works displaying or reacting to the experience of value-loss and lack of orientation in a world of change have taken on many forms. As Friedman notes, the recourse to the poles of traditionalism or primitivism in the identity space of the modern individual is a common phenomenon, when the forward-looking cult of modernism is felt to lead to a crisis in moral identity. As a conspicuous example of that I now turn to a book that on the immediate level may not have much to do with the predicament of the individual in contemporary society. However, its way of addressing the theme of individual and group and its reactivation of the issue of national character, together with its vast popularity and impact in terms of related publications, point to other currents in Chinese society than those highlighted in the very personalized trend of semi-autobiographical writing in contemporary settings. *Wolf Totem* (*Langtuteng* 狼图腾) by Jiang Rong (pseudonym) (Jiang 2004) was published in 2004, by September 2005 it was in its 14th printing, and in 2006 it was estimated to have sold more than seven million copies. While the book is set in another time, the late 1960s early 1970s, takes place on the inner Mongolian plains, far from central China and its metropolises, and certainly does not feature troubled citizen or peasant individualities of the reform period, it clearly had a message for contemporary readers, judging from its popularity and the controversy it provoked. It is a book about man and nature, about the ecological and spiritual disasters of political interference, but also about individual nature and freedom, and about interactions within a group. Much discussion has centred around the book's overall message, grossly expounded in the author's postscript, about the weak culture of the dragon (the agriculture-based Han Chinese) versus the strong culture of the wolf (the nomad culture of the Mongolians), and the text is thickly sprinkled with ethnographical detail to support this as well as quotations from classical works and historical research, which seem to confirm the idea of the superiority of the Mongol over the Han mentality. Here I will leave out this aspect and concentrate on what the book has to say about individuals and collectives.

The individual–group motif is played out as interrelating processes within the community of humans and the community of wolves, and thus unfolds on two intersecting levels. On the level of men we follow the protagonist Chen Zhen and his interaction with the Mongol inhabitants on the Elun plain, where he arrives as a sent-down youth during the Cultural Revolution. On the level of wolves the reader, along with Chen Zhen, step by step gets to know and understand their behaviour and Darwinian fight for survival as pack and as 'individuals' within the group. The first level tells how the young Han-Chinese comes to this faraway place, learns to adapt to the group of Mongolians, and becomes a member of the new community by interiorizing the values and norms of the group. Gradually, making many mistakes, he learns and changes. First considering the wolf an enemy, the 'other' of human civilization, he gets to understand that its skills, intelligence and morale are superior to humans. His adaptation takes on religious overtones as he worships *Tengeli* (Mongolian Heaven) and the wolf totem. The wolf totem is emblematic of the symbolic construction of the community of the Mongolian nomad-herdsmen of which he comes to feel himself a part, despite the fact that he is Han.[19] This is confirmed by the sense of difference Chen Zhen feels when he is confronted with representatives of the central Han culture to which he ethnically and culturally belongs. His sense of symbolic community is with the nomads, and as the story progresses more and more with the wolves. We may say that his nominal identity is Han while his actual identity becomes more and more Mongol. Yet the protagonist does not display any wolf-like characteristics himself. On the contrary, even though his sympathies are clear and he mentally opposes the Han Chinese authorities and their wolf extinction campaign, he does not really fight for his ideas. And in an almost Lu Xun-like postscript we learn that he later in life became a well-adapted Chinese researcher, a part of the system – by analogy the same type of system that caused the destruction of the wolves and the grasslands. But apart from this faintly ironic final twist, the narrative itself is marked by a total absence of ambiguity or irony, mixing magnificent descriptions of nature and minute ethnographical detail with a great deal of hollow pathos.

As many critics have pointed out, the real protagonist of the book is the wolf (Zhao 2005). It appears in the novel both as an 'individual' and as a member of the pack, indeed the reader is left in little doubt that the inter-actions within the pack of wolves represent an ideal relationship between individual and group. Each member is independent, wild and free at the same time as loyal to its pack and willing to be sacrificed if needed for the survival of the group. It is a strictly hierarchical formation with a strong and wise leader, whose authority is unquestioned. The book includes many minute descriptions of how the wolves organize for attack and of their ritual sharing of meals after killing the sheep, all showing them as proud and rational beings. A large part of the book is dedicated to Chen Zhen's attempts to catch and bring up a wolf cub, which he even plans to mate with a dog.[20] He keeps the animal on a chain, but of course the whole idea of taming the free animal is bound to end with its death, and the symbolic implication of a Han Chinese fascinated by the wolf, but wanting to tame and domesticate it, is more than obvious. Other parts of the story could also be interpreted allegorically, for instance the destruction of the wolf by the CCP cadres, thereby upsetting the whole ecological system of man/nature/culture, corresponds to the ideological and social destruction of the free individual in a rigid socialist society.

Extreme and simplified or distorted versions of the novel's message about the human being learning from the wolf appeared in a series of short popular books on the theme of *Langdao* (狼道) – the Way of the Wolf. They are guides to success in business and in life, and the following quotation is typical: 'The world belongs to the strong, all the weak can hope for is compassion and pity but the wolf pack teaches us how to become strong in life', so there is hope for the weak because 'the weakest may become the strongest because its stubborn desire for life makes it endure more hardships and accumulate more skills'.[21] Careful not to advocate unbridled freedom, these books stress that freedom must always be within a structure 'the social structure of the wolf pack is very strict, each member understands its own place and function . . . but when they howl out together all demarcations disappear, as if they would tell us: we are one collective, but each individual is different from the group, so you had better not interfere with us' (Long 2004).

How are we to explain the success of this rather bombastic return of the focus on national character and relentless cultural critique linked to a worship of a primitive pre-modern lifestyle? Most Chinese critics, whether negative or positive, point to the general decline in spiritual civilization, the lack of stable values in contemporary commercial society, but also to the dissolution of central Chinese culture in the face of globalization. All of this makes the individual search for something beyond the here and now, for an authenticity that relates to an original nature rather than to a traditional culture felt to be inadequate. Some, like Hou Rui and Hou Ying chose a culturalist approach by seeing the book as in fact a Confucian way of saving and reinvigorating Han civilization by incorporating marginal cultures as has been done throughout Chinese history (Hou and Hou 2006). Lei Da writing in *Guangming Ribao* openly deplored the moral vacuum which made possible this kind of *Ersatz* worship of the wolf (Lei 2005). Others went on to call it highly dangerous in its mixture of fascism, narrow nationalism and old-fashioned Nietzschean ideas of superman (Li L. 2005). At the other end of the spectrum, placing the book in its contemporary literary context, and implicitly referring to literature's time-old obligation to act as moral guide, one critic said: 'At a time when novels highlight characters turned into materialist, desire driven "bodies", or "lower body parts", then the wolf appears on the scene as the perfect signifier of life and a forceful symbol of human dignity (*rengehua* 人格化). That is to say when some people are about to write human beings into wolves, then the wolf enters the novel endowed with lofty "human nature" (*renxing* 人性)' (Yan 2005).

So to Chinese critics Jiang Rong's novel represents either an answer, an explanation, or a solution (or all three at once) to a crisis in literature as well as in the spiritual climate. And there is no denying the book's huge readership compared to that of the so-called individualized writing (*gerenhua xiezuo* 个人化写作) discussed above. Seen from the point of view of the identity space of the modern individual, as set up by Friedman, *Wolf Totem* reflects the tendency towards the two poles of traditionalism and primitivism, often activated in times when modernism is perceived by the individual to be in crisis. Since '[traditionalist identity] is fixed and ascribed, it provides a medium for engagement in a larger collectivity, and provides a set of standards, values and rules for living.' (Friedman 1994: 243). 'The traditionalist tendency tending towards the culture side may entail emphasis on concrete values and morality and cultural practises, sometimes with religious overtones or tied to ethnicity connected to distinct cultural practises and beliefs. Closely connected to this could be the ecological strategy, basing itself in nature, in the correct relation of man and the eco-system' (Friedman 1994: 191). In choosing to subscribe to the values, religion and cultural practises of the non-Han Mongolian nomads Jiang Rong appeals simultaneously to the poles of primitivism and culturalism. But it is a culturalism based on a view of life alternative to the one prescribed by traditional Han ethics. Furthermore, especially as we see it developed in the *Langdao* books, he thereby – perhaps unwittingly – provides certain social trends of competitive capitalism with a kind of justifying Darwinist ethic.

The Individual versus Life

'The core of wolf nature is to protect one's rights and beliefs, and not to give in even in the most difficult of times, to possess an indomitable wildness which means that one is always prepared to fight for freedom. Even when put into a cage or under numerous restrictions the wolf will stick to its standpoint. And as soon as you let it out of its cage, the wolf is still a wolf, not an adaptable pliable dog' (Li H. 2005: 75). This quotation, obviously inspired by the general wolf-fever, is neither a comment on *Wolf Totem* nor an extract from a *Langdao*-guide, but an attempt to characterize the writer Can Xue. Since her debut in the mid 1980s Can Xue (born 1953) has been known as one of the most consistently individual voices in contemporary fiction, stylistically unique with her surrealist narrative universe, and thematically persistent in addressing the predicament of individuality in contemporary China. A prolific literary outsider, she commands a limited yet highly profiled readership.

Almost simultaneously with the appearance of *Wolf Totem*, Can Xue published the short novel 'The Work Team' (*Mingongtuan* 民工团) (Can 2004), in which she deals with the issue of individual versus group from a very different perspective. As I argue below, the story may be read both as an allegorical reflection on the human condition, and more specifically as a picture of (Chinese) life with a focus on the relationship between the single individual and the collective, and on the individual's overwhelming need to be part of a community, even of the most negative kind, entailing suffering and extreme hardship. The story is told in a focalized first person and played out in drab urban surroundings sometime in between forever and a very recognizable present. The first part of the text reads like a very realistic description of the hard life of migrant workers in today's Beijing. The narrator, a younger man with wife and children back home, arrives on a cold winter's night together with other temporary workers in this grey desolate city where they are put up in the deepest part of a damp concrete basement. He is an honest and decent man who simply wants to do his work well, in order to earn money for his family back home. He does not want to participate in the general informing on and slandering of others, prefers to be alone and reacts naturally with anger and amazement at the rude and insolent behaviour of other members of the work team. However when he is invited to take a day off from the hard and dangerous work and go to a faraway 'leisure park' to relax, the I, just like the reader, is gradually torn out of his normal expectations. The park turns out to be in fact a reform through labour camp (*laogai* 劳改) which is somehow at the same time an extension of the domain of the work team. Later other weird things happen: he witnesses bizarre nightly sado-masochist scenarios involving the team-leader, and a lump protruding on the chest of a young worker from his home village turns out to be his heart. Things get still bleaker and more difficult and the atmosphere increasingly ominous with men groaning and weeping at night, along with deadly dangerous work in the day-time and the constant threat of being sent away. The narrator is happy when he is offered a very special job, simply to occupy a room on the 26th floor in total isolation. However, on the fourth day of his residence up there, a dog suddenly appears, it bites him in the leg and he beats it savagely to death. After this event he has to return to hard labour despite excruciating pain. When a new team of temporary workers arrive, the leader presents the narrator as the 'babe' (*baobei* 宝贝) of the work team. In the last paragraph the narrator realizes that he will never leave, the wound will not heal or change, the pain will go on. What has changed is simply his own adaptability. He is now part of the collective.

As the title indicates it is about a *tuan* (团), about the group and how it affects the single individual. How *zhei yige* (这一个) (the single unique individual, in Kierkegaardian terms 'hin enkelte') is transformed into *mingong-tuan de baobei* (民工团的宝贝) (Lin 2004). The scene on the top floor is central to Can Xue's presentation of the predicament of the individual. Staying in solitude, raised far above the group whose work he can still follow through the window, symbolically expresses the ability to rise above his situation and reflect on it. The dog (with wolf-like eyes) appears as an ambiguous symbol of his free will, the as yet unadapted forces of individuality, but also as a catalyst of aggression and cruelty. The fact that it bites him severely and that he ends up killing it marks the final destruction of his own individuality, his surrender to the collective and its debased way of life. So on the immediate level the novel is a very negative vision of the problematics of individuality in today's China, with specific reference to the hardships of migrant workers in the urban building boom. In the early part of the story the narrator still cherishes memories of his home village, contrasting images of warm colours and a naïve kind of idealism and ambition, as when the villagers once tried to build an aeroplane out of clay. But these memories along with the link to his family recede more and more and gradually fade, till he no longer feels connected to them except through the fact of his still harder work to earn money for them. The physical and mental disembedding thus completed, the conditions are there for re-embedding into a different kind of collective.

The *mingongtuan* is described as a closed, even claustrophobic space, which nevertheless extends everywhere, horizontally and vertically, from 'leisure park'/*laogai* to torture room, from the deepest basement to the top floor in a high-rise. As such it becomes an image of life itself, of inescapable existence. As the narrator arrives at the workplace he is greeted by a woman in a bread-stall as 'death convict' – perhaps an ironic reference to the hard, prison-like and deadly dangerous (we learn that many workers lose their lives) labour. But this can also associate to the human condition: from birth we are all sentenced to death. This dual meaning is reinforced throughout the text, for example in the play on the word *huo* (活) which means both to work and to live, and *wang* (网) – net –, which is both referred to as something in which the narrator feels caught, and as the safety net used during work and operated by colleagues whom he doesn't trust. It also denotes the all-encompassing network of mutual suspicion, envy and power-struggle. Thus the work team becomes an allegory of life and the conditions under which the individual joins the group. As we arrive in life, the community is already there and we have to negotiate our individuality, to adapt or perish. Solitude in the sense of freedom from others has positive value for the narrator (he feels that as long as he keeps to himself he is able to preserve his honesty and dignity). But this turns out not to be an option, and what was in the beginning presented as a choice (though he is criticized for 'separation from the masses'), to join the group or go back home, turns out to be not really a choice. And at the end of the story the adaptation is complete. What is left is pain and debased normalization as the necessary price of integration. Or, in other words, the urge for the single individual to be recognized as part of the collective in which he has invested so much hard work is stronger than everything else.

Conclusion

Can Xue's vision of individual agency vis-à-vis an existing collective, whether interpreted as the great collective of life or as the concrete realities of a present day work team, is indeed negative. As such it may not be representative of the hopes or aspirations of, say, a young entrepreneur in today's Shanghai or even a temporary worker in Beijing counting on other opportunities later in life. In fact, I would not claim any of the texts analysed above to be representative, in the sense that they directly reflect objective realities of social life. They are, as with all serious literature, expressions of the subjective consciousness and imagination of sensitive individuals, who register the times they live in from each their own uniquely individual point of view. And that alone is a significant phenomenon in China, where the previous pressures towards conformity emanating from the party apparatus have been followed by the more complex but likewise mass-oriented mechanisms of the commercial market.

What the texts presented here have in common are three things: a concern with the loss of fixed values, an experience of discrepancy between self and social role, and a strong desire to be part of a community. In the early part of the reform period writers in the still centralized literary discourse seemed engaged in a search for alternative values to be found either somewhere in the depths of Chinese history or culture, or located as a resource within the single individual, yet still within the implicit context of the grander narratives of nation and society. The sense of the inadequacy or failure of this search is reflected in a number of literary texts in this and the ensuing period, and also in nation-wide debates, starting from the mid 1990s and continuing into the new century, on the lack of humanist spirit (*renwen jingshen* 人文精神).[22] From the beginning this groping for values has been tied to a growing sense of the distance between inner self and outer social identity, or at least to a feeling of unease or incompleteness with regard to the latter. Already in the 1980s the awareness of self as role was activated, but mostly, with few exceptions, without the feeling of being able to choose freely among alternative identities (Friedman's principle of alterity). By the 1990s, roles are experienced as possibilities, but often as a cover up for, or undermined by, the urge to find 'the real me'. Or else they are flaunted as expressions of a hedonistic, superficial life-style in no need of permanent values. Nevertheless nearly all of the texts, more or less explicitly, evince the desire on the part of the narrator or protagonist to be part of a community, to belong somewhere. But, notably, this desire is rarely directed towards existing, established collectives. A great number of stories deal with characters who are disembedded from the previous clear-cut social structures of family or work-place and seek re-embedding into alternative communities, be they real or imaginary. From the marginal cultures of roots writers or Wang Shuo's community of friends to Chen Ran's virtual community of writing and Jiang Rong's almost utopian fictional recollections of a 'natural' community of wolves and humans.

Jonathan Friedman's theory of modernity as an identity space, available to the individual subject following the breakdown of holistic structures, works well to illustrate various tendencies discussed in this chapter. The four poles in this space, modernism, traditionalism, primitivism and post-modernism, have all been activated in varying degrees as ways of orientation in the reality of the literary text. According to Friedman, in periods of rising hegemonic status in the global system (certainly the case with China in recent years) the pole of modernism tends to be the dominating one. Modernism is characterized by a sense of progress and the experience that meaning is to be found within the I itself, with previously fixed cultural identities seen as more or less arbitrary. As shown above, while protagonists or main characters in a prominent part of Chinese literature in the reform period certainly perceive given identities as constructed or unstable, meaning (whether positive or negative) often has to be sought by way of connecting to the poles of traditionalism or primitivism. To Friedman this is what happens when the forward-looking cult of modernity, as experienced by the individual consciousness, is felt to be in crisis. The roots literature of the 1980s is an obvious case, tending towards the traditionalist side, but this could also be said of Yu Hua's novels from the 1990s, with their celebration of family values. The immense popularity of and controversy about the novel *Wolf Totem* from its publication in 2004 and on testifies to the appeal of primitivism as cultural critique. Primitivism is here associated with something closer to nature, more authentic and true, a forceful – or desperate – gesture reaching for a human dignity rooted in a pre-modern community, now that such dignity is seen as lost in the maelstrom of a modernity, dominated by the principle of alterity.

The principle of alterity, the individual's recognition of the possibility of taking on different roles or identities, is explicitly focused on in a vast number of post-Mao Chinese texts, notably in stories by for example Liu Suola, Wang Shuo, Chen Ran and many of the youngest generation. Implicitly it is at work as early as Bei Dao's novel *Waves* from the late 1970s.

To Friedman, 'modernity is fundamentally the emergence of alterity as a permanent situation, where the self is never defined, where there are always other possibilities of identity and existence' (Friedman 1994: 241). This corresponds to what Steven Lukes, quoted at the beginning of this chapter, calls the 'role distance' which characterizes the modern (Western) individual: 'confronting all possible roles, he may in principle adopt, perform or abandon any at will'. But while this notion, or at least the awareness of its existence, runs through the various literary currents discussed here, Lukes's extended portrait of the modern individual as also a 'sovereign chooser' and an 'autonomous, self-directing, independent agent who relates to others as no less autonomous agents' is hardly the most conspicuous of the characters that have appeared in recent Chinese literature. On the other hand, the contrasting image of the traditional person to whom 'conceptions of the good are not seen as subject to individual choice' and 'who I am is answered both for me and for others by the history I inherit and the social positions I occupy' is even more difficult to find. Perhaps we should simply conclude that, rather than trying to define *the individual* in the Chinese literature of the last thirty-five years, all we can do is to approach and discuss a selected number of *individuals* as they grope their way in the literary reality of a complex and rapidly changing society.

Notes

1　There are of course numerous discussions of the relationship between the concept of modernity and the individual. Here I would like to refer to Friedman 1994, see esp. p. 215 ff. For discussions about the concept of the individual in China in the early 20th century, see the chapter by Svarverud in this volume.

2　Friedman 1998: 235. I thank Margrethe Ellegaard Hansen for calling my attention to Friedman.

3　Here not to be confused with modernism as a literary ism.

4　Focus on the individual was particularly strong during later phases of the May Fourth Movement and particularly repressed during the Cultural Revolution.

5　See my discussion of the novel *Wolf Totem* later in this chapter.

6　See Kong 2005.

7　A look at the changes in the literary media in the period would offer a further perspective on the role of literature and the individual. In short: in the 1980s most literature was still published in a limited number of magazines and periodicals, hence mostly short stories and novellas, with a common readership. By the 1990s more long novels appear, sold as individual books to be bought individually, thus creating a more private reading space, and by the late 1990s the internet is emerging as on the one hand the most private of media with everyone surfing individually with almost infinite choice, on the other hand the most public and potentially common of all, combining intimacy and publicity and offering virtual communities of various sorts.

8   'Lun wenxue de zhutixing', *Wenxue pinglun*, vol. 6, 1985, and vol. 1, 1986, reprinted in Liu 1988: 72–127.

9   See for example J. Wang 1996 and Wedell-Wedellsborg 1994.

10 Zhao 1981. English translation – see Zhao 1985. For a detailed analysis of this novel see Wedell-Wedellsborg 1994.

11 *Nineteen Eighty-six* was originally published in 1986 and *One Kind of Reality* in 1987.

12 See J. Wang 1996 for a good discussion on the group mentality in these novels.

13 See McDougall 2005 for a discussion on the changing connotations of words for privacy.

14 Yu Hua's recent long novel *Brothers* (Yu 2005–2006) takes the family theme into the present, but shows it as more fragile and influenced by change.

15 It is no coincidence that these texts are referred to as *xiezuo* (writing), rather than *wenxue* (literature), which denotes something more serious.

16 'Individualization is understood as a historical process that increasingly questions and tends to break up people's traditional rhythm of life – what sociologists call the normal biography. As a result more people than ever before are being forced to piece together their own biographies and fit in the components they need as best they can. They find themselves bereft of unquestionable assumptions, beliefs or values and are nevertheless faced with the tangle of institutional controls and constraints which make up the fibre of modern life (welfare state, labour market, educational system, etc.). To put it bluntly, the normal life history is giving way to the do-it-yourself life history' (Beck and Beck-Gernsheim 2003: 88).

17 Chen 1996: 247–277. See also Han 2005.

18 Wei Hui's famous *Shanghai Baby* (1999) is an optimistic – and perhaps somewhat ironic – picture of this. Julia Lovell has translated some stories by Zhu Wen into English – Zhu 2007. See also Friedman 1994: 191.

19 Richard Jenkins in his discussion about the individual's construction of social identities refers to Anthony Cohen's concept of symbolic community. The community generates a sense of belonging through symbols and shared rituals which allow people to imagine a degree of conformity without total conformity in behaviour and values. Cohen also stresses the importance of boundaries, the sense of difference that creates arenas of distinctiveness. This could also apply here to Chen Zhen's reactions towards the Han authorities. See Jenkins 1996: 104 ff.

20 A separate book dealing with the story of the wolf cub came out one year later – Jiang 2005.

21 Long 2004. It is interesting that in most *Langdao* books, the difference between Mongol and Han is downplayed, indeed the message seems to be the nationalist one that China can be 'the wolf of the world'.

22 See for example Wang Xiaoming 1996.

Bibliography

Ah Cheng (阿城) (1984) 棋王 *Qiwang* [King of chess]. Beijing: Zuojia chubanshe.

Ba Jin (巴金) (1979) 随想录 *Suixiang lu* [Random thoughts]. Hongkong: Sanlian shudian.

Beck, Ulrich and Elisabeth Beck-Gernsheim (2003) *Individualization: Institutionalized Individualism and its Social and Political Consequences.* London: Sage.

Cai, Rong (2004) *The Subject in Crisis in Contemporary Chinese Literature.* Honolulu: University of Hawaii Press.

Can Xue (残雪) (2004) '民工团' Mingongtuan [The work team]. *Dangdai zuojia pinglun*, vol. 2, pp. 44–65.

Chen Ran (陈染) (1996) 私人生活 *Siren shenghuo* [A private life]. Beijing: Zuojia chubanshe.

Feuerwerker, Yi-tsi Mei (1998) *Ideology, Power, Text. Self-Representation and the Peasant 'Other' in Modern Chinese Literature.* Stanford: Stanford University Press.

Friedman, Jonathan (1994) *Cultural Identity and Global Process.* London: Sage.

—— (1998) 'Transnationalization, socio-political disorder, and ethnification as expressions of declining global hegemony'. *International Science Review*, vol. 19, no. 3, pp. 233–250.

Han Shaogong (韩少功) (1985) '归去来' Guiqulai [Going home]. *Shanghai Wenxue*, vol. 6, pp. 30–47.

Han Yanbin (韩彦斌) (2005) '论 20 世纪 90 年代个人化小说的创作倾向' Lun 20 shiji 90 niandai gerenhua xiaoshuo de chuangzuo qingxiang [On the tendency towards creating individualized fiction in the 1990s]. *Nei Menggu daxue xuebao*, vol. 37, no.1, pp. 31–35.

Hong, Jiang (2003) 'The personalization of literature: Chinese women's writing in the 1990s'. *The China Review*, vol. 3, no.1, pp. 5–27.

Hou Rui and Hou Ying (侯睿，侯颖) (2006) '狼图腾狂飙之后的文化反思' Langtuteng kuangbiao zhihou de wenhua fansi [Cultural reflections after the storm created by Wolf Totem]. *Shehui kexue zhanxian*, vol. 3, pp. 306–307.

Jenkins, Richard (1996) *Social Identity.* London: Routledge.

Jiang Rong (姜戎) (2004) 狼图腾 *Langtuteng* [Wolf Totem]. Wuhan: Changjiang wenyi chubanshe.

—— (2005) 小狼小狼 *Xiao lang xiao lang* [Wolf cub, Wolf cub]. Wuhan: Changjiang wenyi chubanshe.

Kong, Shuyu (2005) *Consuming Literature. Bestsellers and the Commercialization of Literary Production in Contemporary China.* Stanford: Stanford University Press.

Laughlin, Charles (ed.) (2005). *Contested Modernities in Chinese Literature.* New York: Palgrave Macmillan.

Lei Da (雷达) (2005) '狼性与羊性。姜戎"狼图腾"的再评价与文化分析' Langxing yu yangxing. Jiang Rong Langtuteng de zai pingjia yu wenhua fenxi [Wolfishness and sheepishness. A reevaluation and cultural reflections on Jiang Rong's Wolf Totem]. *Guangming Ribao*, vol. 6, no. 12, p. 4.

Li Hongxia (李红霞) (2005) '狼性与神性的对话。残雪的文学世界' Langxing yu shenxing de duihua. Can Xue de wenxue shijie [A dialogue between wolf nature and divine nature. Can Xue's literary world]. *Jinan Xuebao*, 2, pp. 75–80.

Li Lianjun (李建军) (2005) '是珍珠还是豌豆' Shi zhenzhu haishi wandou [Pearl or pea?]. *Wenyi zhengming*, vol. 2, pp. 60–64.

Lin Chuan (林舟) (2004) '权利与欲望。精神强力的形势 – 对民工团的一种解读' Quanli yu yuwang. Jingshen qiangli de xingshi – dui 'Mingongtuan' de yizhong jiedu [Power and desire. The state of spiritual force – an interpretation of the work team]. *Dangdai zuojia pinglun*,vol. 2, pp. 66–70.

Liu, Kang (2004) *Globalization and Cultural Trends in China.* Honolulu: University of Hawaii Press.

Liu Suola (刘索拉) (1986) '寻找歌王' Xunzhao gewang [In search of the king of singers]. In 你别无选择 *Ni bie wu xuanze* [You have no other choice]. Beijing: Zuojia chubanshe, pp. 130–186.

Liu Zaifu (刘再复) (1988) 刘再复集 *Liu Zaifu ji* [Collection of Liu Zaifu's writings]. Harbin: Heilongjiang jiaoyu chubanshe.

Long Zimin (龙子民) (2004) 狼道 *Langdao* [The way of the Wolf]. Dilei chubanshe.

Lukes, Steven (1985) 'Conclusion'. In Michael Carrithers, Steven Collins and Steven Lukes (eds), *The Category of the Person.* Cambridge: Cambridge University Press, pp. 283–300.

McDougall, Bonnie S. (2005) 'Discourse on privacy by women writers in late twentieth-century China'. *China Information*, vol. XIX, no.1, pp. 97–119.

Visser, Robin (2005) 'Urban ethics: modernity and the morality of everyday life'. In Charles A. Laughlin (ed.), *Contested Modernities in Chinese Literature.* New York: Palgrave Macmillan, pp. 193–216.

Wang, Jing (1996) *High Culture Fever*. Berkeley: University of California Press.

Wang, Lingzhen (2005) 'Reproducing the Self: consumption, imaginary, and identity in women's autobiographival practise in the 1990s'. In Charles A. Laughlin (ed.), *Contested Modernities in Chinese Literature.* New York: Palgrave Macmillan, pp. 173–192.

Wang Shuo (王朔) (1987) '顽主' Wanzhu [Masters of mischief]. *Shouhuo*, vol. 6, pp. 24–52.

—— (1989, reprint of 1988 edition) 玩得就是心跳 *Wande jiu shi xintiao* [Playing for thrills]. Beijing: Zuojia chubanshe.

Wang Xiaoming (王晓明) (1996) 人文精神寻思录 *Renwen jingshen xunsi lu* [Reflections on humanist spirit]. Shanghai: Wenhui chubanshe.

Wedell-Wedellsborg, Anne (1994) 'The changing concept of Self as reflected in Chinese literature of the 1980s'. In *Mémoires de l'institut des haute etudes chinoises*, vol. XXXVI, pp. 227–247, Paris: Collége de France.

—— (2009) 'Literary solitude in traditional and globalized China'. In T. Lodén, H. Löthman and L. Rydholm (eds), *Chinese Culture and Globalization: History and Challenges for the 21st Century*. Proceedings from the Nordic Association for Chinese Studies Conference in Stockholm, 2007. Stockholm and Uppsala University.

Wei Hui (卫慧) (1999) 上海宝贝 *Shanghai baobei* [Shanghai baby]. Shenyang: Chunfeng wenyi chubanshe.

Xie Nandou (谢南斗) (2005) '个人化写作与艺术发生学' Gerenhua xiezuo yu yishu fashengxue [Individualized writing and the study of artistic formation]. *Zhongguo wenxue yanjiu*, vol. 1, pp. 1, pp. 3–6.

Yan Jingming (阎晶明) (2005) '文学成功便捷之门' Wenxue chenggong bianjie zhi men [Gateway to literary success]. *Xiaoshuo Pinglun*, vol. 2, pp. 4–10.

Yu Hua (余华) (1989a) 一九八六年 *Yi jiu ba liu nian* [Nineteen eighty-six]. Reprinted in Yu Hua (余华) 十八岁出门远行 *Shiba sui chu men yuanxing* [Leaving home at eighteen]. Beijing: Zuojia chubanshe.

—— (1989b)现实一种 *Xianshi yizhong* [One kind of reality]. Reprinted in Yu Hua (余华) 十八岁出门远行 *Shiba sui chu men yuanxing* [Leaving home at eighteen]. Beijing: Zuojia chubanshe.

—— (1991) 在细雨中呼喊 *Zai xiyu zhong huhan* [Cries in the drizzle]. Nanjing: Jiangsu wenyi chubanshe.

—— (1992) 活着 *Huozhe* [To live]. *Shouhuo*, no. 6, pp. 5–181.

—— (1996) 许三观卖血记 *Xu sanguan mai xue ji* [Chronicle of a bloodseller]. Shanghai: Shanghai wenyi chubanshe.

—— (2005–2006) 兄弟 *I–II Xiongdi I–II* [Brothers I–II]. Shanghai: Shanghai wenyi chubanshe.

Zhao Zhenkai (赵振开) (Bei Dao 北岛) (1981) '波动' Bodong [Waves]. *Changjiang wenxue congkan*, vol. 1, pp. 21–78.

—— (1985) *Waves*. Hong Kong: Hong Kong University Press.

Zhao Zhunsheng (赵准胜) (2005) ' "狼图腾": 从沉默到宣泄以及"别一种另类" ' Langtuteng: Cong chenmo dao xuanshi yiji ling yizhong linglei [Wolf Totem – from silence to drainage and yet another kind of alternative writing)]. *Dongbei shida xuebao*, vol. 16, pp. 57–68.

Zhu Wen (2007) *I Love Dollars and Other Stories from China*. Translated by Julia Lovell. New York: Columbia University Press.

6 Individual Self-Discipline and Collective Freedom in the Minds of Chinese Intellectuals

Rune Svarverud

In their book *Individualization*, Ulrich Beck and Elisabeth Beck-Gernsheim propose a theory of modernity where the processes of individualization are seen as having developed during the last half of the twentieth century from individualization for and by a few, presumably an intellectual elite, to democratic processes where the basic conditions of society enforce and favour individualization (Beck and Beck-Gernsheim 2003: 8). Beck and Beck-Gernsheim refer to this later stage of modernity as 'second modernity', characterized by a society in which institutionalized individualism becomes the social structure itself. For the first time in history, 'the individual is becoming the basic unit of social reproduction'. Individualization is no longer a mere subjective reality in the objective orientation of the individual towards society, class and collectives but has in fact become the objective social structure. Individualization means the disembedding without re-embedding of the individual. The stereotyped image of a highly individualized society is one in which individuals are only concerned with themselves and assert their freedom by neglecting the social structure of family and other collective and social entities. In their book, Beck and Beck-Gernsheim show, however, that in spite of a 'me-first' trend in second modernity society, there 'are also signs that point toward an ethic of "altruistic individualism". Anyone who wants to live a life of their own must also be socially sensitive to a very high degree' (Beck and Beck-Gernsheim 2003: xxii). Ulrich Beck also briefly discusses the development in China during these last 50 years, referring to the processes of individualization that can be observed in the shift from the collectives and the iron rice-bowl of the 1950s and 1960s to the highly individualized contemporary Chinese society.

Yunxiang Yan, in his Introduction, and a number of the other chapters in this book address the processes of individualization and collective belonging and identity in contemporary Chinese society. They ask whether Chinese society is indeed following a path parallel to the development of a kind of second modernity that Beck and Beck-Gernsheim find unfolding in Europe and the West.[1] Beck and Beck-Gernsheim also raise this issue in their Foreword to this book. In this chapter, I point out some of the main tendencies in the development of ideas about the individual and the collective in what we may identify as China's first modernity, a period that began in late imperial China with strong intellectual influxes from the West in the late nineteenth and early twentieth centuries. I do this assuming that questions about the relationship between the individual and society in China today are intrinsically linked to ideas of individual rights and responsibilities, altruism, human equality, autonomy and self-discipline as they were understood and expressed in China's first intellectual modernity. In Europe the philosophy of Enlightenment postulated that the autonomous and free individual acknowledged nothing but pure reason and its laws. But, the society of Enlightenment Europe was not one characterized by the autonomy and freedom of every individual. The European Enlightenment is characterized by a process of individualization for and by a social and intellectual elite alone.

I address the notion of an autonomous individual and his/her relationship to society as it was conceived by the intellectual elite in China during her first intellectual modernity from the early years of the twentieth century. I discuss the Chinese discourse on the role and position of the individual in relation to collectives in society by focusing on notions of the freedom, autonomy, morality and self-discipline of the individual. I show that a type of 'altruistic individualism', referred to by Beck as a characteristic of Western second modernity, is in some respects also characteristic of the type of individualism we find being formulated in China in the early part of the twentieth century, although in a fashion somewhat different from the altruism referred to by Beck and Beck-Gernsheim. This envisioned Chinese type of individual 'altruism' is understood as a form of social and collective responsibility and strongly attached to age-old ideas about a strong state in China, ideas that historically may be traced back to the Warring States period and the Qin and Han Dynasties. The notion that individual prosperity and happiness rest entirely on the prosperity and harmony of the state has been exceedingly strong throughout the history of the Chinese state and its political philosophy, the latter for simplicity often referred to as Confucianism. This philosophical tradition has defined individuals in terms of inescapable social categories that define their duties towards collect-ives and society at large. It may be argued that traditionally in China we find no explicit ideas about the basic equality of all humans, about human dignity, and about the infallible autonomy of the individual, even though it has been argued that some of the basic ideas of Confucianism involve some similar ideas of the individual. When the intellectuals of the early Chinese modernity addressed questions of individual autonomy and freedom, their intellectual framework was profoundly coloured by this state-focused intel-lectual tradition.

It is generally recognized that the individual gained a prominent position in the literature and political discourse of China after the May Fourth and during the New Culture Movements, thus into the 1920s. In this discourse we are familiar with arguments in favour of the absolute and infallible value of individual autonomy and freedom.[2] The individualism of the May Fourth Movement was, however, also balanced by national interests and ideas of an altruistic individual contributing to the good of society at large. Chow Tse-tsung concludes in his book on the intellectual revolution of the May Fourth Movement that:

> The trend towards the emancipation of the individual, however, did not mean the same as the exaltation of individualism as in the West, nor was liberalism promoted exactly in the Western sense. To many young Chinese reformers, emancipation of the individual was as much for the sake of saving the nation as upholding individual rights. The value of individual and independent judgement was indeed appreciated more in the May Fourth period than ever before, yet the individual's duty to soci-ety and the nation was also emphasized.   (Chow 1960: 360)

I show that the dependency between the individual and the collective in China became the focus of intellectual discourse in the early twentieth century through the negotiation of a national Chinese identity and the merging importance of the notion and role of citizenship in China.[3] A focus on the nation as a new collective entity in China caused intellectuals to seek to disembed the individual from previous social categories and attitudes attached to the Confucian tradition, such as the ethics of family relations, and envision a project where the Chinese individual as a citizen was to be re-embedded in an imagined national collective, in line with strong historical currents for a focus on the state in China. In a process of intellectual liberalization, the individual was simultaneously strongly attached to the aspirations of the nation through the idea of individual self-discipline. The attachment of the individual to the nation through collective demands of self-discipline not only characterizes the early phase of modernity and individualization in China but is in fact also a distinct aspect of the socio-political discourse of the 1910s and 1920s, when the ultimate and indisputable value of the individual was at its strongest in pre-communist China. I thus reveal the strong intellectual currents of the interpretation of the individual running from the early years of the twentieth century, into the May Fourth Movement, with obvious relevance for the interpretation of the relationship between individual and collective in the socialist era from the 1920s. I do this by focusing on ideas of individual autonomy and self-discipline, terms that prove to be particularly fruitful in our attempt to understand the intellectual interpretation of the relationship between individual and collective in modern China. These ideas of the relationship between the individual, society and the state have their roots in the early eras of the Chinese empire. Trends in the changing conception of the relationship between the individual and the state in China in the minds of modern Chinese intellectuals have an interesting parallel in the changing practices prescribed by the legal system in China, as discussed by Mühlhahn in his chapter in this book.

From the early 1920s, liberal ideas of the freedom and autonomy of the individual were replaced by a leftist discourse that argued against currents of individualism. Chen Duxiu (陳獨秀) and others attacked individualism as irresponsible, nihilistic and bourgeois, an outdated idea that should be replaced by socially responsible ideals of the individual as promoted by socialism.[4] Hence, my account of ideas of the autonomy and self-discipline of the individual ends with the strong currents of leftist ideology in China. The questions raised by the intellectuals in China in the first decades of the twentieth century regarding individual agency and the relationship between the individual and collectives, such as the family and the nation, are however still current issues in contemporary China, as is clear from a number of the chapters in this book.

Chinese Individualism, Liberalism and the Freedom of the Individual

If we assume that China's first modernity brought new perspectives on the individual and his relationship to collectives, we must postulate that the individual had a fundamentally different role and position in pre-modern China. Were ideas of the individual and his autonomy current in China in any form before the early twentieth century? It has been argued that the Chinese language, as a conceptual structure, as opposed to the language(s) of the West, lacks the means with which to express anything but individual parts being precisely that, parts of a whole rather than a one–many structure (Hansen 1985). This has been held as an argument against the autonomy of the individual in traditional China. In a similar fashion it has been argued that Confucian ethics only describe and prescribe the individual in his social context and never as an autonomous being. Contrary to these views we find arguments in favour of individual moral autonomy as a central aspect of the Confucian interpretation of man in China (Chan 2002). Different approaches and positions yield different outcomes with regard to interpretations of man and the autonomy of the individual in traditional China, as becomes clear from the various contributions to the volume *Confucianism and Human Rights* edited by Wm. Theodore de Bary and Tu Weiming (De Bary and Tu 1998). Nevertheless, the intellectual currents that reinterpreted the individual in the Chinese society of the early twentieth century were innovative and fresh in their environment. As Ambrose King has argued, the autonomous individual 'is unequivocally affirmed by Confucians. To be a gentleman (*chün-tzu*) one must be able to assert oneself against all kinds of pressure, both from within and without.' Indeed, he argues that 'Confucians never see the individual man as an isolated entity; man is defined as a social being.' The idea of the individual and the self as autonomous entities is to be found at the very centre of traditional Chinese social relations, and the relations are not to be interpreted as simple relations between individual and group. Thus, King argues that 'this singular fact defies the simplistic application of the Western terms "individualism" and "holism" (or "collectivism") to the Chinese phenomenon' (King 1985: 57). It is only with the introduction of liberalism and individualism from the West that we may begin to apply these terms, in their particular Chinese forms, to the Chinese intellectual currents of the late nineteenth and early twentieth centuries.

Late Qing China was a battleground of new terms and new ideas on society, on the nature of man, on the role of the Chinese citizen, on relations between China's ethnic groups and on China's position in international relations. In most areas of the Chinese discourse, ideas and terms translated and imported from abroad played some role. This is particularly true for the period after the Sino–Japanese War and the treaty of Shimonoseki in 1895, when the current discourses on man and society in Japan also had a great impact upon the invention of new meanings in China. Both in the period before the Japanese influence and during his years in exile in Japan from 1898, Liang Qichao (梁啟超) played an important role as mediator in the introduction of ideas from abroad, not least in the invention of new meanings of the individual and his role as citizen in China under the influence of these foreign ideas. Liang Qichao owes much of his thinking on the individual and society during his early years in Japan to British liberalism, social contract thinking, German statism and Darwinian evolutionary theory through Japanese translations. In a distinctive mix of Western philosophy, Western political theory and Chinese new text Confucian ethics Liang constructed a particular programme for the individual and his relationship to collectives in the late Qing Chinese context, framed within a programme for the 'renewal of the role of the citizen' (*xinmin* 新民). The survival of China as a nation in the fierce Darwinian battle for existence is a recurring theme, and the interpretation of the individual in Liang's thinking is very much influenced by this perspective. Jerome Ch'en concludes that Liang's aim 'was not so much individual freedom and individual happiness, as Huxley and Spencer insisted, but the power and wealth which could bring freedom and independence to the Chinese nation' (Ch'en 1979: 181). Individualism was not introduced wholesale to China through Liang Qichao,[5] but the central ideas of individualism were nevertheless brought to China through his writings. Liang Qichao is pivotal in the first modernity interpretation of the individual in China because of his pervasive influence both in China and in the rest of East

Asia. The budding of a Chinese first modernity may, however, be discerned already before Liang's Japanese period.

The translations by Yan Fu (嚴復) of important works on evolution theory, liberalism, economy and sociology were the most important sources of influence on China from the West in the late nineteenth century and the early years of the twentieth century. Yan translated Thomas Huxley's *Essays on Evolution and Ethics*, Adam Smith's *Wealth of Nations*, John Stuart Mill's *On Liberty*, Herbert Spencer's *Study of Sociology* and Mill's *System of Logic*, works that subsequently served as sources of inspiration for liberal intellectuals and scholars such as Liang Qichao. These works also inspired Yan himself, who also wrote on progress, evolution, reform and education. Yan was primarily concerned with the wealth, power and future of the Chinese nation, and he saw liberty as a means to secure China's survival as a nation. To Yan, wealth and power are in the best interest of the people. The best interest of the people is secured through a suitable policy and based upon the incontestable freedom of that people. 'And the precondition for acquiring freedom is the self-government of each individual, lest freedom should lead to chaos' (Yan Fu translated in Ch'en 1979: 180). He prescribed three strategies for strengthening the Chinese people: enhancement of physical strength, development of the intellect and renewal of the morality of the people (Ch'en 1979: 179–182).[6] Yan Fu applied notions of a free and self-governed individual. The freedom of the individual and of the people is the means with which to secure the strength of the Chinese nation. Freedom is a precondition for evolution, but self-government, a sort of self-restraint of the individual, is a restriction on the freedom that otherwise would lead the nation into chaos. Liang Qichao further developed these perspectives in his interpretations of the relationship between the individual and the nation.

Liang Qichao's deliberations on the freedom of the individual may be divided into three stages: one early stage (around 1899) when he is directly influenced by Western liberal ideas and less concerned with national Chinese questions, one middle stage (1902–1903) when his concern for China's national survival in a Darwinian theoretical framework overshadows his earlier conviction about the infallible free nature of man, and one later stage (1903–) when he lost confidence in the Chinese individual in terms of forming a concerned and vigorous national body of citizens, and turns to Bluntschli and German statism for political inspiration. The scattered writings collected under the heading *Notes on freedom* (*Ziyoushu* 自由書) (Liang 1996e), for the most part published in 1899, may serve as a source for the first stage. Liang's exposition on the renewal of the Chinese citizen published in the *Xinminshuo* (新民說) (Liang 1998b) is the main source for our understanding of Liang's interpretation of the freedom of the individual in the second stage. The last three chapters of the *Xinminshuo*, written upon his return from the United States in 1903, published first in 1906, represent the third stage in his development of a strengthening strategy for China, when he had concluded that China was far from ready for democracy (Chang 1971: 149–219, 238–271; Huang 1972: 80–81, 182; Zarrow 1998: 222). We are here primarily interested in the first two stages as a platform for debate on the liberal individual in China.

From the articles of the *Ziyoushu* it is clear that Liang at this time was mainly concerned with the notion of freedom as the means with which to safeguard one's room for action in the Darwinian struggle for survival. In the sub-chapter written in 1899 entitled 'The harm of abandoning freedom' ('Fangqi ziyou zhi zui' 放棄自由之罪) (Liang 1996a), Liang claims that the greatest of all harms is to abandon one's own freedom and hence open up for infringement on one's own freedom, and by doing so create a potential threat to one's option for survival.

> If there were no one under heaven who abandoned his freedom then there would be no one to infringe on that freedom. What is infringed upon is nothing but that very freedom the other person has abandoned.
>
> (Liang 1996a: 23)

Man will opt for strength and existence and in order to reach such a goal he will necessarily attempt to extend his right of freedom. Such extension of one's own freedom will often involve infringement on the freedom of others, from the side of the strongest onto the freedom of the weakest. The one who commits the greatest harm is in fact he who leans back and is satisfied with being in an inferior position, letting others infringe on his own freedom. 'Therefore we say that if there were no one who would abandon his freedom, then there would necessarily not be anyone to infringe on the freedom of others' (Liang 1996a: 24). The notion of freedom applied by Liang in 1899 is not particularly attached to individuals. Rather, freedom in this essay is the freedom of action that every social entity, be it an individual or a collective, possesses in order to maintain its own option for survival. Without a naturally-endowed right to freedom for individual struggle, the order of natural selection would make no sense. Man is free and must make use of that freedom in order to survive.

Three years later, in a chapter entitled 'On Liberty' ('Lun ziyou' 論自由) in the *Xinminshuo* (Liang 1998a), Liang's interpretation of freedom has become more sophisticated and has shifted its focus. Freedom of the individual is at the core of his programme for the new citizen. That freedom is, however, no longer described as the unfettered freedom to act in order to safeguard one's own survival. It is described as a limited freedom of the individual who has the survival and the benefit of the collective group as its aim rather than that of the singular individual or social entity.

> Liang made clear why he asked for assertive and intellectually free 'citizens' – such persons were necessary for China's progress and for her national survival. 'Liberty', in other words, was desirable not only in and of itself, but because it would contribute to national power and survival. Such a conception of 'liberty' suggests at once that a wide gulf separated Liang from his liberal mentors. (Huang 1972: 70)

In these deliberations on the fate of the Chinese nation and the nature of the individual there appears to be an inherent contradiction. Liang is on the one side primarily concerned with the evolution and strength of the collective of which the individual is a member, and on the other side insists on the liberty and independence of the individual. He appears to be liberating the individual from social responsibilities when what he in fact seems to need in order to strengthen the Chinese nation is a band of dedicated, energetic citizens that have the common welfare of society in mind. Philip C. Huang dichotomizes Liang's liberty with the interest of the nation; given

> (. . .) Liang's preoccupation with the fate of the Chinese nation, he no doubt would not have espoused 'liberty' so fervently if he had thought that 'liberty' would conflict with his nationalistic aims. The question remains: why did Liang assume that representative institutions and liberty of thought and discussion were relevant to his nationalistic concerns? (Huang 1972: 76)

The sources of this thinking are easily identifiable. The first and most power-ful source of intellectual inspiration from the West on social thinking in both Japan and China in the early twentieth century is a particular form of social Darwinism interpreted and developed mainly by Katô Hiroyuki and Liang Qichao. Central to Liang's Darwinian theory both in 1899 and in 1902 is that competition and liberty are the main forces that may safe-guard one's survival in a world where natural selection is working day and night on all levels of nature and society. Only by actively working against the potentially destructive outcome of competition may one's future be se-cured. Darwinism in Liang's interpretation was not deterministic. A group's fate could in fact be influenced through an active strategy. One could and should actively struggle for existence and hence make oneself more fit for survival. A dynamic society consisting of energetic individuals fostered through liberty would secure the future of that group, in ways similar to how Katô and Liang saw that British and American liberalism had fostered the international positions of Britain and America. These ideas were also consistent with Liang's interpretation of John Stuart Mill (Huang 1972: 76–77). The core of Liang's program in 1902 was the fostering of a new Chinese citizen, and the liberty of man was central in this programme.[7] Liang was apparently not concerned about the weakness of his argumentation. 'What if it could be shown to Liang that representative government and the liberty of thought and discussion would not in fact contribute to national power?' (Huang 1972: 77)

In his 1902 designation of freedom Liang applied Kang Youwei's evo-lutionary stage theory to make a distinction between the significance of different *kinds* of freedom at different stages in evolution. According to Liang's scheme, there are differences between the freedom of the individual and the freedom of the group. Whereas the freedom of each individual played the most important role in the early (barbarian) stages of social evolution, the group is more important at this advanced stage, according to Liang. The fundamental definition of freedom is that every man is free and the limitation to that freedom is that one may not infringe on the freedom of others. But if one may not infringe on the freedom of others, is that not a token of non-freedom, Liang asks himself. In a barbarian age the freedom of the individual will be the victorious force and the freedom of the group will fail. In a civilized age, however, the freedom of the group will be strong and the freedom of the individual will be weakened. There must be a balance between these two. Liang argues that the nation and its people will suffer under excessive individual freedom. Barbarian freedom is a parasite on civilization. Civilized freedom is freedom under the law. In the eternal (Darwinian) struggle every group must gather all its vitality. When the freedom of the group is jeopardized it will not be able to maintain independence, and will hence be made the slave of another group. How free, then, is this group in the end?, is Liang's rhetorical question. That is why true freedom is to have an ability of submission to the law. Laws are established in order to protect man's freedom but also to restrain it (Liang 1998b: 102–103). Hence, Liang defines freedom as a basic quality of every individual. That freedom may only be protected through the group at a civilized stage in evolution. When the group is free, then every individual belonging to that group is also free. The individual is only free when he subjects himself to the laws and restrictions laid upon him by the group. Licentious freedom of the individual belongs to a barbarian age and will not be the quality that ushers the collective ahead in evolution. That does not, however, encroach upon the fundamental freedom of the individual:

> Then, if this is the meaning of freedom, does that mean that freedom may not be practised by the individual? No, what kind of talk is that? Collective freedom is the accumulation of individual freedom. The individual may not leave the collective and exist on his own, and if the collective is not able to protect its freedom then there will be other collectives coming from the outside to infringe on, suppress and seize this collective. And then, what about the freedom of the individual?
>
> (Liang 1998b: 104)

According to Liang, man has two selves. One is the physical body that contrasts with the collective body of the crowd. The other is the self that opposes this physical body, this is the mental self. The individual may be free from slavery at two different levels. At a political level the individual is free when he submits to the laws of the collective and hence protects his physical freedom as an individual. At a mental level the individual can only be free when he frees himself from the slavery of his own desires, of ancient customs and traditions and of the environment (Liang 1998b: 104–108; Huang 1972: 65–70). The individual must learn to master himself at two different levels, both a mental and a social level. To master oneself means 'to have self-discipline' – 'to be autonomous' (*zizhi* 自治). This quality of the individual is the most important component in Liang's program for checking and balancing the freedom of the individual.

Liang on Kant, Rousseau and the Relationship between Individual and Collective

The translations by Yan Fu of central works by British liberal thinkers were important sources on individualism and liberalism. Liang Qichao was influenced by (and indeed modelled many of his own ideas on liberty, the new citizen, public interest and representative government on) Bentham, Mill, Spencer and others (Huang 1972: 68–83). For Liang Qichao, however, Kant and Rousseau had a much greater impact on his way of conceiving the individual and his relationship to collectives, and on the relationship between the free individual and the restriction of that freedom when man lives in a society in the early years of the twentieth century. An essay on the social contract theories of Rousseau precedes Liang's major prescriptions for the new citizen and the Chinese national character in 1902–03. The essay entitled 'The Teachings of Rousseau' ('Lusuo xueshuo' 盧梭學說) published in 1901 introduces the social contract theories of Kant and Rousseau, fused with elements of Liang's interpretation of evolutionism. In this essay, Liang again makes use of Kang's evolutionary theory, claiming that in a primitive age mankind lives together in societies based on the strength and power of certain individuals. But time passes and man unconsciously realizes the existence of the freedom of each individual and hence protects it. Contracts at all levels of society are based on this innate freedom of the parties involved. Society at large and the nation are all composed of these contracts at various levels. Families unite into greater collectives such as villages through similar social contracts, and these villages unite into collectives as states on the same principles. These social contracts are non-juridical, non-verbal contracts entered into by common consent (Liang 1996d).

Liang's interpretation of Kant's theories of the self and the immanent quality of the freedom or autonomy of the individual is further examined in an essay published two years later. Here Liang addresses the philosophy of Immanuel Kant in an essay entitled 'The Teachings of Kant, the Most Important Philosopher in Recent Times' ('Jinshi diyi dazhe Kangde zhi xueshuo' 近世第一大哲康德之學說), mainly dedicated to Kant's critique of pure reason (Liang 1996b). The individual in Kantian philosophy is explained as consisting of two selves, one 'phenomenal' (*xianxiang* 現象) and one 'noumenal' (*benzhi* 本質) where Liang has identified Kant's solution to the problem of the apparent antagonism between man's freedom and the determinism of nature. Human morality belongs to the free self. There is nothing in our morality that is restricted or fettered by others, it has no past and no future and is always present. The 'true self' (*zhenwo* 真我) is free and may be observed to be of a different nature from our limited and fettered physical self. We are freely able to choose between being good or being evil, and when the decision is made, our free self orders the physical self to make the necessary moves to accomplish the will of the true self. This is how these two selves cooperate and integrate the constrained and the free dimensions of our selves (Liang 1996b: 60). This qualified freedom of human morality is what Kant refers to as autonomy, the quality that makes man independent of the causality and determinism of nature.

The notion of autonomy is one of the central terms in the philosophies of Kant and Rousseau. The idea is originally related to the religious sphere where it refers to the individual's responsibility towards God alone and not towards other humans. The great challenge to Kant was to reconcile the Newtonian natural-scientific mode of explaining cause-and-effect relations with moral and religious ways of understanding human freedom from determination. He solved this apparent contradiction by ascribing all causal relations of the phenomenological world to a realm separate from the world of 'noumena', or 'things in themselves', a realm inaccessible to science where moral freedom could exist in itself. In this way Kant was able to leave human actions potentially free from scientific determinism. In order for moral reason to be able to direct human action by determining the will there must be a principle of purposiveness in nature, Kant concluded. Hence, beneath the phenomena of nature there is a principle of purposiveness effectively determining human actions in Kant's philosophy. 'Only if the world can be assumed to be organized toward such an intelligible end, instituted by a rational being, can we expect reason and reflection to have power over our material urges, needs, and desires' (Seigel 2005: 296). Humans realize their freedom from determination, their autonomy, by following self-made laws. These laws, which are human morality, are directed by their own rational nature. This human morality to Kant is therefore grounded in reason, and determines the direction of human actions according to the purposiveness of nature. So even if man's noumenal self is free from the determinism of nature, it is isomorphic to nature through human morality directed by the purposiveness of nature.

Kant owes many of his ideas of autonomy to Rousseau who was, however, not fully able to solve the question of personality in his social contract theory. Rousseau developed the notion of autonomy within the political sphere where

> (. . .) it described the freedom of the citizens who were at once sovereign and subject in the politics they created. Political freedom did not solve the problem of personal wholeness for Rousseau, since the social contract still left individuals divided between their existence as 'citizens' and as 'men', and Jean-Jacques never looked to reason as a power able to integrate the personality and ground individual moral autonomy in the way Kant did.
>
> (Seigel 2005: 299)

Kant turned Rousseau's notion of autonomy from the political realm to the moral realm of the individual. Man was morally free from determinism but still directed by the purposiveness of nature. Autonomy of the individual to Kant was therefore a freedom restricted by this purposiveness and the self-made laws directing morality. To Kant the autonomy and morality of the individual take precedence over the autonomy of the citizen in society (Seigel 2005: 295–331). In Liang Qichao's expositions on Rousseau and Kant he has fused their theories with elements from Chinese tradition, and he has presented human freedom as synonymous with the notion of autonomy in their philosophies. The question then remains to what degree the Kantian notion of autonomy is the prevailing interpretation of the freedom of the individual in Liang's own description of the Chinese citizen. In the following, I further address the fate of these concepts in Liang's writings in the Chinese discourse on the individual following Liang's own deliberations on the freedom and autonomy of the individual.

Liang on the Self-Discipline and Autonomy of the Individual and the Nation

To be able to employ mastery of one's mental and physical self, 'to have self-discipline' (*zizhi* 自治), is an ability that separates man from birds and beasts, according to Liang Qichao. When someone is unable to maintain order by him or her self then another force will inevitably take control and re-establish order. This is the inevitable order of nature (Liang 1998b: 112). Human nature has dispositions that may be contrary to the best interest of the individual itself as well as the collective. It is unruly in a fashion similar to the 'evil' human nature (*xing'e* 性惡) described by Xunzi (荀子) in the third century BC. If man follows his unruly nature he will not be able to form groups, and for the same reason laws must not be made by single men alone according to their human nature. Laws must be established by the group and for the group and must be based upon the 'reason' (*liangzhi* 良知) of man. Only then may the laws accord with human principles, and only then may they protect the freedom of the individual from infringement by others. According to Liang, self-discipline is when man is able to control his nature without external pressure or encouragement.

In Liang Qichao's discussion of Kantian philosophy and the autonomy of the individual in Western philosophy he applies the term 'freedom' (*ziyou* 自由), while we find that 'autonomy' in a political sense is translated *zizhi* (自治). Autonomy in the Kantian sense points to man's innate disposition and freedom of moral self-legislation based on his pure reason, only limited by the purposiveness of nature directing human morality, as discussed above. Liang claims that freedom is also restricted by man's morality, a morality that ties him to his collective and thus secures his freedom. The kind of self-legislation that man places upon himself is by Liang also termed *zizhi* – autonomy or self-discipline. In this chapter I prefer to translate the term *zizhi* as 'self-discipline' on the individual level and as 'autonomy' on the political level, in order not to confuse Liang's ideas of freedom and self-discipline with Kantian terms. We notice the obvious correlations between these two sets of interpretations of the self-legislation of the individual and the way Kant and Rousseau have influenced Liang's thinking, but we also recognize the differences.

By making creative rhetorical use of the term *zizhi* Liang correlates individual self-discipline with the autonomy of the nation and the state.

Semantically and in early Chinese written sources, the term *zizhi* points to ruling or mastering oneself and is commonly defined as the ability to master one's own affairs without the influence of others, and hence is a particular and very limited aspect of freedom from control by others. In these early sources the term also carries connotations of nourishing one's own moral standards, to exert self-discipline, and to master oneself by suppressing any undesired urge or aspiration for action (*Hanyu dacidian* 1986–1989, 8: 1318–1319). The term *zizhi* for autonomy and self-government in the political sense is a modern adaptation from Western languages.[8] Liang is able to make an immediate ontological and semantic projection from the self-discipline and self-legislation of the individual to the autonomy and independence of the nation. The rhetorical device Liang makes use of is that if the Chinese individual were to be able to discipline his desires and be self-legislated according to the morality desired by the nation (and not the purposiveness as Kant would argue), the group would also collectively acquire this quality, and the nation would inevitably become autonomous. That ability of *zizhi* refers on the one hand to the political ability of self-legislation and self-government of the group and on the other hand to detachment from other groups and their infringement. Hence, from the individual's ability to discipline himself Liang is able to deduce the collective freedom from infringement of the group on the collective level.[9] There are indeed major ontological differences between Liangist *zizhi* and Kantian autonomy when we consider their motivations for infusing the individual with a free but partly restricted nature of morality. To deny Kantian influence on Liangist *zizhi*, would, however, also be to ignore an all too obvious current of ideas.

Liang on Morality

Liang argues that traditional Chinese ethics have left the Chinese national character weak and dependent. In his 1902 exposition on the new citizen he maintains that throughout Chinese history one has focused upon the other rather than on the self. Liang claims that the Chinese have been mostly concerned with 'benevolence' (*ren* 仁) while people in the West have mainly been concerned with 'righteousness' (*yi* 義). Liang argues further that benevolence is concerned with the other. When oneself benefits others, then the others will also benefit me, is the principle that has governed Chinese thinking. Importance in China has thus always been on the other. Righteousness, on the other hand, is concerned with oneself. Oneself should not harm others, and then others will also not harm me. The emphasis in the West has thus always been on oneself, according to Liang. When the Chinese people merely rely on the benevolence of others, they may avoid infringing on the liberty of others. Liang however argues that the result is that the freedom of the Chinese individual itself is compromised (Liang 1998b: 92). When the individual is not independent, but merely acts as a member of a group, and only establishes his basis for morally good deeds in the image of the other, then he will always be dependent on others. This dependency, however, is not of a sociable kind and does not lead to the formation of stable collectives. This sort of dependency does not serve society at large. In the mind of Liang Qichao the Chinese individual in the early twentieth century is conceived as dependent in his life, slavish in his mind, and without an independent character as a person (Liang 1998b: 141).

Self-discipline is what enables man to submit to the laws of a society. Liang does not establish any explicit relationship between morality and laws. Self-discipline is only indirectly related to morality, and he does not discuss in further detail the elements or characteristics of morality. He is more concerned with how the morality of each individual adds up and becomes the morality of a collective, and with the relationship between private morality and public morality.[10]

> Liang's efforts after 1900 were directed toward the preservation and progress of China as a nation-state. 'Public morality' (*gongde*) he defined in terms of its ability to strengthen group cohesion, while 'private morality' (*side*) referred to the means of creating individuals of use to the group.   (Zarrow 1998: 219)

According to Liang, morality is in essence one and only one thing, but when it is expressed in deeds it takes two different forms: 'private morality' (*side* 私德) and 'public morality' (*gongde* 公德). Without private morality individuals will not be independent. Without public morality individuals will not be able to unite. Even with a large number of trustworthy, self-controlled and polite individuals they will still not be able to form a nation (Liang 1998b: 62–63).

Morality is henceforth one singular idea when speaking of its philosophical significance in Liang's ontological universe. Practice, however, will have to change with changing time and place. Practical morality is not one invariable thing (Liang 1998b: 65). The consequence of this observation was also that Liang changed his rhetoric on the requirements for the Chinese nation after his trip to the US in 1903. In the chapter on private morality from 1903, Liang has left his primary focus on public morality and has shifted his focus onto the apparently distorted private morality of the Chinese people. In Liang's new perspective ancient Confucian ethics are no longer sufficient to serve as basis for a private Chinese morality, and indeed insufficient as a unifying force for the Chinese nation. The new Chinese citizen also requires a new private morality of the Chinese individual.

> Therefore, if one aspires to form [new] citizens, then one must take the task of nourishing the private morality of the individual as one's first task. If one wishes to take part in the process of forming [new] citizens, then one must take the task of nourishing one's own private morality as the first task.
>   (Liang 1998b: 197)

The Reaction to Liang's Interpretation of Freedom and Self-Discipline

To sum up, to Liang Qichao the individual is by nature free. In order for man to fulfil his human character, different from that of animals, he needs to live in societies. These societies, the groups at various levels of human society, are man's only guarantor for his freedom. This implies that man will have to sacrifice some of his individual freedom in order to safeguard his natural freedom. This sacrifice involves a degree of 'self-discipline' (*zizhi*) exercised by each individual directing his motivation for action according to the laws agreed upon by society and the public morality of the given group. If man is unable to exert self-discipline and thus safeguard his freedom, his group will not be able to withstand the forces of evolution and may ultimately suffer extinction in the battle for survival. The nation is the ultimate group for the protection of the individual in a civilized age, thus Liang's emphasis on the nourishment of a new citizen for China. When the individual citizen is self-disciplined and self-legislated, then the nation and the state will of necessity be self-legislated and autonomous, a correlation between the individual and the nation that Liang implies in his writings on the new citizen. To Liang, private morality is insufficient to bolster social cohesion. Private morality must be harmonized with public morality in order to support the cohesive forces in society necessary for the strength of the group. Liang's initial faith in Confucian morality as a basis for the private morality for a new China was later exchanged for the need for a new Chinese morality without making any explicit recommendations for the substance of the new morality.

The intellectual debate on the freedom, autonomy and self-discipline of the individual and on private and public morality in China in the first decade of the twentieth century owes most of its arguments to Liang Qichao. The main controversy is related to the question of the application of Confucian moral standards in individual self-discipline. Should private morality, and hence also public morality, continue to build on the ethics prescribed by Confucius and Mencius, or does China need an entirely new, possibly imported set of ethical values, in order to nourish a new self-disciplined individual for a new China?

Liang Qichao's assumption that the excessive freedom of the individual and his lack of self-discipline are the main obstacles to social and national cohesion is one of the main topics on the relationship between the individual and the collective in this discourse. Song Jia (頌嘉) engaged in the debate on freedom and its Chinese interpretation in Liang's own periodical *Xinmin congbao* in 1904 (Song 1904). He argues that the term freedom or liberty (*ziyou*) is commonly misunderstood in China as meaning to be free from all social, moral and individual restrictions. The liberty of a nation and a state builds upon the liberty of its people and all individuals in that state. His argument, easily recognizable from that of Liang, is that in order for China to become free the individual must first obtain freedom through self-discipline. Freedom means self-discipline and self-cultivation without external influence or force, according to Song Jia. Only when one is able to cast off the yoke of external limitations on one's life and become a self-disciplined individual may one be free in the true sense, reflecting an interpretation of freedom somewhat closer to the sense of Kantian moral autonomy than what we find in Liang's expositions on the new citizen.

Song Jia has not made the relationship between the self-discipline of the individual and the autonomy of the nation explicit. The anonymous author of another contemporary article (Anonymous 1905) claims, however, that state autonomy in the West, compared to the dependency of the Chinese nation, is obtained through the autonomy of the individual in the West. China's miserable fate is caused by the Chinese inability of the individual to discipline himself:

> There is self-discipline of the individual. There is self-discipline of the group. There is self-discipline (autonomy) of the nation. Only after the individual is self-disciplined may the group be self-disciplined. And only after the group is self-disciplined may the nation be self-disciplined (autonomous). The nation is the congregation of all its citizens. The existence of the state is entirely dependent upon the ability of individual self-discipline. And the ability of the individual to be self-disciplined is entirely dependent upon the mental state between barbarianism and civility of the individual.   (Anonymous 1905: 123)

Laws, according to Song Jia, are instituted in order to assist man in his endeavours to become morally autonomous, and do not constitute restrictions on man's genuine freedom. On the contrary, laws are in accordance with civilized man's road to discipline.[11] The question of what kind of moral system should be nourished remains. Song Jia is not explicit on this question in his article but refers to Confucian moral standards in the introduction to the article:

> Freedom means to be able to be 'humane' (*ren* 仁) and follow 'righteousness' (*yi* 義) without instructions from others, without the rule of law, without force, and without embellishments. The one who is free aspires to become a sage or a saint and [subsequently] attains 'self-cultivation' and 'self-discipline' (*zizhi* 自治).   (Song 1904: 1)

Both the laws of a society and Confucian morality in general constitute the main directional means in man's endeavours on his way towards the perfection of his character and the realization of genuine autonomy.

In line with Song Jia and Liang Qichao, Zhong Kan (重堪) is also distressed by the lack of self-cultivation of the Chinese individual, expressed in his article 'On self-discipline' ('Zizhi pian' 自治篇).[12] Zhong Kan claims that the individual in Chinese society has become degenerate through excessive care and cruelty:

> The government has protected the individual through the law, society has motivated the individual through affection, and the family has given the individual a platform through education. The government of this time has taken the aspirations from the individual, society has treated the individual with shallowness, and the family has deprived the individual of its life-motivation, either through excessive care and devotion or through cruelty and malice. 400 million compatriots live in a situation of apathy and maliciousness.   (Zhong 1903: 6)

Zhong Kan is more explicit than Song Jia on the role of morality, and he is clearly more critical of traditional Chinese moral standards. He claims that the old morality, pointing to Confucian moral standards, is about to disappear, but a new morality for a new time has failed to manifest itself. Freedom, to Zhong Kan, means a moral life obtained through self-cultivation according to new standards of morality. The morality he prescribes is not a Kantian individual autonomous morality but rather a prescribed morality for the sake of social cohesion. The basis for morality consists of two elements, one objective and one subjective. The objective element is what is given man from heaven and comes from the inner nature of his dispositions. The subjective element is developed in one's responsibilities in social relations and is the result of active endeavours (Zhong 1903: 2–3). In addition there are social morals and psychological morals. According to Zhong Kan, Germany may serve as a standard for the self-discipline of social order and England may serve as a standard for the self-discipline of the mind. Germany has been able to unite many different states into a common social order ruled by one common law. This is based upon basic education and self-discipline. In England people are able to discipline themselves even without written laws (Zhong 1903: 3–5). To Zhong Kan the new morality should be patterned upon the social and psychological standards of the West and not on ancient Chinese ethical standards.

Throughout most of these contributions to this early discourse on freedom, self-discipline and morality we find that China's time-honoured ethical system that developed through the pre-Qin writings of Confucius,

Mencius and other disciples of the Confucian, or *ru* (儒), tradition, are discredited. New morality is commonly seen as being equal or parallel to morality in the West, without tangible examples of the substance of this morality. The anonymous author of the article 'Explication on the individual' ('Geren shuo' 個人說) (Anonymous 1906) is equally concerned about the lack of public morality, and also interprets the individual as a constituent in society who will have to exert his duties of self-discipline in order to benefit the group and thereby benefit himself. This author disclaims, however, the assertion that Confucian morality primarily consists of aspects of private morality. The author finds that the ethical teachings of Confucius and Mencius indeed also emphasize societal morality, such as 'humaneness' (*ren* 仁), 'righteousness' (*yi* 義), 'loyalty' (*zhong* 忠), 'empathy' (*shu* 恕), 'politeness' (*gong* 恭) and 'frugality' (*jian* 儉). All these six are related to private morality in their inner state, but when practised in life they are in fact aspects of public morality. According to the author, morality may be divided into old and new morality. New morality is based in the family, in society and in the nation, while the old morality was based in the relations between master and minister, between father and son, between husband and wife, between elder and younger brother, and between friends. The scope of old morality was narrow while a new morality must be wide and more public in its range. In a manner similar to the other contributions to this debate, this author sees a need for a new Chinese public morality. He finds the answer, however, in a reformation of the Confucian tradition of morality rather than in Western import.

The Autonomy of the Individual, the Minor and Greater Self

This notion of the individual attaching himself to national and state interests through morality was to be radically challenged by the dawn of individualism in the second decade of the twentieth century. *Dongfang zazhi* (東方雜志, *The Eastern Miscellany*) had been published as an organ for political and social debate since 1904. From 1911 the periodical was under the supervision of its new editor-in-chief Du Yaquan (杜亞泉), who introduced radical changes to its content. Du was himself engaged in debates on the relationship between the individual and the state, as displayed in a series of articles on questions related to the individual and his role and position. Du Yaquan's main argument in the article entitled 'Reform of the Individual' ('Geren zhi gaige' 個人之改革) published in June 1914 (Du 1914) is that reforms will be superficial as long as they are only directed at the political and educational structures of society. Reforms must start from the individual, and changes must be initiated at this basic level of society if they are to become effective. His arguments resemble the positions of his predecessors of the previous decade. Du is not merely concerned with the morality of the individual but rather with the autonomy of the individual as such. As Lydia Liu has pointed out, however, the

> (. . .) mere fact that Du Yaquan stresses the centrality of the individual in the reform program does not imply that he endorses the Enlightenment notion of individualism. On the contrary, it is the limits of the individual that he sees and addresses here.   (Liu 1993: 175)

We find in his writings that the form of individualism proclaimed by Du is compatible with both socialism and Confucianism. It is a premature form of the kind of individualism brought to the forefront during the May Fourth and New Culture Movements, but it carries an important distinction compared to the notion of the individual during the preceding decade. The individual is taking on an absolute primacy over the interests of the state – the autonomy of the individual is transforming from a qualified freedom tied to the interests of the nation towards a notion of the individual autonomous from national and group obligations. The movement towards this new form of individualism was only brought to full fruition during the New Culture Movement, but we discern its heralding in the *Dongfang zazhi* in 1914. The demise of this kind of individualism is found during the latter half of the 1920s, when individualism was conceived in polar opposition to socialism, 'when individualism had acquired the negative status of bourgeois ideology and was opposed to socialism' (Liu 1993: 176). In the following I draw attention to some of the contributions to the discourse on freedom, autonomy, morality and limitations to individual freedom in the periodicals during this period.

In Du Yaquan's particular form of socialism, a Confucian type of individual is found at the fundamental level of society. Reforms must start with the individual, and socialism is to be built upon the reformed strong and active individual with abilities to be self-reliant, with a moral obligation to cultivate himself, and a self-discipline to conform to the laws (Du 1914: 3). His form of individualism corroborates with the individual described in the teachings of Confucius and Mencius. Individualism in Du Yaquan's form does not depart from Chinese concerns for social and political reforms and change. His endeavours to turn to the individual rather than to society, the nation and the state as a focal point for reform are only partly successful as an attempt to liberate the individual from social obligations and turn him into a morally autonomous individual. In a series of articles in the same periodical in 1916, however, we find more successful attempts at constituting the individual as an autonomous entity. Lydia Liu argues that the individual was 'beginning to evolve into something of an absolute value' with the publication of Min Zhi's (民質) article 'Myself' ('Wo' 我) (Min 1916) and with Jia Yi's (家義) article entitled 'Individualism' ('Gewei zhuyi' 個位主義) in 1916 (Jia 1916). Jia Yi juxtaposes the individual with social collectives. Social collectives are established to provide a basis for the individual, and to ensure and safeguard his development. The individual takes absolute precedence over the collective.

> The case of individualism is borne out, moreover, by established modern disciplines such as psychology, sociology, and ethics, all of which are designed, in his view, to assist in the 'development of the individual' and his 'self-realization'.   (Liu 1993: 177–178)

Individualism is taking form in China. Paradoxically, in this somewhat premature form of individualism, Jia Yi is unable to disentangle the individual from his role as a cure for China's social problems. Gao Yihan (高一涵) seems to be aware of this contradiction and introduces a division of the individual into two levels of individuality, one personal and one societal.

Gao applies the term *xiaoji* (小己), 'lesser self', for the individual in contrast to the 'greater self', *daji* (大己), visualizing the self in society at large.[13] Lydia Liu argues that Gao Yihan by this gesture is in fact tying the individual to the state rather than distinguishing him from it. She argues that Gao by his terminology is maintaining a hierarchical order between the individual and the state rather than establishing an antithetical distinction (Liu 1993: 179–180). In the article entitled 'Self-discipline and freedom' ('Zizhi yu ziyou' 自治與自由) published in January 1916 (Gao 1916) Gao specifically discusses the freedom of the individual and the limitations to that freedom, and confirms Lydia Liu's assumption. The smaller self is intrinsically linked to the fate and development of society. To Gao Yihan, true freedom of the self may only be obtained through self-restraint, echoing Liang's arguments from *Xinminshuo*, when the individual is able to sacrifice his smaller self and strive for the larger self. Freedom is conditioned by self-discipline. According to Gao, man is born neither good nor bad. After one is born the struggle for life starts, and through one's life the individual applies the forces of diligence or indolence in all matters. To be self-disciplined means to apply diligence in one's life in order to overcome indolence. If the individual is able to eradicate his indolent character and develop his diligence, then both his physical and mental self will be sound and strong, and progress will inevitably follow. Conversely, if the individual follows his indolence and neglects his diligence, then both his physical and mental self will be dull and muffled, and decline will inevitably follow. According to Gao Yihan's arguments, the strength or weakness of any nation is the fruit of the use of this force of self-discipline among its people.

Gao Yihan has not successfully been able to detach the individual and his morality from the fate of the nation. The autonomy of the individual, of the lesser self, is interpreted as a duty on the individual to restrain his indolence, apparently for the sake of the collective, the greater self. Freedom of the individual is only obtained through a morally prescribed framework that evidently attaches the lesser self to the larger self, making him dependent upon it for the realization of freedom. Individualism was gradually taking form in China. Contributors to the debate on the relationship between individual and collective in China envisioned a morally autonomous individual. It was, however, only with the New Culture Movement that the individual became detached from his moral duties towards the collective. Chen Duxiu argues that the existence of the state can only be justified in terms of its function as a protector of individual rights and happiness (Lin 1979: 61–62). Chen's emphasis on national interests and nationalism may, however, be explained precisely in these terms, with the result that there seems to be a tension between individualism and nationalism in the writings of Chen, and indeed in that of many his fellow May Fourth iconoclasts. Chen never took the nation as the highest good or ultimate end, but he was deeply concerned with the question of Chinese national survival. He attacked traditional, Confucian ethics in order to emancipate the individual, and simultaneously saw this as a means to save the nation in quite straightforward social Darwinian terms.

> His individualism, which was mainly concerned with the emancipation of the individual from the shackles of traditional Chinese culture and society, was functionally related to his nationalism. The emancipated individual, he believed, can contribute to both his own good and the good of the nation.   (Lin 1979: 67)

Individualism in the literature of the New Culture Movement is well known and discussed by Lydia Liu (Liu 1993) and others. Fu Sinian (傅斯年) discusses the place of the individual in modern society in the inaugural issue of *Xinchao* (新潮) in 1919 (Fu 1919), arguing for the necessity of a free development of the individual for the common good. This liberal interpretation of the individual was, however, very soon replaced by a leftist discourse on the role of the individual in society, which refuted the liberal interpretation of the individual (Liu 1993: 183–184). I here consider two examples of how the notions of autonomy and self-discipline of the individual were conceived in the framework of the discourse in China in the 1920s.

Self-government (*zizhi*) was an important political issue in China in the latter half of the 1910s and in the 1920s as a part of the call for a democratization of the Chinese government and a movement for greater regional self-government (Twitchett and Fairbank 1978 – 12: 213–225, 13: 335–340). This debate brought back to life the ideas about how the self-discipline of the individual collectively brings about the autonomy and self-government of the state. The movement for self-government was criticized for being a top to bottom movement. Jian Hu (堅瓠) maintains in the article 'The steps in the progress of self-government' ('Zizhi jinxing zhi buzou'自治進行之步驟) (Jian 1921) that only if the people are self-governing (*zijue* 自決) and support local officials submitting to public will is it possible to establish political self-government with success. According to Jian Hu, self-government on a political level must be established upon the self-government of the individual and the will of the people from bottom and up and not vice versa. These concerns are also the central focus in an article by Kang Baiqing (康白情) entitled 'Self-governed unity and united self-government' ('Zizhi de tongyi yu tongyi de zizhi' 自治的統一與統一的自治) (Kang 1922). According to

Kang, individual freedom and state power are the two opposite forces that must be balanced in order to secure the safety and well-being of the people in the state. State power is expressed through unification, while individual freedom is expressed through self-government/autonomy. That is why the forces of unification and the forces of self-government must be maintained in a balanced condition if an ordered state is to be maintained. Kang Baiqing argues further that self-government is one aspect of individual freedom. This self-government (or autonomy) represents the individual's ability to govern himself, also in moral terms, and this ability of each individual sums up to become the self-government of the people in a state. In this way, Kang argues, the state applies limitations on individual freedom. The state is, however, the only way to secure that individual freedom. Balance between state power and individual freedom is the key to success. Kang Baiqing's article shows that the idea of self-discipline and self-governing of the individual adding up to the self-government and autonomy of the collective inherited from Liang Qichao's *Xinminshuo* was still very strong in the 1920s, in spite of the focus on individual autonomy and sovereignty during the New Culture Movement. In the political discourse the individual was still very much seen as an agent of the collective, an idea that was easily integrated into the leftist discourse to follow. The absolute freedom and autonomy of the individual was brought into the literature of the New Culture Movement, while political concerns for the self-discipline of the individual and the morality of society still attached the individual to his role in the building of the nation in a parallel discourse that echoed the arguments from Liang Qichao in the early years of the twentieth century.

Conclusion

The interpretation of the individual and his relationship to collectives in China's early intellectual modernity was inspired by a current of ideas from the West, but took on shapes that were particularly Chinese. Liberalism was an important source of inspiration in the Chinese discourse on the freedom of the individual, while Social Darwinism and Kant and Rousseau were important intellectual resources when the individual was interpreted in his social context. The Confucian tradition and indigenous Chinese interpretations of the nature of man were also vital elements in the particular interpretation of the individual in China in this discourse during the first three decades of the twentieth century. The vital position of the state in securing the prosperity and security of man in early Chinese philosophy is particularly prominent in the modern Chinese interpretation of the relationship between the individual and society. The individual was from the early contributions to this discourse strongly attached to his social duties as citizen and a member of the Chinese nation through the notion of self-discipline (*zizhi*). That the individual is free by nature but his freedom may only be secured through collective freedom is a common argument put forth by the intellectuals of this period. Collective freedom is obtained through individual self-discipline. This self-discipline (*zizhi*) of the individual adds up to the autonomy (*zizhi*) of the nation. Thus, the individual must exert self-discipline in order to maintain his freedom. This form of 'altruism' is in fact interpreted as a means to maintain individual freedom, with some analogy to Beck's descriptions of second modernity altruism. Beck's altruism is, however, related to a described form of social sensibility issuing from the disembedded individual, whereas the early modern Chinese altruism in fact represents a prescribed programme for attaching the individual to the nation rather than to the traditional ethics of the Confucian family. In spite of a generally acknowledged focus on the absolute primacy of the autonomous individual during the May Fourth and New Culture Movements, the attachment of the individual to the collective through demands of self-discipline is also surprisingly strong in the discourse throughout the 1910s and 1920s. The individual in China during this time is often found by intellectuals to be too selfish and concerned with personal profit and gain, social tendencies working contrary to the common good of a strong nation. When these intellectuals agree on the need for Chinese self-discipline, their disagreement is commonly attached to the basis for a new morality, indigenous Chinese or imported Western. These deliberations on the individual in China were curbed by the socialist discourse from the 1920s. The chapters in this book analyzing trends in the choice, agency and identity of the individual in contemporary Chinese society indicate to what extent the early modern Chinese intellectual drive to conduct a self-disciplined life sacrificing family ethics for the sake of a strong state and nation has in fact had any impact on individual agency as it is lived and experienced in China today.

Notes

1 See the chapters by Thøgersen and Ni; Hansen and Pang; Delman and Yin; Li; and Rolandsen in this book.

2 See for instance Chow 1960; Lin 1972; Lin 1979; Liu 1995; Schwarcz 1986; Fogel and Zarrow 1997; and Zhang 2004.

3 As also pointed out by for instance Huang 1972; Liu 1995; Zarrow 1998; and Zhang 2004.

4 Liu 1993: 184–186. Chen had earlier been a fervent supporter of the value of individual freedom, as in an article in the first issue of *Xin qingnian*, see Chow 1960: 295.

5 Lydia Liu has described the very interesting fate of individualism in Chinese discourse. She finds that the term *geren zhuyi (*個人主義) as a neologism, along with many other new terms for new ideas in China, was introduced into China from Meiji Japan at the turn of the century, but only brought about a debate on individualism as an ideology in periodicals such *as Dongfang zazhi (*東方雜志, The Eastern Miscellany) from 1914, see Liu 1993.

6 See also Schwartz 1964.

7 See also Fogel and Zarrow 1997

8 The dictionary of new terms in modern Chinese claims that the term was first used in this meaning in the text *Sizhouzhi (*四洲志) in 1844 (*Jin-Xiandai Hanyu xinci ciyuan cidian* 近現代漢語新詞詞源詞典 2001: 355). Later it is used for autonomy or self-government in W.A.P. Martin's 1864 Chinese translation of Henry Wheaton's *Elements of International Law*, see *Wanguo gongfa* 萬國公法 1: 25b. See also Liu 1995: 306; Masini 1993: 222.

9 For an explicit reference see the article 'Lun duli' 論獨立, Liang 1996c: 9.

10 Two chapters of the *Xinminshuo* are dedicated to these topics, one entitled 'On public morality' (*Lun gongde* 論公德) and one entitled 'On private morality' (*Lun side* 論私德), the former written as an early part of the *Xinminshuo*, the latter after the 1903 trip to the US, see Chang 1971: 272–295.

11 For further considerations on the role of law in relationship to the individual in late imperial China, see Mühlhahn's chapter in this volume.

12 Zhong 1903. The Chinese periodical *Zhejiangchao* 浙江潮 was published by Chinese students in Japan in the early twentieth century.

13 These terms are Gao's translations of the terms 'individual' and 'greater self' from chapter six in Bernard Bosanquet's *Philosophical Theory of the State*, Bosanquet 1925.

Bibliography

Ameriks, Karl (2000) *Kant and the Fate of Autonomy. Problems in the Appropriation of the Critical Philosophy.* Cambridge: Cambridge University Press.

Anonymous (1905) '論中國個人之不能自治' Lun Zhongguo geren zhi bu neng zizhi [On the inability of the Chinese to be self-disciplined]. 東方雜志 *Dongfang zazhi*, vol. 2, no. 6, pp. 123–126. Reprinted from 同文滬報 *Tongwen hubao*.

Anonymous (1906) '個人說' Geren shuo [Explication on the individual]. 東方雜志 *Dongfang zazhi*, vol. 3, no. 10, pp. 205–208. Anonymous reprint from 南方報 *Nanfangbao*.

Beck, Ulrich and Elisabeth Beck-Gernsheim (2003) *Individualization: Institutionalized Individualism and its Social and Political Consequences.* London: Sage.

Bosanquet, Bernard (1925) [1923] *The Philosophical theory of the state.* London: Macmillan.

Chan, Joseph (2002) 'Moral autonomy, civil liberties, and Confucianism'. *Philosophy East & West*, vol. 52, no. 3, pp. 281–310.

Chang, Hao (1971) *Liang Ch´i Ch´ao and Intellectual Transition in China, 1890–1907.* Cambridge: Harvard University Press.

Ch'en, Jerome (1979) *China and the West. Society and Culture 1815–1937.* London: Hutchinson.

Chow, Tse-tsung (1960) *The May Fourth Movement: Intellectual Revolution in Modern China.* Cambridge: Harvard University Press.

De Bary, Wm. Theodore and Tu Weiming (eds) (1998) *Confucianism and Human Rights.* New York: Columbia University Press.

*Dongfang zazhi (*東方雜志*)* (1904–1948) [The Eastern Miscellany]. Taibei, Shanghai: Shangwu yinshuguan.

Du Yaquan (杜亞泉) (1914) '個人之改革' Geren zhi gaige [Reform of the individual]. 東方雜志 *Dongfang zazhi*, vol. 10, no. 12, pp. 1–4.

Fogel, Joshua A. and Peter G. Zarrow (eds) (1997) *Imagining the People: Chinese Intellectuals and the Concept of Citizenship, 1890–1920.* Armonk: M.E. Sharpe.

Fu Sinian (傅斯年) (1919) '人生問題發端' Rensheng wenti faduan [Introduction to the problem of human life]. 新潮 *Xinchao* [New Tide], vol. 1, no. 1, pp. 5–17.

Gao Yihan (高一涵) (1916) '自治與自由' Zizhi yu ziyou [Self-discipline and freedom]. 青年雜志 *Qingnian zazhi* [Youth Magazine], January 1916, pp. 102–105.

Hansen, Chad (1985) 'Individualism in Chinese thought'. In Donald J. Munro (ed.) *Individualism and Holism: Studies in Confucian and Taoist Values.* Ann Arbor: University of Michigan Press, pp. 35–56.

*Hanyu dacidian (*漢語大辭典*)* (1986–1989) [Great Chinese Dictionary]. Hubei and Sichuan: Hubei cishu chubanshe, and Sichuan cishu chubanshe.

Huang, Philip C. (1972) *Liang Ch'i-ch'ao and Modern Chinese Liberalism*. Seattle: University of Washington Press.

Jia Yi (家義) (1916) '個位主義' Gewei zhuyi [Individualism]. 東方雜志 *Dongfang zazhi*, vol. 13, no. 2, pp. 6–10.

Jian Hu (堅瓠) (1921) 自治進行之步驟 Zizhi jinxing zhi buzou [The steps in the progress of self-government]. 東方雜志 *Dongfang zazhi*, vol. 18, no. 12, pp. 1–3.

Jin-Xiandai Hanyu xinci ciyuan cidian 近現代漢語新詞詞源詞典 (2001) [Etymological dictionary of neologisms in the modern Chinese language]. Shanghai: Hanyu dacidian chubanshe.

Judge, Joan (2002) 'Citizens or mothers of citizens? Gender and the meaning of modern Chinese citizenship'. In Merle Goldman and Elizabeth J. Perry (eds), *Changing Meanings of Citizenship in Modern China*. Cambridge: Harvard University Press, pp. 23–43.

Kang Baiqing (康白情) (1922) '自治的統一與統一的自治' Zizhi de tongyi yu tongyi de zizhi [Self-governed unity and united self-government]. 東方雜志 *Dongfang zazhi*, vol. 19, no. 11, pp. 1–4.

King, Ambrose Y. C. (1985) 'The individual and group in Confucianism: a regional perspective'. In Donald J. Munro (ed.), *Individualism and Holism: Studies in Confucian and Taoist Values*. Ann Arbor: University of Michigan Press, pp. 57–70.

Liang Qichao (梁啟超) (1996a) '放棄自由之罪' Fangqi ziyou zhi zui [The harm of abandoning freedom]. In Liang Qichao 梁啟超 (1996) [1936] 飲冰室合集 *Yinbingshi heji* [Collected works from the Ice-Drinker's studio]. Beijing: Zhonghua shuju, '專集' Zhuanji [Monographs Collection] 2, pp. 23–24.

—— (1996b) '近世第一大哲康德之 學說' Jinshi diyi dazhe Kangde zhi xueshuo [The teachings of Kant, the most important philosopher in recent times]. In Liang Qichao 梁啟超 (1996) [1936] 飲冰室合集 *Yinbingshi heji* [Collected works from the Ice-Drinker's studio]. Beijing: Zhonghua shuju, '文集' Wenji [Essays Collection] 13, pp. 47–66.

—— (1996c) '論獨立' Lun duli [On independence]. In Liang Qichao 梁啟超 (1996) [1936] 飲冰室合集 *Yinbingshi heji* [Collected works from the Ice-Drinker's studio]. Beijing: Zhonghua shuju, '文集' Wenji [Essays Collection] 14, pp. 5–10.

—— (1996d) '盧梭學案' Lusuo xue'an [The teachings of Rousseau]. In Liang Qichao 梁啟超 (1996) [1936] 飲冰室合集 *Yinbingshi heji* [Collected works from the Ice-Drinker's studio]. Beijing: Zhonghua shuju, '文集' Wenji [Essays Collection] 6, pp. 97–100.

—— (1996e) '自由書' Ziyoushu [Notes on freedom]. In Liang Qichao 梁啟超 (1996) [1936] 飲冰室合集 *Yinbingshi heji* [Collected works from the Ice-Drinker's studio]. Beijing: Zhonghua shuju, '專集' Zhuanji [Monographs Collection] 2, pp. 1–112.

—— (1998a) '論自由' Lun ziyou [On liberty]. In Liang Qichao 梁啟超 (1998) 新民說 *Xinminshuo* [On the New Citizen]. Zhengzhou: Zhongzhou guji chubanshe, pp. 98–111.

—— (1998b) 新民說 *Xinminshuo* [On the new citizen]. Zhengzhou: Zhongzhou guji chubanshe.

Lin, Yü-sheng (1972) 'Radical iconiclasm in the May Fourth period and the future of Chinese liberalism'. In Benjamin Schwartz and Charlotte Furth (eds) *Reflections on the May Fourth Movement*. Cambridge: Harvard University Press, pp. 23–58.

—— (1979) *The Crisis of Chinese Consciousness: Radical Antitraditionalism in the May Fourth Era*. Madison: University of Wisconsin Press.

Liu, Lydia H. (1993) 'Translingual practice: the discourse of individualism between China and the West'. *Positions – East Asia Cultures Critique*, vol. 1, no. 1, pp. 160–193.

—— (1995) *Translingual Practice. Literature, National Culture, and Translated Modernity – China, 1900–1937*. Stanford: Stanford University Press.

Lukes, Stephen (1973) *Individualism*. Oxford: Basil Blackwell.

Masini, Federico (1993) *The Formation of Modern Chinese Lexicon and Its Evolution Toward a National Language: The Period from 1840 to 1898. Journal of Chinese Linguistics Monograph Series*, no. 6. Rome: Department of Oriental Studies, University of Rome.

Min Zhi (民質) (1916) '我' Wo [Myself]. 東方雜志 *Dongfang zazhi,* vol. 13, no. 1, pp. 13–16.

*Qingnian zazhi (*青年雜志*)* (1999) [1915–1916] [Youth Magazine]. Shanghai: Qiuyi shushe. In *Xin qingnian* 新青年 (1999). Zhengzhou: Zhongzhou guji chubanshe.

Schwarcz, Vera (1986) *The Chinese Enlightenment: Intellectuals and the Legacy of the May Fourth Movement of 1919*. Berkeley: University of California Press.

Schwartz, Benjamin (1951) 'Ch'en Tu-Hsiu and the acceptance of the modern West'. *Journal of the History of Ideas*, vol. 12, no. 1, pp. 61–72.

—— (1964) *In Search of Wealth and Power: Yen Fu and the West*. Cambridge: Harvard University Press.

Seigel, Jerrold (2005) *The Idea of the Self. Thought and Experience in Western Europe since the Seventeenth Century*. Cambridge: Cambridge University Press.

Song Jia (頌嘉) (1904) '自由解' Ziyou jie [Explication of freedom]. 新民叢報 *Xinmin congbao* (1902–1907) (*Sein min choong bou*) [New People's Gazette], Yokohama, 16, pp. 1–5. (Reprinted in *Dongfang zazhi* 2.5.1905).

Twitchett, Denis and John K. Fairbank (eds) (1978–) *The Cambridge History of China*. London: Cambridge University Press.

*Wanguo gongfa (*萬國公法*)* (1864) [Public law of all nations]. Beijing: Chongshiguan.

*Xinchao (*新潮*)* (1919–1922) [New Tide]. Beijing: Beijing daxue xinchaoshe.

*Xinmin congbao (*新民叢報*) (Sein min choong bou)* (1902–1907) [New People's Gazette], Yokohama.

Zarrow, Peter (1998) 'Citizenship and human rights in early twentieth-century Chinese thought: Liu Shipei and Liang Qichao'. In Wm. Theodore De Bary and Tu Weiming (eds) *Confucianism and Human Rights*. New York: Columbia University Press, pp. 209–233.

Zhang Qing (章清) (2004) "胡適派學人群"與現代中國自由主義 *Hu Shi pai xue renqun yu xiandai Zhongguo ziyou zhuyi* ['Academics of the Hu Shi School' and Modern Chinese Liberalism]. Shanghai: Shanghai guji chubanshe.

*Zhejiangchao (*浙江潮*)* (1983) [Zhejiang Tide]. *Zhonghua minguo shiliao congbian* 中華民國史料叢編. Taibei: Dangshi shiliao bianzuan weiyuanhui.

Zhong Kan (重堪) (1903) '自治篇' Zizhi pian [On self-discipline]. 浙江潮 *Zhejiangchao* [Zhejiang Tide], no. 6, pp. 1–9.

7 'Friendly Pressure': Law and the Individual in Modern China

Klaus Mühlhahn

We must affirm anew the discipline of the Party, namely:
  (1) the individual is subordinate to the organization;
  (2) the minority is subordinate to the majority;
  (3) the lower level is subordinate to the higher level; and
  (4) the entire membership is subordinate to the Central Committee.
Whoever violates these articles of discipline disrupts Party unity.

> Mao Zedong, 'The Role of the Chinese Communist Party
> in the National War' (Mao 1968, vol. 2: 203–204)

In a political and legal sense the term 'individualism' refers to the concept that all values, rights and duties originate in individuals. Such an approach relates individualism less to a cultural or behavioural level than to a political and ideological level. Individualism in law basically describes a 'rights-claim' (Franck 1999: 3) that is meant to empower the individual, allowing him or her to confront claims on loyalty or subordination made by collectivities such as states or communities. It is in this sense, then, that the role of the individual in law and politics poses a critical issue for the state. All governments must in fact address and answer the question of how to define the status of the individual and how to determine its relationship to the state. A whole range of answers to this crucial question is possible and imaginable, varying from positions that stress the dependency and subordination of the individual to a position that highlights the primary rights of individuals. The fundamental question has been whether political authorities are willing to accept a position that stresses individual rights as inalienable and of primary importance, or whether they deny legitimacy to this concept.

There is a broad range of sectors where questions of the individual and his rights vis-à-vis the state are negotiated. Among them, criminal justice is the sector where state and individual interact in the most intimate and intricate way and where any acceptance or denial of individual rights is most visible. It is in the criminal justice system where state and society, through laws and legal procedure, indicate what level of intrusion into the individual's life is considered acceptable or justifiable. In this context, legal scholars distinguish between two approaches (Reichel 2002: 56ff): the legal rules can be activated to emphasize repressing rule violation (the crime control model), or to contain the system's level of intrusion into the life of the citizenry (the due process model). The former emphasizes the precedence of the state over the individual, while the latter stresses that states need to respect individual rights. These approaches shape the criminal process and penal treatment which then in turn reflect the status, rights and conception of the individual in a society in a most clear and unequivocal manner.[1]

In the modern period, the Chinese legal system underwent several far-reaching changes. In the course of this process, law and criminal justice in China were produced, administered and upheld in ways that were completely different from the administration of justice in imperial times. Although traditional legal thinking and rhetoric have to a certain extent found their way into the new legal systems and fused with new, mostly Western-derived, law modules, the overall legal system went through a process of tremendous transformation (Bünger 1950). Three legal systems can be distinguished in modern China that were based on different legal conceptions of the individual.

The imperial system was in place until 1911. In its fundamental outlook, focusing on family and social hierarchy, it failed to explicitly take note of the individual, although there were implicit regulations concerning, for instance, the treatment of individuals in a court. During the Republican period, the legal system systematically and explicitly 'discovered' the individual in many ways and on various levels. This was especially true in the field of criminal justice, where 'individualization' in sentencing and punishment was the order of the day. After 1949 and until the beginning of the reform policy in 1978, the socialist government reversed the tendency of individualization and brought the collective back in, but in a new form: instead of the family, so called 'small groups' (*xiaozu* 小組) appeared as the fundamental reference point and framework to which individuals should relate themselves.

While the overall legal position of the individual in twentieth-century China was subject to considerable change, there is nonetheless one commonality: for most of the time under discussion in this chapter, the individual appeared to various Chinese governments as a potential threat and fundamental security problem. Therefore, Chinese governments were willing to limit the legal status of the individual and struggled against efforts to assert individual rights. On the most general level, when it came to legal issues almost all twentieth-century Chinese governments viewed the individual less as a bearer of rights than as the subject of duties – a small cog in the larger collective machinery of the nation, in need of supervision and discipline.

This chapter thus approaches the changing perception of the individual in relation to collectives as seen from the operations of the state through the legal system. The underlying goal is to clarify the status of the individual in Chinese law by looking into how delinquents were treated in court and in penal institutions. Specifically, I am interested in exploring the willingness of state agencies in modern China to accept limits to state power and to assert the existence of boundaries that shield the individual from infringement and potential abuse. Since law and criminal justice are broad topics that cannot be comprehensively dealt with in the framework of one essay, the following discussion must be narrowed down using concrete examples from and aspects of Chinese criminal justice. For the most part, I am interested in the treatment of convicts in prisons and labour camps in China from the early 1900s to the beginning of the reform policy in 1978. This development must be linked to the preceding imperial period. Here, however, we are confronted with a problem: the lack of incarceration as a legal punishment in imperial Chinese law makes it necessary to change the focus of the discussion. For the imperial period, the legal concept of *criminal intent* is best suited for a discussion of the ambivalent status of the individual in Chinese law.

The Individual in Imperial Chinese Law

The individual's relationship to the state in imperial China has been extensively debated among scholars studying traditional Chinese philosophical and political thought. Conventional wisdom has it that traditional Chinese thinking is group-oriented and essentially hostile to individualism (Pye 1991: 444f). In this view, the individual in imperial China has been conceived primarily as a member of a larger group, and the group's interests are assumed to take precedence over those of the individual, as also discussed by Svarverud in the preceding chapter. The relationship between the state and the individual was described as one of dependency and not one based on the rights of individuals. Traditional Chinese thinking lacked any notion of individualism, and the individual was always conceptually placed in relation to a larger group of which the individual was a part (Hansen 1985; King 1985). A number of scholars, however, most prominently Wm. Theodore de Bary (1970), have held a different opinion. De Bary has argued that one can find at least in Ming neo-Confucianism a well-articulated defence of the role of self in society and the importance of the individual. While de Bary admits the general dominance of the state in imperial China, he maintains that Confucian thinkers, especially in the late imperial era, argued for a 'balance of public and private' (*gong si yiti* 公私一體) (De Bary 1998: 29), and consequently rejected any subordination of the person or the individual to the collective and the state. To him and others, the dominance of the state was certainly not uncontested in imperial China.[2]

It is interesting to note, however, that this debate stopped short of looking for answers in Chinese law.[3] If a significant notion of the individual existed in imperial China, it has to be found in the law; otherwise it would be a mere theoretical (or philosophical) concept with little practical relevance. As we will see, the role of the individual in law reflects the ambivalence we find in philosophy. While the law clearly recognized the individuality of criminals and their deeds, the Chinese empire ceded little autonomy to the individual in law. However, it was less the state than the family in which the claims on loyalty and subordination of individuals originated.

In imperial Chinese law, crime was mainly understood as damage done to the existing social order. The criminal act itself was, therefore, the actual object of the law and much effort was devoted to assuring that the punishments fitted the damage caused by the crime. Punishments were usually measured not on the basis of individual guilt, but on the basis of the damage done to social order (MacCormack 1996: 209). The judge was supposed to follow the rule that the greater the disturbance caused by a criminal act, the greater the punishment. Murder of a superior or senior person was punished more severely than the murder of an inferior or junior person. The status of any offender (as well as of the victim of a crime) was defined in relation to others rather than in individual terms. He was seen as part of a group and his membership in this group defined his status. This went so far as to include the concept that responsibility for a given act extended beyond the individual actor (Waley-Cohen 2000). Chinese law from Qin times onward offered the judge the possibility to punish not only the single person who had committed a crime, but also many others, such as family members, neighbours and community leaders, who were held to be guilty merely by virtue of their association with the accused. Inasmuch as the insistence on group or collective responsibility reinforced the political power of the collective and the family, it also weakened the status of the individual and foreclosed any possible recognition of rights an individual might claim.

It would be wrong however to assume that the individual was completely absent from the law. Consider for instance numerous categories of homicides (*liusha* 六殺) specified in the Chinese Law Code (*Da Qing Lüli* 大清律例) of the Qing Dynasty (1644–1911). It is worthwhile to list here some of the categories as they demonstrate the extent to which the consideration of individual motives entered the administration of criminal justice. (1) *mousha* (謀殺): intentional killing by premeditated or preconcerted design, punishable by decapitation after imprisonment pending the autumn assizes; (2) *gusha* (故殺): intentional killing without previous design, punishable by decapitation; (3) *dousha* (鬥殺): killing in an affray, punishable by strangulation; (4) *xisha* (戲殺): killing at play (involving a dangerous game or sports), punishable by strangulation after imprisonment pending autumn assizes but typically punished one degree less, by 100 heavy bamboos and banishment of 3,000 li; (5) *wusha* (誤殺): killing by mistake or mishap (for instance, when one, fighting with another in an affray, were to hit and kill a third party with whom he had no quarrel and to whom he intended no harm), punishable by strangulation after imprisonment pending autumn assizes; (6) *guoshisha* (過失殺): killing by misadventure or pure accident, which was 'beyond what one could hear, see, or foresee in judgment,' punishable by a fine of 12.4 taels of silver for the victim's family (see articles 282, 290, 292 of the Qing Law Code in Jones 1994: 268–278). Overall, it seems that imperial Chinese law operated on the fundamental principle that '[i]ntent was conceived along a finely graded continuum of severity beginning at the high end with malice aforethought, and continuing through a diminishing scale based on when the intent was formulated vis-à-vis the commission of the crime' (Neighbors 2004: 6–7).

The above-mentioned categories were only some of the major statutory distinctions in Chinese law, and judicial practices were, of course, far more nuanced and complex. Likewise, the stipulated punishments were also frequently commuted to lesser ones (such as exile, labour servitude, and so on) in the local courts (for lesser crimes), or at the central level of judiciary after the autumn assizes, when allowed by mitigating circumstances. Though defined in part based on the circumstances surrounding the crime, these statutes gave weight to the question of individual intention behind the crime. Major homicide categories, such as killing in affray or killing at play, therefore serve to illustrate the status of the individual in Qing law, whereby individual intent was conceptualized in tandem with concrete situations, allowing detailed differentiation of individual motives and a detailed scale of homicide offences.

Based on the regulations outlined above, there is hardly any evidence for the frequent statement that Chinese law did not require any consideration of the individual in meting out criminal punishments. Chinese criminal law operated along an extremely finely graded scale of individual culpability, which involved looking at the individual person and his or her intention. However, even if we concede that Chinese law in imperial times reckoned with individual factors (intent) when deciding on the category or section under which a case was to be tried, one cannot overlook that overall, these individual factors were clearly given minor weight. A judge would first determine the harm caused by the crime by looking for the appropriate paragraph in the law code. He would then decide on the social and familial status of an offender based on group membership, and only thereafter consider individual circumstances such as intent, motives and background. While it would be a distortion to deny the appearance of the category of the individual in the administration of justice, it is beyond doubt that the notion of the individual remained conceptually subordinate to social order and the larger group membership, which functioned as the more decisive criteria.

This leaves us with the conclusion that imperial Chinese law was predominately oriented toward the group or the collective, although it could give consideration to individual motives on a secondary level. However, this concern never gave rise to the notion of a right the individual could claim in court. Group membership and social relations to others were the basic principles not only of the law. Rather, this principle reflected the larger pattern of social and political organization in imperial China. While it recognized the individual implicitly, it viewed it as part of a dense hierarchical web of social relations which defined a person's position, social role and the obligations towards others that such a role carried with it.

Individualization and Power in Republican Law

In the twentieth century, reforms were introduced that changed the Chinese legal system profoundly. Criminal justice was one of the sectors where the legal reforms were particularly ambitious. This change concerned both fundamental philosophical principles and the concrete administration and techniques of jurisdiction. Many reforms were linked to shifting conceptions concerning the role of the individual in law.

The development of criminal law in Republican China can be characterized by the general tendency to redirect the focus of criminal justice away from the criminal act and group membership, and toward the personality of the criminal or the individual behind the criminal act. Between 1905 and 1907 several leading officials of the Qing Dynasty proposed the abolition of all five corporal punishments listed in the old Code of the Qing Dynasty and proposed prisons be built instead (Dikötter 2002: 27–52). The prison in Europe has always combined two goals. It was intended, on the one hand, as a place to lock away convicts and troublemakers and keep them busy by work. At the same time, the official mission was to correct and rehabilitate the inmates. The latter idea was received with great interest by Chinese legal reformers of the late Qing and the early Republic. They saw the real benefit of the punishment of custody in its assumed capability to correct the individual and transform his or her state of mind. This is evident in a memorandum on prison reform presented by Shen Jiaben (沈家本), a leading legal reformer. He wrote, 'Use the prison location to apply the method of instruction (*jie jianyu zhi di, shi jiaohui zhi fang* 借監獄之地,施教誨之方)' and '[t]he key principle in setting up prisons is not to cause suffering and bring disgrace, but to change the inmates' (Shen 1988). The positive aspects of imprisonment for delinquents as well as for society as a whole would be a change and transformation in the individual convict. Crime was seen as a kind of social illness that affected the individual, who could be cured through proper treatment while confined in a closed environment. Compared to the corporal and painful punishments of imperial law, imprisonment would not only be more humane and devoid of suffering, but would also be more effective, since the transformation of criminals would undoubtedly promote social stability. The prison was expected to release good citizens.

In Republican criminal law, emphasis was thus laid on the principle that the criminal process and the punishment both related to the specific condition of each criminal. This principle was called the 'individualization of punishment' (*xingfa de gerenhua* 刑法的個人化) (Wang 1919). In accordance with this principle, the new criminal laws all acknowledged individual mitigating circumstances (§ 62 of the 1919 criminal law, § 59 of the 1935 criminal law). The judge was directed, before passing sentence, to consider the state of the offender's mind, his motives, his past conduct, his general intelligence and also his conduct subsequent to the offence. In the imposition of fines, too, the judge was instructed to take into account individual circumstances, namely the economic and mental condition of the offender.

A prison law (*jianyu guize* 監獄規則) was issued by the Republican government in 1913. It remained in effect with only a few modifications until 1949 (reprinted in Dikötter 2002: 380–391). In general, imprisonment as explicated in this legislation was fully in accordance with the principle of the individualization of punishments mentioned above, because it allowed the individual treatment of the convict by taking into account his or her specific individual deficiencies, needs and responses. Consequently, such concepts also dominated the prison law. But still, the law especially noted the duties of convicts and the necessity of their subordination. Article nine of the prison law, for instance, read: 'The punished must be induced to respect the dignity of national law and to whole-heartedly value national law. After being released, the former prisoner must be able to lead an ordered life in accordance with the law.'

These discourses formed the epistemological basis for new concepts regarding the purpose and forms of punishment. New normative rationales emerged which underpinned the birth of the criminal justice system in China and structured its operation. The courts and prisons became places where new social relationships between the individual and state authority could be trained. The process of individualization was initiated by state authorities with the goal of transforming the individual mind in order to shape mentalities that conformed to the new social order of the Republic. The law codes were mainly concerned with the question of how to best re-educate deviants, but they did not explore the necessity of protecting the convicts in prison from abuse. A closer look at the practices and rituals implemented in the prison reveals the close connection between individualization and state power.

On entering a Chinese prison, a set of rituals was performed upon the prisoner with the goal of assaulting his personality (see Mühlhahn 2007). Some of the treatments intended to clean the convict. Prisoners were washed on arrival, had their heads shaved, and underwent a medical inspection to detect contagious diseases or mental disorders (Commission on Extraterritoriality 1925: 102). A second set of measures dealt with the identity of the convict. All personal property was impounded, to be returned upon release, and prisoners were handed grey uniforms. The status of the inmate was recorded, in particular his occupation, conduct, preferences and medical history. His picture and fingerprints were taken, and any identifying individual characteristics were noted. Prisoners were also given numbers. Instead of their names these numbers were used to identify the convicts during their time in prison. Writing about similar practices in the US in the 1950s the sociologist Erving Goffman has argued that such admission procedures and purifying rituals have an important effect. The point is that the nakedness (washing, medical examination) marks a midpoint between leaving off an earlier identity and taking on a new role. The inmate is stripped of his previous civil roles, which of course provided him with his identity in civil life. Goffman (1961: 18) wrote, 'Admission procedures might better be called "trimming" or "programming" because in thus being squared away the new arrival allows himself to be shaped and coded into an object that can be fed into the administration machinery of the establishment, to be worked on smoothly by routine operations.' The dispossession of personal effects basically brought upon a deculturation which amounted, in Goffman's words, to a 'civil death'. The loss of the prisoner's name and all other belongings effectuated a curtailment of the convict's self and identity. By stripping him of any individual attributes, he became part of a social category. In a similar way, the Chinese prison produced a uniform object to work upon – the inmate. Individuality here is only recognized in order to be removed and redefined.

Admission procedures were the first step in erecting a community of power. It was followed by the organization of space and time further intended to augment the reach of power. The activities in which prisoners in Republican China were engaged in prison were thoroughly controlled by way of a set of innovative technologies, such as timetables, training, observation and examination. Space and time were broken into ever smaller and more useful segments. Such a disciplinary control of activity produced, in Foucault's words, 'a positive economy; it poses the principle of a theoretically ever-growing use of time: exhaustion rather than use; it is a question of extracting, from time, ever more available moments and, from each moment, ever more useful forces' (Foucault 1979: 154).

The useful forces that were to be extracted pertained to training and work. Imprisonment as the main legal punishment in Republican China should above all serve the purpose of reformation (*ganhua* 感化). The three main tools of reformation were considered to be forced labour (*laoyi* 劳役), moral instruction (*jiaohui* 教誨) and basic education (*jiaoyu* 教育). In the Republic's new prisons, the life of the inmates was increasingly dominated by industrial work and work training. So important was labour in the new prisons that they gradually developed into industrial complexes. The Beijing First Prison (formerly Beijing Model Prison) had facilities for lithography, type-printing, woodblock printing, type making, typesetting, book-binding, sewing, weaving, metal foundry, rice preparation, washing, making rattan goods, masonry, carpentry and agriculture (Commission on Extraterritoriality 1925). All prisoners were to be assigned manual labour whereby supervisors had to take into consideration the age of the prisoner, nature of the crime the prisoner had committed, length of sentence, social standing, handicraft expertise, future profession and physical condition of the inmate. Working hours varied between seven to twelve hours a day, seven days a week. Prisoners were not supposed to receive remuneration, but financial rewards up to one-third of the income derived from prison labour could be given to the prisoner and paid upon release.

According to Article 48 of the prison law, all prisoners were to receive instruction. For juvenile inmates, basic education in reading, writing, arithmetic and composition could be offered. Three methods of instruction were applied: prisoners were taught together, mostly on Sunday afternoons. There was also individual instruction as well as special instruction upon entering and leaving the prison, again provided individually. Collective instruction was held in the instruction hall. The prison instructor would give a talk to all prisoners assembled in the hall. He told the delinquents how to behave and how to become good and useful. For example, a lesson in the Beijing Second Prison began with the following words: 'Heaven and earth gave birth to man. Man's nature is good. Originally he did not have an evil nature. It is only when he is exposed to all kinds of social circumstances that he becomes infected with evil. Those who become accustomed to evil are evil. Those who are accustomed to good are good' (Liang 1919). The talk then proceeded to explain that someone who is infected by evil in his mind would easily engage in criminal activities. What stands out in this talk is the medical metaphor. The individual prisoner is seen as an object for therapeutic action. The criminal appears as a maladjusted individual. To rectify such a maladjusted individual was part of an effort of social prevention for securing public order.

The set of innovative techniques applied in the prison, such as use of space and time, curtailment of the self, training and programming, instruction, observation and working together formed a social technology of control, which could be used in other institutions, such as the school or the factory. Modern Chinese individuality was defined by these new power relationships in which it was constrained, and which became most visible in the prison. Power was no longer reduced to extrinsic coercion or confinement; it also included a whole array of intrinsic techniques to persuade and manipulate the individual and to intervene in the production of subjectivity and self. In the legal system, the Republican Chinese nation-state structured a new system of representation and set new terms of individualized self-representation. In other words, the individual was 'discovered' and developed mainly as an object of state intervention and a resource for the nation.

Socialism and Collective Discipline, 1949–1979

The establishment of a new and revolutionary system of justice administration ran equally high on the political agenda of the Chinese Communist Party (CCP) from the 1930s onwards. The CCP perceived the Republican legal system from the new courts to the new prisons as an instrument of the ruling class, used to suppress and exploit the Chinese working masses.[4] For the CCP, the system of criminal justice established in the Chinese Republic possessed a clear-cut 'class character'. For this reason, every effort to overthrow the Chinese Republic invariably also implied an attack against the justice system in general and the Republican prison in particular. In the early 1930s, at a time when the Republican system was not even fully developed, the CCP already started to look for alternative forms of administering justice. Based on Marxist theories and on Soviet experiences, a new system of criminal justice was tested in the revolutionary base areas: new definitions of criminality were developed, new processing formats were applied, and new treatments for offenders were explored. After 1949, these formats and techniques were implemented nation-wide.

Many of the ideas that influenced the Chinese Communist legal system were received from the Soviet Union. Prominent among them were concepts that touch upon the status of individual, such as the exceedingly important concept of the *kollektiv*. Perhaps most influential in this respect were the writings by Anton Semyonovich Makarenko (1888–1939).[5] Makarenko conceptualized and theorized his practical experiences with the treatment of juvenile delinquents in several books that circulated widely throughout the socialist world. His work and theories were also studied intensively in China. This pedagogue and educator influenced the Chinese Communist legal system more than any other legal expert or political thinker.[6]

Like the early European Socialists, Makarenko regarded labour as fundamental to intellectual and moral development. All convicts should therefore be assigned tasks requiring labour and should be given positions of responsibility in order to learn the limitations of their individual rights and privileges. Makarenko spoke of labour as an almost mystical process of beauty, satisfaction and fulfilment. He used descriptions like 'the symphony of labour' and compared a railway factory to a 'fairytale castle' (Adolphs 1962: 18–42). Overall, his education focused on the instilment of discipline, which demanded that the juvenile offenders understand and accept limits in individual freedom. Makarenko ascribed the greatest importance to the collective. To him, any effective education had to be 'education in and by a group – a *kollektiv*' (Koutaissoff 1953: 133).

The over-reaching goal of his social experiments was to set up strong communities that shared a certain code of behaviour. He expected that communities always would try to impose their norms of behaviour on the newcomer. Rewards or punishments should therefore represent the approval or disapproval of the group. When the group norms were accepted and internalized by group members, 'friendly pressure' to conform to those norms would arise, the authority of which rested with the *kollektiv* and would not be questioned or resisted. Collectivism thus meant that each member should act in accordance with the norms of the *kollektiv* through his or her own will. Makarenko considered what he called the 'friendly pressure' of the collective to be a new Soviet style of discipline. He saw discipline not as a result of extrinsic training and surveillance (as practised in the Republican prison), but as coming from the pressure and broad educational influences exercised by the collective. He wrote,

> Discipline is a product of the sum total of the educative efforts, including the teaching process, the process of political education, the process of character shaping, the process of collision – of facing and settling conflicts in the collective, the process of friendship and trust, and the whole educational process in its entirety, counting also on such processes as physical education, physical development and so on.
>
> (Makarenko 1965: 56)

Makarenko also tried to develop a new socialist understanding of punishment. He saw the goal of punishment in 'settling and eliminating a conflict' (Makarenko 1965: 82). In his commune, punishment should not produce moral or physical suffering: 'What then is the meaning of punishment? Knowing that the collective condemns your action. The culprit must not feel crushed by the punishment, but it will make him think over his mistake, and ponder on his estrangement, however slight, from the collective' (Makarenko 1965: 83). Makarenko also asserted that punishment is only effective if it is carried out and supported by collective pressure. The main goal should be to isolate the offender from the collective so that collective pressure could come to bear on the offender.

These remarks point to a form of discipline overlooked by Michel Foucault. For Foucault, discipline in the modern age was individualized and individualizing. Yet here we see discipline produced within and through the collective. One could describe it as an alternative strand of discipline and social organization which would eventually fully emerge in state socialism.

Emphasis on the collective and the group at the expense of the individual marked the criminal justice system in China as it emerged after 1949. The socialist system in China was based on the ideal that individual interests and the interests of the group should converge and be in harmony. Mao wrote, 'The individual is an element of the collective. When collective interests are increased, personal interests will subsequently be improved' (quoted in Nathan 1986: 64). The individual should subject himself to the higher interests of the larger group such as the Party, the class, the nation. In principle, the general interest of the group had to be defined in a process of open discussion and then wholeheartedly implemented by every member of the group. Public goals could only be achieved meaningfully by collective effort, whereby members had to unite to pursue the common good. In this line of thinking, individualism or an emphasis on individual rights denoted disunity, selfishness and privatism. The CCP therefore considered that the outright promotion of individual rights could potentially undermine state unity and group coherence, and was thus likely to help to restore class exploitation. Such behaviour was generally suspected to be counter-revolutionary.

After assuming power, the CCP carried out several campaigns to re-educate Chinese citizens and propagate the primacy of collective interests. So-called 'thought reform' (*sixiang gaizao* 思想改造) or ideological re-education was at the centre of many campaigns in the 1950s and 1960s. Citizens all over the country were asked to hold study and discussion sessions that would help them to identify wrong individualistic thinking and to bring the thinking of all members in line with the interests of the collective. Thought reform was conducted in small groups (*xiaozu* 小組). Work and/or residential units were supposed to set up regular political courses, cultural programs, discussion sessions and reading activities.

Thought reform and re-education was particularly prevalent in the legal system. According to criminal theory at that time, crime was caused by wrong thinking which was acquired by an offender's social background. Crime was thus always understood as resulting from individualism and false consciousness. Accordingly, the state's response was to re-educate the offender and re-integrate him or her into the collective. The offenders should be forced to remould themselves through hard labour and become 'new persons' (*xin ren* 新人). Mao also described this process as 'turning rubbish into something useful' (Mao 1992: 57). Officially, this penal treatment of deviants was called 'labour reform' (*laodong gaizao* 劳动改造). Here, too, thought reform was applied to subordinate the individual to the collective. Overall, thought reform consisted of two elements: first, a confession that should result in 'the exposure and renunciation of past and present evil', and second, re-education that led to the instilment of new values and 'the remaking of man' (Lifton 1961: 5).

Soon after their arrest, convicts and suspects were called upon to write self-examinations (*fanxing zi zhuan* 反省自傳). The self-examination had two functions (Li 1984: 18f). It should, on the one hand, deliver a confession of the crimes an offender had committed, yet on the other, it went well beyond a confession. It should start from early childhood and cover the whole life prior to the arrest. POWs, war criminals and high profile political prisoners were often asked to provide chronological charts of their official and private lives, which listed all-important events for every year and every month. In this way the self-examination resembled a full and detailed autobiography in which the prisoner was supposed to reflect critically upon the entire life he had led up to the time of his arrest. The goal of the self-examination was to demonstrate to the offender where exactly the hidden reasons for and remote origins of his transgressions were. 'Their aim is not so much to make you invent nonexistent crimes, but to make you accept your ordinary life, as you led it, as rotten and sinful and worthy of punishment, since it did not concord with their own, the police's conception of how a life should be led' (Bao and Chelminski 1973: 40). Self-examination meant re-examining one's individuality with the goal of expounding where selfishness and egoism led a person to violate the interest of the collective. A clear acknowledgment of one's errors and crimes should be produced and, at the same time, the hidden origins of the crimes in life habits or wrong beliefs were to be highlighted. Self-examination was seen as a prerequisite for thought reform. It tended to qualify individuality *per se* as something wrong or harmful. By bringing these relationships to one's attention, a first step towards reform was made.

The self-examination was verified by an officer. It served as the basis for the interrogations that followed as the next step. The first version was usually judged as insufficient and sketchy. Pressure and coercion were used if inmates did not comply or cooperate. These measures varied from threats to the use of shackles and handcuffs, to solitary confinement (see below on punishments). In general, prisoners were informed that refusal to fully cooperate would result in harsh treatment and long sentences, while compliance would be rewarded by light sentences. The next steps in a normal process of thought reform were political study and criticism.

Political study meetings (*xuexihui* 學習會) were conducted in the camps and prisons on a regular basis (Williams and Wu 2004: 110–118). Frequency depended on local conditions. If there were many tasks to do in the camps for harvests or production, political study was scheduled only once a week. But in winter or at other times when there was less to do, political study was carried out daily, for periods of two to three hours. At the meetings, texts of political content were collectively read and debated. The following sources were frequently used: articles from the *People's Daily*, and selected texts from Mao Zedong as well as from Marx, Engels, Lenin and Stalin. Almost every prisoner, for instance, was familiar with Mao's 'On the People's Democratic Dictatorship', 'On Correctly Handling Contradictions Among the People' and with Liu Shaoqi's 1 May address from 1950, in which he praised the historical significance of physical labour (Zhang 1994: 212f). The study of these texts should instil new norms and values and provide a new moral framework for the remaking of the prisoner's personality.

Criticism was a very important element in the process of thought reform. Criticism and self-criticism served to expose a wrong worldview and debunk false lifestyles. We can distinguish between two forms: public criticism in front of a large audience and criticism conducted in sessions attended by small groups. The small group, be it a *Laogai* (勞改) squadron or a prison cell, was supposed to help its members uncover socially undesirable attitudes and habits. There were different kinds of meetings, such as 'meetings for the investigation and discussion of lifestyle' (*shenghuo jiantao hui* 生活檢討會), 'meetings for the evaluation of thinking' (*sixiang pingbi hui* 思想評比會) or the 'criticism and struggle meeting' (*pidou hui* 批鬥會). In the description of Zhang Xianliang, a meeting for the discussion of one's lifestyle took place in the following way: 'In each small group on Sunday evening, convicts would sit cross-legged on their bunks, and, like true believers, confess their sins. They would recount the mistakes they had committed during the week – mistakes they now regretted' (Zhang 1994: 148). Sometimes a prisoner would come forward and point out mistakes committed by other prisoners. The group would go on and discuss his problems. In general, the officers continually emphasized that every person had to 'hand over', or expose, his own thinking.

The therapeutic character of the meetings could quickly give way to punitive and violent treatment of those accused of having committed an error. The criticism and struggle session was the most severe form. Prisoners also called it 'heat treatment' (Zhang 1994: 210). Prisoners or group members who were accused of refusing reform by being egoistic or individualistic were subjected to the heat treatment several evenings in a row. Every member of the squadron had to utter criticism and to yell accusations. Many eyewitnesses and victims reported physical abuse such as beatings or the use of shackles and handcuffs. But even without violence, many prisoners experienced the public exposition of error and public censure as humiliation, and therefore dreaded to become targets. Criticism sessions were an effective tool for staff to force prisoners to adhere to the norms and rules of thought reform.

Thought reform has received great attention in the West. During the Cold War, it was often seen by Western media as being tantamount to brainwashing. The psychiatrist Robert Jay Lifton (1961: 438–461) has argued that the techniques of thought reform bear resemblance to certain practices of organized religions, various kinds of religious re-education as well as psycho-therapeutic and psycho-analytical forms of treatment, especially in psychiatric hospitals. All these agencies make use of basically the same approaches to change the inner self of a person: coercion, exhortation, therapy and realization (through, for example, punishment and reward; see below). In the case of thought reform, the goal was to exterminate every form of individualism and thus to subdue the individual to the collective.

In Maoist China, the unity of the masses under the leadership of the Party was proclaimed the ultimate political goal (Munro 1977: 158). Unity was also a means to achieve more immediate national goals such as industrialization, defence and strengthening. Without unity among the masses and the leadership of the Party, national goals were unattainable. Unity should be approached by diminishing and eventually liquidating social divisions. It is in this context that law was used as a tool to diminish divisions and to reconcile conflicts between individual and collective interests. This reconciliation took place through re-education under Party supervision. Thought reform aimed to subordinate the individual to the masses led by the party. In Chinese socialism, citizens should be selfless, even to the point of self-sacrifice and the complete neglect of the individual.

Conclusion

All three legal systems under discussion in this chapter recognized the importance of the individual in criminal justice, but no system developed a concept of individual rights or entitlements that shielded the individual from excesses of state power. The basic reference point of traditional Chinese law was not the individual, but the collective. In legal affairs, family, clan, village and state dominated the individual. While there were notions or doctrines that in theory limited imperial power, it is indeed striking that the law failed to develop ideas or consistent rules for addressing the problem of state power. The individual appeared as an object of concern, cure and punishment, but not as a holder of rights. A similar ambivalence concerning the individual still prevailed in Chinese criminal and penal law during the Republican era. In criminal justice matters, officials started to place emphasis on the individual, his past experiences and present situation. An individualized approach in criminal justice and the Chinese prison was supposed to re-educate criminals and train good citizens. Again the individual appeared as an object of penal law rather than the subject of rights. The perhaps strongest assault on the individual was mounted during the Mao years. In law and in penal treatment the individual (and with it crime) were meant eventually to wither away. The goal of criminal law and punishment was the creation of a coherent and unified society in which individual interests were compelled to merge with the interests of state and society.

Therefore, the intent of crime control and of social repression dominated the legal system in China for most of the twentieth century. Despite the obvious importance of legal changes and political divides, the time span reaching from 1900 to 1978 forms a coherent whole. In this time we see continuous efforts to actually expand the realm of the state at the expense of any legal autonomy of the individual. This fundamental approach did not allow the notion of individual rights to be recognized in the legal procedures.[7] The imperial system had elaborate rules to ensure a 'good administration by good officials' (Connor 1998: 189) and displayed a serious concern for justice, yet it was never designed to protect the rights of individuals. When legislators and legal scholars studied Western law intensively during the Republican period, ideas of due process and protection of individual rights remained sidelined and secondary to the overarching concern with social stability and the maintenance of social order. The People's Republic of China was most outspoken in its undisguised and frank neglect of individual rights. Until the 1980s, advocating or promoting individual rights was declared to be an attack on the principles of socialism in China. Of course this is not to say that individualism as a concept was completely absent in Chinese society in all the periods under discussion. Expressions of individualism and privacy practices, especially within the family, have always persisted despite the state's intrusion into individual life (McDougall 2004. See also the chapters by Hansen and Pang; and Thøgersen and Ni in this book). But it is significant, and tells us about the limits of individual expression and of privacy that the individual as right-holder played de facto no role in the legal system until very recently.

Thus, the legal role and status of the individual in twentieth-century China appears as a rather ambivalent phenomenon. Individualism did not so much emerge as an oppositional mode of thinking to emancipate the Chinese subject from a Confucian–imperial system that gravitated towards family and clan, as in the words of Chow Tse-tung (1960: 312) it 'cleared the way for placing the individual in bondage to state, party, or other social and economic organization'. Freed from clan and family, the individual became to be viewed as a resource to be incorporated by the nation-state and to be appropriated for its projects of national strengthening. The legal discourse around the neologism *geren* (个人) both before and after 1949 envisioned the individual as a subject of liberation for the greater cause of the nation, with the goal of preserving national coherence and achieving national salvation. In that way the concept of the individual was brought into complicity with the primacy of the nation-state and of nation-building.

Yet it also needs to be pointed out that the start of economic reforms and the opening up of China in 1978 marked a new turning-point, not only for developments in politics, economics and society but also for law and criminal justice. Since then, some of the currents this chapter has analyzed have been reversed. China altered its policy concerning crime control and the management of justice (although in some areas change was slower or not palpable at all), and a new criminal justice system gradually emerged, along with a new set of laws (Cohen 2007). The Chinese government thus re-established a formal legal system that also recognized the right of the accused to a defence lawyer in criminal proceedings. Under the Law of Criminal Procedure 1979, the court could appoint a lawyer for a defend-ant who did not have someone to act as his or her legal representative. In practice, under this rule a large number of Chinese lawyers were appointed every year by their law firms at the request of the courts, and their fees were mainly paid by the courts or the government, through the law firms.

From 1978 to the late 1980s, it was however unclear how far the legal reforms were supposed to go. On the one hand, China started to partici-pate in and even actively contributed to many relevant United Nations human rights activities, but on the other hand the government continued to condemn concepts in China that were similar to the UN standards for human rights. In the 1980s, for example, presumption of innocence was at least twice officially labelled as a bourgeois principle. Another example: when initiatives were launched to clear up 'spiritual pollution' in 1983 and 1986–1987, scholars were criticized for promoting the concept of human rights. Beginning in the 1990s the pace of legal reform accelerated. Changes included the abolition of the crime of counter-revolution, an enhanced con-cept of judicial independence, redefined roles for prosecutors, new limits on the power of the police, the new right to legal aid, increased independ-ence of the legal profession, enhanced professional qualifications of judges and prosecutors, recognition of the right to defence in pre-trial detention, provision of legality in substantive criminal law, and the abolition of the retroactive application of criminal law. Much progress has been made toward a greater protection of individual rights, yet none of these developments is uncontested. Criminal justice is still the area where the conflict between the state's desire to curb crime and corruption and to protect individual rights is most dramatically played out against the backdrop of Party stewardship.

Notes

1   It is of course possible and even likely that in philosophy, the arts, or in private life different conceptions of the individual prevail in a society. In contrast, the legal system reflects and enforces the official definitions imposed by the state organs.

2   In this context Taoist thinkers such as Yang Zhu or Zhuang Zhou could be mentioned as well. They set the highest value on individual freedom. The German sinologist Rolf Trauzettel (1990) tried to develop a more balanced view that on the one hand accounts for a Chinese recognition of the worth of the individual, while on the other also tries to explain why this did not give rise to the notion of individual rights.

3   This is not true for Chinese scholars who have discussed the role of the individual in imperial law. See for instance Ma 1999 or Wu 1972.

4   In 1949, the 'Instruction to Abolish the Six Codes of the Guomindang and to Define the Judicial Principles for the Liberated Areas' issued by the Central Committee of the Party stated that 'all the Guomindang laws are nothing but instruments designed to protect the reactionary rule of the landlords, the compradors, the bureaucrats, and the bourgeoisie, and weapons to suppress and coerce the vast masses of the people.'

5   Makarenko, a teacher and social worker, was the most influential educational theorist in the Soviet Union. He was the author of several books on education, including *Pedagogicheskaya poema (1933–1935* [The Road to Life, an Epic of Education]), which is an account of his work at the Gorky Colony; and *Kniga dlya roditeley (1937* [A Book for Parents]). In the 1920s, Makarenko organized a rehabilitation settlement for children made homeless by the Russian Revolution, called Gorky Colony. These children and juveniles had roamed throughout the countryside in criminal gangs. In 1931 he was appointed head of the Dzerzhinsky Commune, a penal institution for young offenders. Both institutions were organized along military patterns: inmates were grouped in brigades and troops. Uniforms were also handed out. Newcomers were called 'pupils', who had to strive to become full 'communards'.

6   For the importance of Makarenko for China, see for example the discussion by Sun Xiaoli, 1994: 17–18. In 1954, a selection of his writings was published in Chinese under the title *On Communist Education*. Two years later, in 1956, a second edition of this book was published. Apart from that, several films were shown in China that introduced Makarenko's life and work to the Chinese audience.

7   In contrast, most Chinese constitutions list a number of rights. The point is that these enumerations of rights have for the most part been mere proclamations that were not followed through by implementation in criminal justice.

Bibliography

Adolphs, Lotte (1962) *A. S. Makarenko. Erzieher im Dienste der Revolution – Versuch einer Interpretation.* Verlag Dürrsche Buchhandlung: Bad Godesberg.

Bao, Ruo-wang and Rudolph Chelminski (1973) *Prisoner of Mao.* New York: Coward, McCann and Geoghegan.

Bünger, Karl (1950) 'Die Rezeption des europäischen Rechts in China'. In E. Wolff (ed.), *Deutsche Landesreferate zum III. Internationalen Kongress für Rechtsvergleichung in London 1950.* Berlin: W. de Gruyter, pp. 166–189.

Chow, Tse-tung (1960) 'The anti-Confucian movement in early republican China'. In A. Wright (ed.), *The Confucian Persuasion.* Stanford: Stanford University Press, pp. 288–312.

Cohen, Jerome A. (2007) 'A slow march to legal reform'. *Far Eastern Economic Review*, pp. 20–24.

Commission on Extraterritoriality in China (1925) *Chinese Prisons.* Peking: Commission on Extraterritoriality.

Connor, Allison W. (1998) 'Confucianism and due process'. In Wm Theodore de Bary and Weiming Tu, *Confucianism and Human Rights.* New York: Columbia University Press, pp. 179–192.

De Bary, Wm Theodore (1970) *Self and Society in Ming Thought.* New York: Columbia University Press.

—— (1998) *Asian Values and Human Rights: A Confucian Communitarian Perspective.* Cambridge: Harvard University Press.

Dikötter, Frank (2002) *Crime, Punishment and the Prison in Modern China.* New York: Columbia University Press.

Foucault, Michel (1979) *Discipline and Punish.* New York: Viking.

Franck, Thomas M. (1999) *The Empowered Self. Law and Society in the Age of Individualism*, Oxford: Oxford University Press.

Goffman, Erving (1961) *Asylums: Essays on the Social Situation of Mental Patients and Other Inmates.* New York: Doubleday.

Hansen, Chad (1985) 'Individualism in Chinese thought'. In D. J. Munro (ed.) *Individualism and Holism: Studies in Confucian and Taoist Values*. Ann Arbor: Center for Chinese Studies, University of Michigan, pp. 35–55.

Jones, William C. (1994) *The Great Qing Code*. Oxford: Clarendon Press.

Kiely, Jan (2001) *Making Good Citizens: The Reformation of Prisoners in China's First Modern Prisons*. PhD dissertation, University of California, Berkeley.

King, Ambrose Y. C. (1985) 'The individual and group in Confucianism: a relational perspective'. In D. J. Munro (ed.), *Individualism and Holism: Studies in Confucian and Taoist Values*. Ann Arbor: Center for Chinese Studies, University of Michigan, pp. 57–72.

Koutaissoff, E. (1953) 'Soviet education and the new man'. *Soviet Studies*, vol. 5, no. 2, pp. 103–137.

Li Baiying (李白英) (1984) 回忆我的改造生活 *Huiyi wo de gaizao shenghuo* [Recollections of my life during reform]. Beijing: Qunzhong chubanshe.

Liang Jinhan (梁锦汉) (1919) 京师第二监狱报告书 *Jingshi di er jianyu baogao shu* [Report of the Beijing Second Prison]. Beijing: Jingshi di er jianyu.

Lifton, Robert J. (1961) *Thought Reform and the Psychology of Totalism: A Study of 'Brainwashing' in China*. Chapel Hill: University of North Carolina Press.

Liu, Lydia H. (1997) 'Translingual practice: the discourse of individualism between China and the West'. In T. Barlow (ed.), *Formations of Colonial Modernity in East Asia*. Durham: Duke University Press, pp. 83–112.

Ma, Herbert Han-Pao (1999) *Law and Traditions in Contemporary Chinese Society*. National Taiwan University, Legal Studies Series. Taipei: National Taiwan University.

MacCormack, Geoffrey (1996) *The Spirit of Traditional Chinese Law*. Athens: University of Georgia Press.

Makarenko, Anton Semyonovich (1965) *Problems of the Soviet School Education*. Moscow: Progress Publisher.

Mao, Tse-tung (1968) *Selected Works, 4 vols*. Foreign Languages Press: Beijing.

Mao, Zedong (1986) (edited by M. Kau, and J. K. Leung) *The Writings of Mao Zedong, 1949–1976*, Armonk: M.E. Sharpe.

Mao, Zedong et al. (1992) *Mao's road to power: revolutionary writings 1912–1949*. Armonk: M.E. Sharpe.

McDougall, Bonnie (2004) 'Privacy in modern China'. *History Compass*, vol. 2, pp. 1–8.

Mühlhahn, Klaus (2007) 'Visions of order and modernity – crime, punishment and justice in urban China during the republican period'. In David Strand, Sherman Cochran and Wen-Hsin Yeh (eds), *Cities in Motion: Interior, Coast, and Diaspora in Transnational China*. Berkeley: Institute of East Asian Studies, University of California, pp. 182–215.

Munro, Donald J. (1977) *The Concept of Man in Contemporary China*. Ann Arbor: University of Michigan Press.

Nathan, Andrew J. (1986) *Chinese Democracy*. Berkeley: University of California Press.

Neighbors, Jennifer M. (2004) *Criminal Intent and Homicide Law in Qing and Republican China*. PhD dissertation, University of California at Los Angeles.

Pye, Lucian W. (1991) 'The state and the individual: an overview interpretation'. *The China Quarterly, Special Issue: The Individual and State in China*, vol. 127, pp. 443–466.

Reichel, Philip L. (2002) *Comparative Criminal Justice Systems: A Topical Approach*. Upper Saddle River: Prentice Hall.

Shen Jiaben (沈家本) (1988) [1907] '監獄訪問錄' Jianyu fangwen lu. Preface in 中华人民共和国司法部 Zhonghua renmin gongheguo sifabu (ed.), 中国监狱资料汇编 *Zhongguo jianyu shiliao huibian* [Collected historical materials on the history of the prison in China], vol. 1, Beijing, p. 411.

Sun Xiaoli (孙晓雱) (1994) 中国劳动改造制度的理论与实践：历史与现实 *Zhongguo laodong gaizao zhidu de lilun yu shijian: lishi yu xianshi* [Laogai – the Chinese prison system's theory and practices: history and reality]. Beijing: Zhongguo zhengfa daxue chubanshe.

Trauzettel, Rolf (1990) 'Historical aspects of the individual–society relationship in China'. In C. A. Seyschab, A. Sievers, S. Szynkiewicz (eds), *Society, Culture, and Patterns of Behaviour*. Unkel/Rhein: Horlemann, pp. 25–70.

Waley-Cohen, Joanna (2000) 'Collective responsibility in Qing criminal law'. In K. G. Turner, J. V. Feinerman and R. K. Guy (eds), *The Limits of the Rule of Law in China*. Seattle: University of Washington Press, pp. 112–131.

Wang, Chung-hui (1919) 'Individualization of punishment'. *The Chinese Social and Political Science Review*, vol. 5, no. 2, pp. 91–99.

Williams, Philip F. and Yenna Wu (2004) *The Great Wall of Confinement: The Chinese Prison Camp through Contemporary Fiction and Reportage*. Berkeley: University of California Press.

Wu, John C. H. (1972) 'The status of the individual in the political and legal traditions of old and new China'. *Chinese Culture* (Taipei), vol. 13, no. 4, pp. 1–26.

Zhang Xianliang (长贤亮)(1994) 我的菩提树 *Wo de puti shu* [My Bodhi Tree]. Beijing: Zuojia chubanshe.

Zhongyang zhengfa ganbu xuexiao (1962) *Lectures on the General Principles of Criminal Law in the People's Republic of China* [Zhonghua renmin gongheguo xingfa zongze jiangyi], translated by the U.S. Department of Commerce, Office of Technical Services. Washington: Joint Publications Research Services.

8

Collective Symbols and Individual Options: Life on a State Farm for Returned Overseas Chinese after Decollectivization

Li Minghuan

Individualization is a fate, not a choice; in the land of individual freedom of choice, the option to escape individualization and to refuse participation in the individualizing game is emphatically not *on the agenda.*

(Bauman 2003: XVI)

During recent decades, Chinese society has undergone a gradual process of modernization and reform, and the structural changes caused by the government's reform policies have altered not only the relationship between the state and the individual, but also the ways in which individuals relate to their status and identity as members of different forms of collectives, in this case as residents of Songping Farm – one of the state farms for overseas Chinese returnees. As a result of the gradual disintegration of state collectives since 1978, many individuals whose lives used to be governed and catered for by the state have now been forced to make more individualized life choices. What were once collective responsibilities – such as the provision of housing and a livelihood – have become tasks to be solved by the individual or the family. By focusing on the social consequences of these reforms in one specific collective – Songping state farm for overseas Chinese returnees – I explore how the decollectivization process has prompted people who chose to remain on the farm after decollectivization to renegotiate their identity and develop new collective strategies in order to secure their livelihoods.

The historical trajectory of Songping Farm serves as an illustration of the process of what Ulrich Beck and Elisabeth Beck-Gernsheim have called 'institutionalized individualization'[1] in contemporary China. I argue that the 'liberated' individual continues to be shaped by the institutional: while the policies of the Chinese reform era have resulted in a withdrawal of the state's direct control over farmers' lives, farmers are to an increasing degree dependent on the workings of the market. In response to these challenges, the farmers who have suffered most from involuntary individualization – resulting from the break-down of the collective – have sought to build a new collective based on their special status as 'patriotic returnees'. The process by which the responsibilities of a crumbling collective is transferred to the level of the individual, and by which individuals choose to regroup in the form of new collectives, makes this case study an instructive illustration of the process of institutionalized individualization in a Chinese context.

The State-Owned Institution Seen from a Perspective of Individualization

Songping Farm is one of 84 overseas Chinese farms (*huaqiao nongchang* 华侨农场) that were set up by the Chinese government in response to the changing conditions in both China and Southeast Asia between the end of the 1950s and the late 1970s. It is a unique collective in the sense that it is an institution founded on a collective political symbol, a shelter for the so-called 'patriotic returnees' in mainland China.

Although the farms for returned overseas Chinese have existed for more than half a century and have undergone several waves of reform, few efforts have been made to explore the implications and social consequences of the reforms from an academic perspective. Between 1994 and 2007 Chinese academic journals published approximately 15 papers on the topic of these farms, in addition to the four papers published by a research team organized by myself. A well-known phenomenon that attracted attention is the fact that almost all the farms are in debt, which creates a situation in which they are completely dependent on government subsidies (Investigation Team of Zhigongdang in Yuxi City 2006: 45). For instance, in the case of the four farms on Hainan Island alone, from the time they were established and up until the year 2000 the government had provided a total of 227 million Yuan in subsidies.[2] Since most farms had suffered considerable losses in business, the major concern addressed in studies is how to deepen the reform by modifying the management system in order to allow the farm to become a profitable industry.[3]

My own study of these farms started in the spring of 2001, and has continued for six years. Together with two colleagues and three students I organized a research team to study a farm near Xiamen city.[4] In order to respect the interviewees' privacy, I have chosen a new name for the research target – Songping Farm. Unlike the other research that focuses on the reform and management of similar farms, this study takes an individualization perspective. The following analysis focuses on how the altered relations between individuals and state, in terms of governance and subsidies, have promoted new understandings of individual responsibility among the residents of Songping Farm, and the differing ways in which they have responded to the structural changes. My study focuses on those who had to remain on the farm, and who therefore experienced what constitutes an example of involuntary or forced individualization.

A process such as this gives rise to a new type of symbolic collective: as the state-imposed farm collectives disintegrated, the farmers' reinterpretation of their collective identity as 'patriotic returnees' became instrumental in their bargaining with the state for continued, and even renewed, privileges. Because all of the relevant farms have had similar reactions towards the reform, preferential treatment has occasionally been renewed and implemented. A decision made by the central government in October 2007 illustrates this: new, state-financed housing is to be built for all returnees who still remain on the farm. Because the price of housing is increasing dramatically in China today, the impact of this decision cannot be overstated. As I demonstrate in the following, the case of Songping Farm contributes to our understanding of the negotiations between the individual, the collective and the state during the process of individualization in contemporary China.

The Development of Songping Farm: From a Comprehensive Umbrella to Organized Irresponsibility

The unique process of re-grouping we see in these farms today, however, cannot be fully understood without a more detailed account of their origins and development.

(i) The emergence of a social enclave: the inception period (1960–1965)

In May 1959, the Indonesian authorities announced an injunction whereby the trading licences of all Chinese below the Kabupaten (regency) level in rural areas were revoked. The force used in the execution of this ban led to social unrest, and consequently to the exodus of approximately 120,000 Chinese to China by ships and boats (Tan 2004: 806). Noting the political tension in Indonesia, the newly established People's Republic of China government sent ocean liners to Indonesian harbour cities to offer to bring back the Chinese immigrants who had been hit by the Indonesian policies. The Taiwanese government also expressed compassion for their compatriots' suffering, and because of the enmity between the Chinese Communist Party and the Kuomintang government in Taiwan at the time, those who voluntarily chose to return to the PRC rather than to Taiwan were given an especially warm welcome as 'patriotic returnees'.

Many of the forced returnees had lost all private belongings and arrived in mainland China empty-handed. Realizing that ethnic Chinese returnees were pouring into the port-of-entry cities in South China, the PRC government decided to establish dozens of state-owned farms to settle them. Songping Farm was founded in March 1960, and was one of the first such farms in Fujian Province. It is located in Tongan county, a rural area near Xiamen city, on a hilly flank of Beichen Mountain. The government of Fujian Province had delimited an area of approximately 6949 *mu*[5] for the farm. The area was covered with wild, dense bush, and only approximately 50 *mu* was cultivated as rice paddies. Originally, it had been the property of three villages (at that time three production teams). In June of 1960 the first group, composed of 50 returned households consisting of 210 family members, was brought over to the farm. From that time and up until the year 1963, Songping Farm was home to approximately 800 returnees, and all adults became wage-earning farmers paid by the state while their children enrolled in the farm's own school.

During the first years after its establishment Songping Farm developed into an independent unit that clearly differed from the surrounding villages. Politically, in terms of the administrative chain of command, the farm was under the direct command system of the Overseas Chinese Affairs Office, which linked the farm to the central government in Beijing. As a consequence, the head of Songping Farm ranked higher in the bureaucracy than the head of the Tongan county government. This made it possible for the head of Songping Farm to send reports and requests directly to the provincial or even central government, rather than through the ordinary local county government structure.

Economically, Songping Farm became secure enough for all farmers to rely completely on it for their livelihood. Under the *hukou* (戶口) system,[6] officially, all returnees belonged to a rural system. They lived in a rural area and engaged in farm work. It was difficult for them to migrate to urban areas, which had been their preference upon their return. One of the questions on the registration form that needed to be filled out when the returnees arrived at their Chinese port concerned what sort of work they wanted to do in China. Many reported that they had a certain skill: trader, driver, plumber, carpenter, tailor and so on. All expected to settle in a city in southern China. In about one hundred such forms that are kept in the archive of Songping Farm, I found that no one had expressed a wish to become a farmer. However, as farmers of a state-owned institution, they were state employees entitled to regular wages, regardless of whether or not the farm turned a profit. Although the wages were low, they were enough to cover the basic needs of a family. Moreover, the farmers enjoyed certain special services. For instance, the houses in which they lived, although very simple, were free of charge. The farm established its own kindergarten, primary school and junior high school exclusively for the state farmers' children. A dispensary was established to treat minor ailments, and all could enjoy free medical and hospital care. Moreover, when goods such as cooking oil, meat, sugar, soap and cigarettes were in short supply throughout mainland China in the economic crisis period (1960–1962), the Songping farmers and their peers on other farms for returned overseas Chinese could use special vouchers to purchase goods in the farms' special shops. Seen from this point of view, all farmers experienced remarkable preferential treatment as compared to their village neighbours.

Culturally, most farmers, consciously or unconsciously, retained the living customs to which they had been accustomed in Indonesia. For instance, some families planted palm trees, coffee trees and tropical trees in the area around their houses. Unlike the native peasants who spoke the local dialect of Hokkian, the Songping farmers preferred to speak with each other in one of the Indonesian dialects they had used before their return. Their dress was more colourful than that of the local peasants. They showered daily, and often cleaned the furniture and washed the floors in their homes. Whenever there was a festival, or occasionally during the short breaks from working in the fields, they enjoyed singing and dancing to Indonesian music.

Therefore, since its establishment in 1960 and up until the year 1965, right before the start of the Cultural Revolution, Songping Farm was not only labelled as a collective institution for returned overseas Chinese, it was also recognized as an alien enclave among the native peasants in the surrounding villages. All returnees came back of their own accord, but were now organized as a closed and close-knit community and collective.

(ii) Contradiction runs parallel with development: the expansion period (1966–1980)

During the 1960s, Tongan County was still an economically backward and rather conservative rural area. Songping Farm attracted quite a bit of local attention, and the living habits of the Songping farmers, not to mention the special treatment to which they were entitled, became a subject of gossip among the local peasants. Almost from the very beginning, the contrast between the Songping farmers and the native peasants had run parallel with the development of the settlement.

Most male adult returnees had been peddlers before their return and none of them had wanted to become peasants. Coming to China, all return-ees had to learn how to raise crops, including how to till the ground, trans-plant rice seedlings, cover farmland with fertilizer, and harvest the crops. While hundreds of returnees on Songping Farm were experiencing the hardship of adjusting to the new environment, discontent was developing among the native peasants in the neighbouring villages. The authorities had clearly established a boundary between Songping Farm and the neighbour-ing villages, and the native peasants of the three surrounding villages had never accepted the farm and its inhabitants. In the minds of the natives, the Songping farmers were an alien group who had occupied their land. Some angry natives crossed the border to steal crops, vegetables and even clothing that the Songping farmers dried outdoors. When the farmers attempted to stop them, the natives shouted insults at them: 'You barbarians go away! We have the right to everything from our own land!' The tension between the returnees/farmers and the natives grew. Ethnic feuds caused the authorities to reconsider how to define the borders of the farm. At the beginning of 1966, just a few months before the start of the Cultural Revolution, the authorities made an important decision: from that time on, the three villages that had given up part of their land to Songping Farm were to become a component of the farm. This entailed that all adults in the three villages would be employed in the same manner as the Songping farmers, and paid wages. This decision greatly excited the villagers, because at that time it was a great benefit to be a salaried employee of the state. Because of this policy, the population and the territory of the farm more than doubled.

The second expansion of Songping Farm occurred in the mid-1970s, when thousands of ethnic Chinese fled conflict and extreme stress in Vietnam. They were known as 'boat people'. Again, as in the 1960s, most boat people who arrived in China were settled in the overseas Chinese farms. From May 1978 and until the end of 1979, Songping Farm accepted a total of 637 returnees from Vietnam. In addition to the returnees from Indonesia and Vietnam, during the first two decades of Songping Farm's existence, dozens of individual returnees from other Southeast Asian countries, such as Cambodia, Thailand, Burma, Singapore, Malaysia and the Philippines, were settled on Songping Farm. Some applied themselves, while others were sent by the local authorities. By the end of the 1970s, the farm had accepted a total of 2,200 returnees from eight Southeast Asian countries.

(iii) Collective disembedding: Songping after 1980

The change within state farms during the reform period is an example of institutionalized individualization in China and its profound impacts on people's lives. The economic reform movement that started in the early 1980s produced great changes on Songping Farm. In the late 1970s, the reform whereby all land was contracted to individual households began in Anhui province and spread quickly throughout China. This reform excited peasants all over China and caused a surge of high production figures. The Songping farmers were, however, affected in a different manner.

Economically, the reform pushed the farmers to become individual labourers, with the effect that they had to start making their living by their own efforts. In the year 1981, Songping Farm started to contract out all land and fruit trees. At that time, thousands of longan trees on Songping Farm were in their production years. Because these trees had been planted by the earlier returnees and their fruit was more profitable than rice, the authorities decided that all longan trees should be contracted out to the returnees, while rice paddies should be contracted out to the native households. After signing these contracts with the farm, the regular wages to the farmers stopped, and they all had to earn their income from the contracted agricultural work.

In the beginning almost everyone was happy to be rid of the comprehensive state control over the farm. 'We had much more freedom and needn't obey instructions from higher authorities', as many interviewees put it. After the longan trees were contracted out individually, the contractors took good care of the trees. Moreover, the weather was beneficial. During the first decade after the reform the returnees earned a much higher income than before: 'At that time, longan trees were really like our private bank', I was told. Although the profit level was different among the contractors, many accepted this fact, and the few who did not earn a reasonable profit from the contracted trees were regarded as lazy or having bad luck.

However, this situation did not last long. Beginning in the mid-1990s, when general inflation and living standards were on the rise throughout China, the market price of longan fruit, as was the case with the price of other agricultural products, stagnated, or even fell in some instances. At the same time, several other factors made the situation of the Songping farmers worse. Firstly, more and more peasants planted fruit trees on their contracted land and started to harvest the fruit after approximately one decade. But after China had become a member of the WTO, the import of fruit from Southeast Asia and Taiwan increased. Being individual farmers, and moreover being returnees without owning the full rights to the land, they were unable to make full use of new methods to increase fruit quality and production. Soon, their income decreased. The first case of peasants asking to be released from their contracts occurred in 2000. After that, every year a few more households requested to be released from their contracts.

Another important reform carried out in the year 1981 by the central government was the abolishing of the recruitment of new farmers to state farms. Under the state farms' system, all children of the farmers had been recruited as salaried employees when they reached the age of 18 years. After the recruiting of new farmers was abolished, a marginalized group made up of these children of farmers emerged and continued to expand on all state farms. They had farm *hukou*, but were not farmers and could not benefit from any policies directed towards the ex-farmers. Consequently, they found themselves living in a rural area on a state farm, but with no land to cultivate. They were given the odd designation 'Farm's non-farmers'. On Songping Farm, by the end of 2006, this marginal group included 888 adults.

Another factor that pushed the individualized differentiation in Songping was the preferential re-emigration policy implemented by the state in the late 1970s and early 1980s. After the introduction of China's open door policy, the Chinese central government implemented a special policy whereby the returned overseas Chinese would have priority to visit their relatives outside mainland China. After learning about the new policy, many returnees sent their applications and had to queue up for the official permission. Those who could prove that their overseas contacts were especially strong would be approved first. By the year 2000, a total of 459 returnees had left Songping for Hong Kong, Macao, the United States, Australia, or Canada, mainly through support provided by siblings abroad.

In addition, another new policy caused 96 returnees to move to urban areas on an individual basis. According to the policy implemented in 1985, returnees who were able to support themselves in urban areas could apply for urban *hukou* for their entire families. They could choose either the nearby city of Xiamen, or other cities if their reasons were good. One prerequisite was that after receiving a one-off subsidy, applicants had to give up their farmer status, and cease to have financial links with Songping Farm. They had to return their homes to Songping Farm and, moreover, they would not receive a pension from Songping Farm when they reached the age of retirement.

Since the mid-1990s, other political reforms have shaken the independent bureaucratic pillar of Songping Farm. The Fujian government implemented a new policy, authorized by the central government, in 1996. Starting on 1 January 1997, all of the 17 farms in Fujian for returned overseas Chinese – Songping Farm being one of them – were no longer affiliated with the overseas Chinese affairs command system, and became subject to their respective local authorities. That is, an independent organizational system for the farms ceased to exist. The social consequences of this policy were more psychological and emotional than practical. A common reaction among the returnees was something like 'babies suddenly lost their mothers', as one interviewee expressed it. It was the 'mother' who had abandoned her burden.

By the late 1990s, except for the salaried officials of the farm, most returnees who had to remain on the farm were economically and socially vulnerable. Moreover, the growing feelings of deprivation among the returnees and their adult children were strengthened after the start of the new millennium when the area was subjected to a new project of developmental planning. Seeing the native peasants claim high compensation when their land was appropriated by the development planning projects, the returnees felt quite strongly that they ought to have the right to decide over the land they had cultivated immediately upon their arrival. One incident in the

Table 8.1. Five groups of Songping Farm

Category	Number	Monthly income	Medical care paid for by the farm	Note
State cadre	46	≈ 3,000	Yes	Some cadres do not have Songping *hukou*.
Retired farmer	439	≈ 350 (pension)	Yes	Returnees would get another 60 Yuan as special subsidy.
Farmer	438	Acquired from market	Yes	Will receive pension when retirement age is reached.
Farm's non-farmer	888	Acquired from market	No	No pension available.
Minor	≈ 650	No income	No	

Source: Neibu ziliao, unpublished.

spring of 2006 became a test case for the Songping residents. After some negotiation between the leaders of Songping Farm and a development company, a section of land in the central part of Songping Farm together with the buildings on it were sold. The Songping residents, including most returnees and their offspring, were incensed when they discovered they would not get any compensation from the deal. They appealed to the municipality and accused a few leaders of corruption. When they were not satisfied with the response, approximately two hundred people representing the returnees held a demonstration in front of the Xiamen Municipal building on 5 June 2006. In addition to claiming the rights to the land, they made it clear that they wished to be treated as a special group, namely as 'patriotic returnees'. All demonstrators were advised to return home late that afternoon and a group of officials were sent to consult with them.

The Intensification of the Reform, and Individual Differentiation

As we have seen above, the shift in state polices has created structural changes in the institution of overseas Chinese farms. The economic reform has also deeply challenged the vested interests of the ex-farmers of Songping, and furthermore differentiated them on an individual level. The farm used to be the pillar on which each individual could rely, but by the new millennium not only had 655 returnees left the farm, but those who remained had become segmented.

The reforms have greatly differentiated the returnees' social status. According to the latest statistics I have collected, in August of 2006 there were 2,426 people who still had Songping Farm *hukou*. Of these, approximately 30 per cent are returnees and their offspring, and the remaining 70 per cent are natives who were recruited in 1966 and their offspring. The government's policy towards ex-farmers makes no distinction between returnees and natives. However, with the expansion of the reform, particularly concerning the question of land rights, the differences between these two groups are increasing.

On the basis of their current links with the farm, five groups can be defined, and the differences become obvious (see Table 8.1). The biggest difference can be found between the first group and the others, and the most dissatisfied group is the fourth group, whose numbers are increasing.

According to the interviewees themselves, the individual's 'luck' (*yunqi* 运气) was one of the factors that affected differentiation among the returnees, while another factor was remittances from abroad. According to a cadre of Songping Farm, approximately one third of the returned families received remittances from abroad, some regularly, but others only during the Chinese New Year or in relation to a particular event (marriage, death of an elder, etc.). During the interviews many mentioned that their greatest expectation was that their relatives would help their children to go abroad. By the year 2006, one of the most obvious signs of social differentiation between farm inhabitants was the residential situation. As mentioned earlier, all returnees had the same living situation when they settled on Songping Farm. In the middle of the 1980s, four new five-storey buildings had been built in the centre of the farm, for which the residents had to pay a certain amount of rent to live in. Also, the earliest returnees had enjoyed preferential treatment when applying for the new apartments. At the end of the 1980s, approximately 80 families had moved to the new buildings. Then, in the mid-1990s, as one of the reform steps, apartments in the first two groups of buildings on the farm were sold to the residing households at a very low price. Subsequently, however, the buyers were required to assume responsibility for all maintenance, at their own cost. Since the first group of houses was built more than forty years ago and constructed in a hurry, many were now in such poor condition that rain would seep through the roofs and walls. Some households reinforced the buildings, and some rebuilt at their own cost. But those who could not afford this had to remain in these dilapidated houses. In January of 1999, a new policy announced by the local authorities triggered bitter debate among the Songping farmers. Right next to the area where four buildings were built in the 1980s, an area of 5,800 square metres was divided into approximately 30 sections, each with the foundation for a house, designed for a three-storey house with a yard. The most important regulation was that only the returnees who were able to pay for the foundation and finance building within one year could apply. Although many farmers, both returnees and natives, expressed anger at this policy, the selling process was in progress. Before the deadline, a total of 33 families had paid for the foundation and completed their respective villas. The farm authorities decided to add three more sections. These newly finished houses have become a collective symbol of the wealthy group on the farm. Today, the weather-beaten houses from the 1960s, the simple but newer buildings of the 1980s, and the modern villas are in sharp contrast to each other.

The last but not the least differentiation is the greatly expanded gap between the salaried farm leaders and the rank and file residents. Not only is the income of the leaders almost ten times the pension of the retired ordinary residents, the leaders also enjoy benefits that are out of reach for ordinary residents. During my early visits, there was one car and a couple of motorbikes parked in front of the administration building. These were to be used when the leaders needed to get around on business. During my later visits in the second half of 2006, however, I saw three cars parked there. Each of the three top leaders has a car to travel between home and office, because they have all bought houses in the nearby city of Tongan. The cars have been fully financed by the state farm, or rather by the development company. Today, the leaders of the farm use the titles of manager or president of the development company, and they have the right to own a car for business and in the name of a company. In the eyes of ordinary people, the subsidies provided by the state for the returnees have been misappropriated. Such a contrast is a major cause of discontent.

Remaking a New Collectivity, and the Efforts of Re-embedment

Having experienced reform for more than a decade and seeing the differentiation among the ex-farmers, those who remain on the farm have developed a deep nostalgic feeling for life in the collective period. The memory of comprehensive protection has been romanticized, and an unexpected wave of fighting back to claim more state protection has been on the rise, and has become a survival strategy. In the process of decollectivization, a new collectivity based on being a group of 'patriotic returnees' has been recreated. This reminds us of an interesting argument: '"Individualization" consists in transforming human "identity" from a "given" into a "task" – and charging the actors with the responsibility for performing that task and for the consequences (also the side-effects) of their performance; in other

words, it consists in establishing a *de jure* autonomy (although not necessarily a *de facto* one)' (Bauman 2003: XV).

In their negotiations with the authorities, both the ex-farmers and the
current leaders of the farm – none of whom are returnees themselves – have
tried hard to emphasize their collective trait of being a unit of 'patriotic
returnees'. Consciously or unconsciously, in order to establish this social
image and common identity, their lives and experiences before return
have been recreated. According to the altered narratives of return by the
returnees and their offspring, they were not directly *forced* to go back to
China; rather, it was their own *choice* to return to the PRC. Moreover, their
motivation was to contribute to their socialist motherland. They repeatedly stress that they do not want the reforms to erase the memories of
their own special contributions to the farm, and thereby the country. The
situation in which they find themselves has caused them to reinvent their
history to support their daily life. The alien language, cuisine and songs
and dances have not only become collective symbols that indicate their
differences from other locals, but have been utilized as practical strategies.
In the early 1990s for instance one woman started to provide Indonesian
cuisine to visitors. Gradually, more visitors came to Songping especially
for this Indonesian food. In the year 2002, a returnee, together with his
wife and two sons, opened a family restaurant at the side of the main road,
and called it 'Indonesian Restaurant'. Soon two more restaurants were
established: one called Bali Island (Indonesia) and the other Vietnamese
Cuisine. In addition, some retired or middle-aged Songping residents met
regularly to perform Indonesian songs and dances as their spare time activity. They are not returnees themselves, and are therefore not familiar with
the Southeast Asian culture. In one of the meetings I observed, an elderly
man acted as the teacher, and a dozen participants learned from him. They
were intentionally re-creating these cultural elements. All of these cultural
recreational activities have enjoyed the support of the new leaders of the
farm.

The most important negotiation between Songping Farm and the
state after the reform concerns the new development project for the
area. In July of 1997, after years of negotiation with Xiamen municipality, Songping Farm received approval to be reorganized as the Songping
Overseas Chinese Economic Development Area. In order to attract foreign

investment, a ten-kilometre concrete road was built in 1998, financed by Xiamen municipality, to connect the farm with the main public road. Finally, Songping Farm was no longer isolated from public transportation. Moreover, in the name of protecting the rights of the returnees, all officials of the farm have since been treated in the same way as the officials affiliated with Xiamen institutions, and all retired farmers have been taken care of by the local social welfare system, which means that their pension has been guaranteed. The extra subsidy to the returnees mentioned earlier comes from the budget of Xiamen municipality as well. From this, both leaders and Songping farmers have recognized how important it is to stress the collective attribute of being an organized returned migrant unit. In the year 2000 a great project developed the area of the farm as a tourist site with Southeast Asian cultural features. As was mentioned earlier, when the returnees had settled down on the farm, some planted tropical trees around their houses. After some years, these trees have become a beautiful symbol of the farm. Also, the Southeast Asian-style restaurants set up by the individual returnees have become a successful advertisement for the area. Similar development ideas have been promoted again and again. The latest programme, presented in the summer of 2007, includes a five-star hotel and an amusement park with tropical views. The plan also suggests a three-storey independent villa for every permanent household. Because the returnees were from eight Southeast Asian countries, the designer used this slogan: 'Visiting Songping is like visiting eight countries in Southeast Asia'. The purpose of this grandiose programme is to seek outside invest-ment. Again, the symbol of a returnee unit has consciously been utilized to attract attention, investments, and to recreate a collective identity.

In the year 2006, when constructing a 'harmonious society' had become the national guiding policy, the central government took some serious social problems under preferential consideration. The returned overseas Chinese living on state farms became a special target because of their close connections and influence abroad. In early 2007, several groups headed by high-ranking national leaders were sent by the central government to visit returnees on farms. While visiting a farm in a distant mountainous area of Guangxi Province, one of these leaders was shocked to see the returnees' poor living conditions. He immediately wrote a special report to the central government, and soon after, the government made an important resolution which was sent to all provincial and municipal governments where overseas Chinese farms were located. Clearly, the government was worried that the poor conditions of overseas returnees might damage the image of China in Southeast Asia. In order to effect radical improvement in the living conditions on the farms, a national project was initiated to build social welfare apartments for returnees on all overseas Chinese farms. The expenses were to be shared by the central, provincial and municipal governments. In Xiamen, in accordance with the instructions, up to 22 million Yuan was budgeted to be used for the 'Songping Farm returnees' housing project'. A total of 234 returnee households remained on Songping Farm at the end of 2007, and the construction of 234 social welfare apartments began. All of the 234 returnee households have been authorized to move to these almost-free apartments in the year 2008. This is a positive indication that a collective preferential policy has been remade and put into practice again.

Conclusion: Individualization in the Political Context of China

The above picture has indicated two contrasting trends in the reform process on farms for returned overseas Chinese, of which Songping Farm is representative. On the one hand, the reform initiated from the top down reduces the state's control and therefore relieves the state of responsibility by pushing the state farm's employees, who had an 'iron rice bowl' in their hands, to make their individual livings in the market economy. While some capable persons have left the farm to exploit the freedom that also comes with being rid of the government's comprehensive control, those who remain are vulnerable, and many have suffered from the involuntary individualization. Experiencing the loss of the state's preferential protection, they tried to regain what they had lost. In the process of negotiation, they made real progress only when they had a political card to play, namely the symbolism inherent in the government's treatment of the 'patriotic returnees' with a potential influence abroad. When the new policy of establishing social welfare housing for all returnees who still remained on the farm was implemented, the returnees' dream of re-embedment had to a certain degree come true.

The case of Songping is a telling example of the changing relationship between the individual farmer and the state-owned farm, and between the farm collective and the state. The process of negotiation and renegotiation on different levels demonstrates '*how* the institutionally shaped collective fate appears in the life context of people in individualized society, how it is perceived and how it is dealt with' (Beck 1992: 165). The Chinese farms set up for the returnees have both symbolic and instrumental significance. The symbolic power cannot be converted to practical benefits without given conditions; that is, the state must have systematic supportive policies towards these communities. This is in the returnees' vested interest, but the state must bear the burden. From an economic perspective, the state need not assume this burden after the reform, but political and moral responsibility forced the state to continue its institutional support. Therefore, the position of these farms in today's China is still wavering between a moral organization and an enterprise whose purpose is to make a profit. This contradiction creates a paradox in the reform of the farms. More than anything, it is an example of institutionalized individualism. The 'unseen' and 'latent' side effects have in fact shaped the individual's decision making. 'Individualization thus means precisely institutionalization, institutional shaping and hence the ability to structure biographies of life situations politically.' Moreover, the newly arising individual situations 'span the separated areas of the private sphere and the various areas of the public sphere. They are no longer merely private situations, but also always institutional' (Beck 1992: 160).

While the policies of the reform have resulted in a withdrawal of the state's direct support of farmers' lives, the 'liberated' farmers however did not accept individualization as their fate, as Bauman, quoted at the beginning of this chapter, writes. Instead, their survival strategy has been to recreate a new collective based on their special status of being a 'patriotic returnee unit'. Their goal is to be taken back collectively under the protective umbrella of the socialist state, in order to enjoy advantages that they cannot hope to obtain on the open market. After making efforts to play the political card, they indeed became a preferential group who enjoy a few supportive policies, and the newest policy – the state's provision of housing – is the most important achievement. The initiation of the reform on the farms is the attempt of the state to transfer its responsibility to the individual via the provision of housing and a livelihood, and has been influenced by the global wave of the market economy in enhancing the efficiency of state-owned industry, of which the state farm is one component. This process reveals that the reform in China is going through a process of what could be described as individualization. The diversity of the ex-farmers and the emergence of independent salary-earners outside the farm suggest that individualization is indeed evolving. Accompanying the intensified reform, the continual implementation of policies pushing the individual into the market, together with the adoption of market principles, imply that the state is moving in a trajectory similar to, though not indistinguishable from, the global tendency of individualization. However, the strategy of individualization as adopted by Chinese authorities is highly instrumental, intended only to improve industrial efficiency, not to cause a fundamental shift in the political system. The Chinese experience should be argued as being the government's attempt to make use of market forces to reduce the state's burden and thereby improve the efficiency of all state industry, rather than being an ideological shift to a free market system. Changing the status of the state farmers does indicate a reduced state role in financing, but this process does not constitute a total withdrawal of the state's responsibility. While political considerations towards 'patriotic returnees' and their overseas contacts have been put on the agenda, the central government has engaged in different forms of state intervention, and it has not entirely given up its responsibility of protecting 'patriotic returnees'. Moreover, it is important for the state to maintain a positive international image of China as a responsible socialist state.

In summary, tracing the trajectory of the reform at Songping farm, we may differentiate the Chinese experience of individualization from the Western practice described by Beck and Beck-Gernsheim. In other words, we should not analyze individualization practices in China simplistically in terms of a one-dimensional movement from the state to the individual. In the case of Songping farm, which is representative of all farms for overseas Chinese returnees, the individual did not accept individualization as his fate. Instead, the option to escape individualization and to refuse to participate in the individualizing game came on the agenda, and moreover has been realized to a certain degree, Though the move to the principle of individual responsibility suggests a withdrawal of the state from provision and subsidy, such practices are compatible with the development of a more effective state role in terms of its political image of a socialist state. Hence, the international phenomenon of individualization should be understood differently in different places, in its special political context. The trend of individualization in China should be understood and analyzed in light of the context of socialism, with its own manner of governance.

Notes

1   Beck and Beck-Gernsheim 2003, and discussed in Yunxiang Yan's introduction in this book.

2   http://hqnc.hainan.net/qk.htm

3   Xia 1994; Zhong 1994; Gong 1995; He and Nong 1996; Lan 1999; Zheng 2003; Jia 2004a; Jia 2004b; Chen 2007.

4   Although this chapter is written by me, the research data have been collected by the research team. I have benefited greatly from discussions with colleagues and students. I wish to thank all of them.

5   A *mu* is a unit of land equivalent to approximately 667 m².

6   As discussed also in Yan's Introduction in this book, the *hukou* system is the system of residence permits introduced by the Chinese central government in the early 1950s as part of the planned economy. The system was set up in order to regulate the movement of the Chinese work force, and functioned as an internal 'passport', which made it difficult to move from the rural areas to the cities, and also hindered people from moving between village areas. Since the 1980s, the system has undergone significant reforms, and although it is not as rigidly enforced as earlier, *hukou* registration still has an impact on the life choices of Chinese individuals.

Bibliography

Bauman, Zygmunt (2003) 'Foreword: Individually, together' in Ulrich Beck and Elisabeth Beck-Gernsheim, *Individualization: Institutionalized Individualism and its Social and Political Consequences*, London: Sage.

Beck, Ulrich (1992) (translated by Mark Ritter) *Risk Society: Towards a New Modernity*. London: Sage.

Beck, Ulrich and Elisabeth Beck-Gernsheim (2003) *Individualization: Institutionalized Individualism and its Social and Political Consequences*. London: Sage.

Berger, Peter L. and Samuel P. Huntington (2002) *Many Globalizations: Cultural Diversity in the Contemporary World*. Oxford: Oxford University Press.

Chen Peiyu (陈佩钰) (2007) '新视角下中国华侨农场的发展思路：以陆丰农场为例' Xin shijiaoxia Zhongguo huaqiao nongchang de fazhan silu: yi lufeng nongchang weili [New considerations on the development of overseas Chinese farms: the case of Lufeng Farm]. *Keji zixun daobao*, no. 27, pp. 105–106.

Gong Fenglong (龚凤龙) (1995) '华侨农场的出路何在?' Huaqiao nongchang de chulu hezai? [What is the future of the overseas Chinese farms?]. *Fujian shuiwu*, no. 5, pp. 8–9.

Hainanese net '海南省华侨农场通览' Hainansheng huaqiao nongchang tonglan [Overseas Chinese farms in Hainan Province] http://www.hainanese.com/hqnc/nongchang.htm. Accessed 28 April 2006.

He Jing and Nong Guixin (何静, 农贵新)(1996) '关于华侨农场经济体制改革的思考' Guanyu huaqiao nongchang jingji tizhi gaige de sikao [On the reform of economic system in the overseas Chinese farms]. *Fujian luntan*, no. 6, pp. 29–31.

Hou Chaorong and Chen Zhihong (侯朝蓉, 陈志宏) (2007) '金坪华侨农场债务化解调查' Jinping huaqiao nongchang zhaiwu huajie diaocha [Investigation on how to clear the debt of Jinping Overseas Chinese Farm]. *Zhongguo nongken*, no. 5, p. 60.

Investigation Team of Zhigongdang in Yuxi City (致公党玉溪市委调查组) (2006) '深化云南华侨农场体制改革的若干思考' Shenhua Yunnan huaqiao nongchang tizhi gaige de ruogan sikao [Deepen the systematic reform in Yunnan overseas Chinese farms]. *Yunnan shehuizhuyi xueyuan xuebao*, no. 1, pp. 44–46.

Jia Daming (贾大明) (2004a) '我国华侨农场管理体制改革探析' Woguo huaqiao nongchang guanli tizhi gaige tanxi [An investigation report on the reform of management of overseas Chinese farms]. *Fujian luntan*, no.10, pp. 20–24.

—— (2004b) '华侨农场管理体制改革调查报告' Huaqiao nongchang guanli tizhi gaige diaocha baogao [Research on the reform of management of overseas Chinese farms]. *Zhongguo nongken jingji*, no. 10, pp. 10–14.

Lan Qiang (兰强) (1999) '从武鸣华侨农场看归侨安置的实践和经验' Cong wuming huaqiao nongchang kan guiqiao anzhi de shijian he jingyan. [Practices and experiences: reviewing the settlement of returned overseas Chinese in Wuming overseas Chinese farm]. *Bagui qiaokan*, no. 2, pp. 52–55.

Li Minghuan, Yu Yunping, Liu Zhaohui and Sun Sheng (李明欢, 俞云平, 刘朝晖, 孙晟) (2003) ' 社会人类学视野中的松坪华侨农场' Shehui renleixue shiye zhong de songping huaqiao nongchang [A study on Songping Overseas Chinese Farm from the perspective of social anthropology]. *Huaqiao huaren lishi yanjiu*, no. 2, pp. 1–25.

Mao Qixiong (毛起雄) ed. (2000) 华侨华人百科全书：法律政策卷 *Huaqiao huaren baikequanshu: falu zhengce juan* [Encyclopaedia of Chinese Overseas: Volume of Laws and Policies]. Zhongguo Huaqiao chubanshe.

Neibu ziliao 内部资料 (Songping Farm's [internal records] at the end of 2006). Unpublished.

PRC State Department (中华人民共和国国务院) (1995) '关于深化华侨农场经济体制改革的意见' Guanyu shenhua huaqiao nongchang jingji tizhi gaige de yijian [Improve the reform movement in the economic system of overseas Chinese farms]. *Zhonghua renmin gongheguo guowuyuan gongbao*, no. 33.

Ru Jin (如今) (1999) '60年代福建安置归侨记实' 60 niandai Fujian anzhi guiqiao jishi [Settle returned overseas Chinese in the 1960s in Fujian]. *Fujian dangshi yuekan*, no. 10, pp. 37–38.

Tan, Mely G. (2004) 'Ethnic Chinese in Indonesia'. In Ember et al. (eds), *Encyclopedia of Diasporas*. New York: Kluwer Academic/Plenum Publishers, pp. 795–808.

Xia Guoxing (夏国兴) (1994) '华侨农场企业政权化的思考：广东部分华侨农场情况调查' Huaqiao nongchang qiye zhengquanhua de sikao: Guangdong bufen huaqiao nongchang qingkuang diaocha [Considerations on the regime of overseas Chinese farms: investigation in overseas Chinese farms in Guangdong Province]. *Jiaoyu yu guanli*, no. 4, pp. 30–33.

Yang Ying, Fu Hanzhang, Zheng Shaozhi and Wang Bing (杨英，傅汉章，郑少智，王兵) (2003) '广东省国有华侨农场体制改革基本思路探索' Guangdongsheng guoyou huaqiao nongchang tizhi gaige jiben silu tansuo [Research on the reform on state-owned overseas Chinese farms in Guangdong Province]. *Zhongguo nongcun jingji*, no. 2, pp. 57–62.

Zheng Shaozhi (郑少智) (2003) '国营华侨农场改革与资产营运模式探讨' Guoying huaqiao nongchang gaige yu zichan yingyun moshi tantao [Research on the reform of capital working system in state-owned overseas Chinese farms]. *Jinan daxue xuebao*, no. 4, pp. 50–54.

Zhong Daqiu (钟大球) (1994) '"小政府"催长了大经济：对珠江华侨农场成立管理区后的调查' Xiao zhengfu cuishengle da jingji: dui zhujiang huaqiao nongchang chengli guanliqu hou de diaocha [Small government developed big economy: investigation on the establishment of Zhujiang administrative zone for overseas Chinese farms]. *Zhongguo nongken jingji*, no. 10, pp. 14–15.

Index

NIAS Press is the autonomous publishing arm of
NIAS – Nordic Institute of Asian Studies, a research institute
located at the University of Copenhagen. NIAS is partially funded by the
governments of Denmark, Finland, Iceland, Norway and Sweden
via the Nordic Council of Ministers, and works to encourage and
support Asian studies in the Nordic countries. In so doing, NIAS
has been publishing books since 1969, with more than two
hundred titles produced in the past few years.

COPENHAGEN UNIVERSITY

Nordic Council of Ministers